CONTENTS

To the Teacher iv

Unit Tour vii

Scope and Sequence xiv

Correlations xx

About the Series Consultants and Authors xxii

Acknowledgments xxiii

PRE-UNIT Getting Started 2

UNIT 1 Making Connections 5

UNIT 2 All in the Family 25

UNIT 3 Lots to Do 45

UNIT 4 Small Talk 65

UNIT 5 At Home 85

UNIT 6 In the Past 105

UNIT 7 Health Watch 125

UNIT 8 Job Hunting 145

UNIT 9 Parents and Children 165

UNIT 10 Let's Eat! 185

UNIT 11 Call 911! 205

UNIT 12 The World of Work 225

My Soft Skills Log 245

Grammar Review 247

Grammar Reference 258

Word List 262

Audio Script 266

Map of the World 276

Map of the United States and Canada 278

Index 279

Credits 282

TO THE TEACHER

Welcome to *Future: English for Work, Life, and Academic Success*

Future is a six-level, standards-based English language course for adult and young adult students. *Future* provides students with the contextualized academic language, strategies, and critical thinking skills needed for success in workplace, life, and academic settings. *Future* is aligned with the requirements of the Workforce Innovation and Opportunity Act (WIOA), the English Language Proficiency (ELP) and College and Career Readiness (CCR) standards, and the National Reporting System (NRS) level descriptors. The 21st century curriculum in *Future*'s second edition helps students acquire the basic literacy, language, and employability skills needed to meet the requirements set by the standards.

Future develops students' academic and critical thinking, digital literacy and numeracy, workplace and civic skills, and prepares students for taking standardized tests. Competency and skills incorporating standards are in the curriculum at every level, providing a foundation for academic rigor, research-based teaching strategies, corpus-informed language, and the best of digital tools.

In revising the course, we listened to hundreds of *Future* teachers and learners and studied the standards for guidance. *Future* continues to be the most comprehensive English communication course for adults, with its signature scaffolded lessons and multiple practice activities throughout. *Future*'s second edition provides enhanced content, rigorous academic language practice, and cooperative learning through individual and collaborative practice. Every lesson teaches the interpretive, interactive, and productive skills highlighted in the standards.

Future's Instructional Design

Learner Centered and Outcome Oriented

The student is at the center of *Future*. Lessons start by connecting to student experience and knowledge, and then present targeted skills in meaningful contexts. Varied and dynamic skill practice progresses from controlled to independent in a meticulously scaffolded sequence.

Headers highlighting Depth of Knowledge (DOK) terms are used throughout *Future* to illuminate the skills being practiced. Every lesson culminates in an activity in which students apply their learning, demonstrate their knowledge, and express themselves orally or in writing. DOK reference materials for teachers, available in the TE, on the ActiveTeach, and from the Pearson

English Portal, include specific suggestions on how to help students activate these cognitive skills.

Varied Practice

Cognitive science has proven what *Future* always knew: Students learn new skills through varied practice over time. Content-rich units that contextualize academic and employability skills naturally recycle concepts, language, and targeted skills. Individual and collaborative practice activities engage learners and lead to lasting outcomes. Lessons support both student collaboration and individual self-mastery. Students develop the interpretative, productive, and interactive skills identified in the NRS guidelines, while using the four language skills of reading, writing, listening, and speaking.

Goal Setting and Learning Assessment

For optimal learning to take place, students need to be involved in setting goals and in monitoring their own progress. *Future* addresses goal setting in numerous ways. In the Student Book, Unit Goals are identified on the unit opener page. Checkboxes at the end of lessons invite students to evaluate their mastery of the material, and suggest additional online practice.

High-quality assessment aligned to the standards checks student progress and helps students prepare to take standardized tests. The course-based assessment program is available in print and digital formats and includes a bank of customizable test items. Digital tests are assigned by the teacher and reported back in the LMS online gradebook. All levels include a midterm and final test. Test items are aligned with unit learning objectives and standards. The course Placement Test is available in print and digital formats. Test-prep materials are also provided for specific standardized tests.

One Integrated Program

Future provides everything adult English language learners need in one integrated program using the latest digital tools and time-tested print resources.

Integrated Skills Contextualized with Rich Content

Future contextualizes grammar, listening, speaking, pronunciation, reading, writing, and vocabulary in meaningful activities that simulate real workplace, educational, and community settings. A special lesson at the end of each unit highlights soft skills at work. While providing relevant content, *Future* helps build learner knowledge and equips adults for their many roles.

Meeting Work, Life, and Education Goals

Future recognizes that every adult learner brings a unique set of work, life, and academic experiences, as well as a distinct skill set. With its diverse array of print and digital resources, *Future* provides learners with multiple opportunities to practice with contextualized materials to build skill mastery. Specialized lessons for academic and workplace skill development are part of *Future*'s broad array of print and digital resources.

In addition to two units on employment in each level, every unit contains a Workplace, Life, and Community Skills lesson as well as a Soft Skills at Work lesson.

Workplace, Life, and Community Skills Lessons

In the second edition, the Life Skills lesson has been revised to focus on workplace, life, and community skills and to develop the real-life language and civic literacy skills required today. Lessons integrate and contextualize workplace content. In addition, every lesson includes practice with digital skills on a mobile device.

Soft Skills at Work Lessons

Future has further enhanced its development of workplace skills by adding a Soft Skills at Work lesson to each unit. Soft skills are the critical interpersonal communication skills needed to succeed in any workplace. Students begin each lesson by discussing a common challenge in the workplace. Then, while applying the lesson-focused soft skill, they work collaboratively to find socially appropriate solutions to the problem. The log at the back of the Student Book encourages students to track their own application of the soft skill, which they can use in job interviews.

Academic Rigor

Rigor and respect for the ability and experiences of the adult learner have always been central to *Future*. The standards provide the foundation for academic rigor. The reading, writing, listening, and speaking practice require learners to analyze, use context clues, interpret, cite evidence, build knowledge, support a claim, and summarize from a variety of

text formats. Regular practice with complex and content-rich materials develop academic language and build knowledge. Interactive activities allow for collaboration and exchange of ideas in workplace and in academic contexts. *Future* emphasizes rigor by highlighting the critical thinking and problem solving skills required in each activity.

Writing Lessons

In addition to the increased focus on writing in Show What You Know! activities, *Future* has added a cumulative writing lesson to every unit, a lesson that requires students to synthesize and apply their learning in a written outcome. Through a highly scaffolded approach, students begin by analyzing writing models before planning, and finally producing written work of their own. Writing models, Writing Skills, and a checklist help guide students through the writing process.

Reading lessons

All reading lessons have new, information-rich texts and a revised pedagogical approach in line with the CCR and ELP standards and the NRS descriptors. These informational texts are level appropriate, use high-frequency vocabulary, and focus on interpretation of graphic information. The readings build students' knowledge and develop their higher-order reading skills by teaching citation of evidence, summarizing, and interpretation of complex information from a variety of text formats.

Future Grows with Your Student

Future takes learners from absolute beginner level through low-advanced English proficiency, addressing students' abilities and learning priorities at each level. As the levels progress, the curricular content and unit structure change accordingly, with the upper levels incorporating more advanced academic language and skills in the text and in the readings.

Future Intro	Future Level 1	Future Level 2	Future Level 3	Future Level 4	Future Advanced
NRS Beginning ESL Literacy	NRS Low Beginning ESL	NRS High Beginning ESL	NRS Low Intermediate ESL	NRS High Intermediate ESL	NRS Advanced ESL
ELPS Level 1	**ELPS** Level 1	**ELPS** Level 2	**ELPS** Level 3	**ELPS** Level 4	**ELPS** Level 5
CCRS Level A	**CCRS** Level A	**CCRS** Level A	**CCRS** Level B	**CCRS** Level C	**CCRS** Level D
CASAS 180 and below	**CASAS** 181–190	**CASAS** 191–200	**CASAS** 201–210	**CASAS** 211–220	**CASAS** 221–235

TO THE TEACHER

The **Pearson Practice English App** provides easy mobile access to all of the audio files, plus Grammar Coach videos and activities, and the new Pronunciation coach videos. Listen and study on the go—anywhere, any time!

Abundant Opportunities for Student Practice

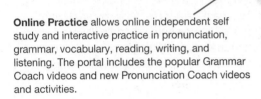

Student

Student's books are a complete student resource, including lessons in grammar, listening and speaking, pronunciation, reading, writing, vocabulary, and Soft Skills at Work, taught and practiced in contextual and interactive activities in the eBook.

Workbook—with audio—provides additional practice for each lesson in the student book, with new readings, and practice in writing, grammar, listening and speaking, plus activities for new Soft Skills at Work lessons.

Online Practice allows online independent self study and interactive practice in pronunciation, grammar, vocabulary, reading, writing, and listening. The portal includes the popular Grammar Coach videos and new Pronunciation Coach videos and activities.

Teacher's Edition includes culture notes, teaching tips, and numerous optional and extension activities, with lesson-by-lesson correlations to CCR and ELP standards. Rubrics are provided for evaluation of students' written and oral communication.

Outstanding Teacher Resources

Teacher

Presentation tool for front-of-classroom projection of the student book, includes audio at point of use and pop-up activities, including grammar examples, academic conversation stems, and reader's anticipation guide.

College and Career Readiness Plus Lessons supplement the student book with challenging reading and writing lessons for every level above Intro.

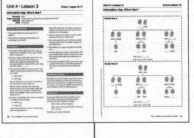

Assessment Program, accessed online with interactive and printable tests and rubrics, includes a Placement Test, multi-level unit, mid-term and final exams, and computer-based Test Generator with additional tests ready-to-use and customizable. In addition, sample high-stakes test practice is included with CASAS test prep for listening and reading.

Multilevel Communicative Activities provide an array of reproducible communication activities and games that engage students through different modalities. Teachers' notes provide multilevel options for pre-level and above-level students, as well as extension activities for additional speaking and writing practice.

Go to the Teacher's Portal for easy reference, correlations to federal and state standards, and course updates. pearsonenglish.com

Preview questions activate student background knowledge and help the teacher assess how much students know about the unit theme.

2 All in the Family

PREVIEW
Look at the picture. What do you see?
Who are these people?

A full-page photo introduces the **unit theme** and provides opportunities for interactive classroom discussion.

UNIT GOALS

- ☐ Identify family relationships
- ☐ Talk about family
- ☐ Talk about what people have in common
- ☐ Ask about mailing services
- ☐ Ask about people

- ☐ **Academic skill:** Retell information
- ☐ **Writing skill:** Use capital letters and commas in names of places
- ☐ **Workplace soft skill:** Separate work and home life

Unit goals introduce the competencies taught in the unit and allow students to track and reflect on their progress.

25

UNIT TOUR

Key **vocabulary** is contextualized and practiced in connection to the unit theme.

Study tips introduce the learning skills and strategies students need to meet the rigor required by the CCRS.

Lesson 1

Vocabulary

Family relationships

A **PREDICT.** Look at the pictures. Find Marta in each picture. Who are the other people in the pictures? What is their family relationship to Marta?

I think Paco is Marta's brother.

B ▶ **LISTEN AND POINT.** Then listen and repeat.

Paco Tina Manuel Ella Marta Lina Tony Delmar

Ben   Marta   Tina Eva Felix

Marta   Ben   Sandra   Tom   Ann

Tommy Liz Marta Ben

Liz   Marta   Ben Mary Tommy Sue Benny

Vocabulary

Family relationships

1. brother	6. cousin	11. nephew	16. sister-in-law	21. grandmother
2. sister	7. uncle	12. wife	17. son	22. grandfather
3. father	8. fiancé	13. husband	18. daughter	23. granddaughter
4. mother	9. fiancée	14. mother-in-law	19. children	24. grandson
5. aunt	10. niece	15. father-in-law	20. parents	25. grandchildren

C **WORK TOGETHER.** Look at the pictures. Student A, ask a question about Marta's family. Student B, answer.

A: *Who is Marta's sister?*
B: *Tina. Who are Marta's grandchildren?*

D **CATEGORIZE.** Which family words are for females? Which are for males? Which are for both? Complete the chart.

> **Study Tip**
>
> **Make connections**
> Write the names of five people in your family and their relationship to you.
> *Marie: niece*
> *Pete: nephew*

Female — *mother*   Both — *parents*   Male — *father*

Show what you know!

1. THINK ABOUT IT. Make a list of your family members. Where do they live?

husband — New York   son — New York   parents — China
daughter — New York   brother — San Francisco

2. TALK ABOUT IT. Talk about your family.

A: *Is your family here?*
B: *My son and daughter are here. My mother and father are in China.*

3. WRITE ABOUT IT. Write about your family.

My children are in New York. My parents are in China.

I can identify family relationships. ■   I need more practice. ■

In **Show what you know!**, students apply the target vocabulary in meaningful conversations and in writing.

Three **Listening and Speaking** lessons provide students opportunities for realistic conversations in work, community, and educational settings.

Pronunciation activities help students learn, practice, and internalize the patterns of spoken English and relate them to their own lives.

Lesson 2 — Listening and Speaking
Talk about family

1 BEFORE YOU LISTEN

MAKE CONNECTIONS. How many family members live with you? Who are they?

2 LISTEN

A ▶ PREDICT. Look at the picture of two new co-workers. What are they talking about? What do people talk about when they meet for the first time?

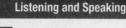

B ▶ LISTEN FOR MAIN IDEA. Choose the correct word.

Amy and Sam are talking about _____.

a. work   b. families   c. cars

C ▶ LISTEN FOR DETAILS. Choose the correct word.

1. Sam doesn't have a _____ family.
   a. big
   b. small

2. Sam has _____.
   a. one brother
   b. two brothers

3. Sam's _____ live in Senegal.
   a. brothers
   b. sisters

D ▶ EXPAND. Listen to the whole conversation. Choose the correct word.

Sam's brother lives _____ Sam.
a. far from   b. with   c. near

Multiple listening opportunities progress from listening for general understanding, to listening for details, to listening to an extended version of the conversation.

Listening and Speaking

3 PRONUNCIATION

A ▶ PRACTICE. Listen. Then listen again and repeat.

I have a brother and two sisters.
We live in the same apartment.
He works in a hospital.

Sentence stress

Some words in a sentence are **not stressed**. These words are very short and quiet.
For example, a, and, the.

B ▶ APPLY. Listen. Circle the words that are not stressed.

1. I don't have a very big family.
2. My sisters live in Senegal.
3. He's a medical assistant.

4 CONVERSATION

A ▶ LISTEN AND READ. Then listen and repeat.

A: Tell me about your family.
B: Well, I don't have a very big family. I have a brother and two sisters.
A: Do they live here?
B: My sisters live in Senegal, but my brother lives here.

B WORK TOGETHER. Practice the conversation in Exercise A.

C MAKE CONNECTIONS. Talk about your own family.

A: Tell me about your family.
B: I have a very big family.
   I have . . .

I can talk about family. ■   I need more practice. ■

Conversations carefully scaffold student learning and build language fluency.

Predict activities focus students on the social context of the conversation.

Checkpoints at the end of lessons provide students an opportunity to reflect on their progress and identify further resources for more practice.

UNIT TOUR

Each unit presents three **Grammar** lessons in a systematic grammar progression. Every Grammar lesson focuses on language introduced in the preceding Listening and Speaking lesson. Additional grammar practice is available in the Grammar Review and online.

Images provide scaffolding for meaningful grammar practice.

Grammar

Lesson 3

Simple present affirmative and negative:
live / work / have

Simple present affirmative and negative: *live / work / have*

Affirmative				Negative			
I You We They	live / work	in the U.S.		I You We They	don't	live / work	in Senegal.
He She	lives / works			He She	doesn't		
I You We They	have	a small family.		I You We They	don't	have	a big family.
He She	has			He She	doesn't		

Grammar Watch

- With *he, she,* or *it,* the simple present verb ends in *-s.*
- *Have* is an irregular verb. With *he, she,* or *it,* use *has.*
- Use *don't* or *doesn't* to make a verb negative. Use the base form of the verb after *don't* and *doesn't.*

For contractions, see page 258.

A **IDENTIFY.** Cross out the incorrect words.

1. My cousin **has / have** a wife and two children.
2. They **doesn't / don't** have children.
3. Her brother **work / works** in a theater.
4. My mother-in-law **lives / live** on South Street.
5. Our grandparents **doesn't / don't** live here.
6. We **don't / doesn't** work on weekends.
7. Pam and Ben **have / has** two boys.

B **COMPLETE.** Write the simple present form of the verbs.

1. Mary (work) ____works____ at a hair salon.
2. His sister-in-law (not have) __doesn't have__ a job.
3. Nina's fiancé (live) _____ near the city.
4. Her husband (work) _____ with her brother.
5. I (not live) _____ with my parents.
6. Our family (live) _____ in Colombia.
7. They (not work) _____ in a big office.
8. Tom (not have) _____ any cousins.

Grammar

C **INTERPRET.** Look at the family tree. Complete the sentences with the simple present.

1. Alba __doesn't live__ in Los Angeles.
   (live)
2. Marcos _____ in Lima.
   (live)
3. Lola _____ a son.
   (have)
4. Marcos _____ a brother.
   (have)
5. Lola and Pablo _____ in New York.
   (live)
6. Sandra _____ three grandchildren.
   (have)
7. Pablo and Marcos _____ a sister.
   (have)
8. Sandra and Paco _____ in Dallas.
   (live)

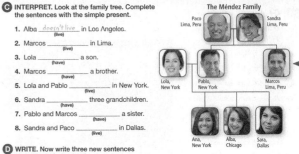

The Méndez Family

Paco, Lima, Peru — Sandra, Lima, Peru

Lola, New York — Pablo, New York — Marcos, Lima, Peru

Ana, New York — Alba, Chicago — Sara, Dallas

D **WRITE.** Now write three new sentences about the Méndez family.

Sara doesn't live in New York. She lives in Dallas. She has two sisters.

Show what you know!

1. **THINK ABOUT IT.** Write two true sentences and one false sentence about your family and life.

   I have _____
   I live in _____
   I work in _____

2. **TALK ABOUT IT.** Play a guessing game with three students. Read your sentences. Guess the false sentence.

   A: *I have four sisters. I live in Oak Park. I work in a hotel.*
   B: *I think the first sentence is false. I don't think you have four sisters.*
   A: *That's right. I don't have four sisters. I have one sister.*

3. **WRITE ABOUT IT.** Write three sentences about someone in your group.

   _____
   _____
   _____

I can use the simple present. ■   I need more practice. ■

Grammar activities progress from controlled to open practice, leading students from understanding to mastery of the target grammar.

Every **Show what you know!** integrates an interactive exchange and a writing task so students demonstrate their mastery of the grammar point using a range of language skills.

Grammar charts present the target grammar point in a clear and simple format.

Workplace, Life, and Community Skills

Lesson 4 — Help wanted ads and job requirements

1 READ HELP WANTED ADS

A IDENTIFY. Read the help wanted ads. Where can you find these ads? Where else can people find out about jobs?

job-ads.com
Home Job Listings Post Resume Career Advice Help

CAR SERVICE DRIVERS NEEDED

Job description: Drivers for evening and weekend airport car service. Experience: 1 year of driving service. Part-time. Pay: $12/hr. For more information, and to apply, please send a letter of interest to Jonna Kern at jkern@carservice.org

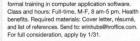

Career.com
Home Post My Resume Job Listings Resource Center Help

Office Assistant

Responsibilities: handle phone calls, greet visitors, and organize customer files. Preferred experience: 1 year of working in a busy office environment and formal training in computer application software. Class and hours: Full-time, M-F, 8 am-5 pm. Health benefits. Required materials: Cover letter, résumé, and list of references. Send to: erinhubs@hroffice.com. For full consideration, apply by 1/31.

B MATCH. Connect the sentence parts.

1. ____ A full-time employee works
2. ____ Responsibilities are
3. ____ A résumé includes
4. ____ A cover letter is
5. ____ Experience is
6. ____ References are
7. ____ Health benefits are

a. people who can describe you and your work.
b. a list of your job experiences and skills.
c. when your company pays some of your health insurance.
d. the activities and things you will do at a job.
e. a way to introduce yourself to your future employer.
f. your past work activities.
g. 40 hours a week.

C INTERPRET. Read the ads again. Answer the questions.

1. Which job is full-time? _____
2. What should someone do to apply for the car service driver position? _____
3. Which job requires evening and weekend work? _____
4. What is the pay for Car Service Drivers? _____
5. What are the responsibilities of an office assistant? _____
6. What kind of experience is preferred for the Office Assistant position? _____
7. When does the Office Assistant need to be able to work? _____

I can read help wanted ads. ■	I need more practice. ■

Workplace, Life, and Community Skills

2 IDENTIFY JOB REQUIREMENTS

A WORK TOGETHER. Look at the résumés. Which job from 1A is each candidate applying for? Write your answers on the lines. How do you know?

Jin Mong
1234 New Moon Road, New Jersey 11112

Education: Jones Community College
Major: Hospitality
Work experience: OMBER Driver, June 2018-present, Moon Gas, gas station attendant, June 2017-June 2018
Languages: English and Chinese
Skills: can operate a cash register

_____

B COMPARE. Look at the résumés. Answer the questions.

Which candidate is best qualified for the Car Service Driver job? Why?

Which candidate is best qualified for the Office Assistant job? Why?

Ann Lopez
42 North Shore Road, Boynton Beach, FL
alopez@gmail.com

Education: Palm Beach High School, currently enrolled in Palm Beach State College, Office Technology
Work Experience: Starland Coffee Shop, server January 2018-present.
Relevant Experience: Work with customers, handle customer problems, train new staff
Languages: Spanish and English
Skills: Can type, order supplies, use a cash register

C ROLE-PLAY. Act out a job interview. Choose a job from 1A. Student A, you are the interviewer. Student B, you are the applicant. Take turns.

Kim Kiska
22 West Lane Street, #3A
Stockton, CA
kimkas@yippe.com

Education: Stockton High School, A.A in Office Systems and Technology.
Work Experience: Office Assistant, Gem Restaurant Supply, March 2017-present
Responsibilities: Handle phone calls, organize file room, work with customers; Office Clerk, Bel Blue Office Systems, October 2015-March 2017.
Responsibilities: Greet customers, enter new data in database
Languages: Polish, Russian, and English
Skills: Fluent in all Office Software Systems

D GO ONLINE. Search for a job posting website. Find a job you are interested in.

What are the job responsibilities? What experience do you need? How can you apply for the job?

_____

Bin Fang
807 Kates Place, #21. Chicago, IL binfang@macro.com

Education: Jones Driving School, C-License
Work Experience: John's Taxi Service, September 2018-present; Roberto's Car Service, December 2015-present
Skills: Can type, use a computer, operate a commercial vehicle

_____

I can identify job requirements. ■	I need more practice. ■

UNIT TOUR

All new informational **Reading** lessons develop academic language and build content knowledge to meet the rigorous requirements of the CCRS.

Close-reading activities require that students return to the reading to find textual evidence of detail, to summarize for general understanding, and to make inferences.

Students develop **numeracy** skills by interpreting numeric information in charts and graphs.

Lesson 7 — Reading
Read about jobs in the U.S.

1 BEFORE YOU READ

A LABEL. Label the pictures with the words in the box.

| agriculture | health care | manufacturing | technology |

1. _____ 2. _____ 3. _____ 4. _____

B MAKE CONNECTIONS. Think about the fields of employment in A. Which fields have the most jobs these days? What kinds of jobs are they?

2 READ

▶ LISTEN AND READ.

Academic Skill: Predict the topic

You can often guess what an article is about by looking at the title and pictures. This will prepare you to understand what you read.

Today's Hot Jobs

The U.S. job market is changing fast. At one time, most workers in the U.S. had jobs on farms. Now, less than 2 percent of workers have agricultural jobs. In 1960, 25 percent of workers had jobs in manufacturing. Now, only 10 percent of workers are making things in factories. So where are the jobs today?

Health Care

Many of the fastest-growing jobs are in health care. The U.S. population is getting older. These older Americans need medical care and help with daily living. The greatest need is for personal care aides. There may be more than 750 thousand new jobs of this kind by 2026. Personal care aides take care of people in their homes or in day programs. They sometimes work with people with disabilities or long-term illnesses. On average, they make about $22,000 a year. There are other

fast-growing jobs in health care, too. For example, by 2026, there may be a need for 437 thousand more registered nurses. On average, they make about $69,000 a year.

Computer and Information Technology

There are also many fast-growing jobs in computer and information technology. By 2026, there may be more than 546 thousand new jobs in this field. Almost 300 thousand of those jobs will be for software developers. Some software developers create programs for computers and cell phones. Others design computer networks (where many computers work together). On average, they make more than $100,000 a year.

Many of today's fastest-growing jobs are in these two fields. Where will tomorrow's jobs be?

Source: U.S. Department of Labor

Percentage of Growth in Jobs

Home health aides	47%
Physical therapist assistants	31%
Application software developers	31%
Occupational therapy assistants	29%

Reading

3 CLOSE READING

A IDENTIFY. What is the main idea?

The fastest-growing jobs in the United States _____.
a. are in health care and in computer and information technology
b. are some of the highest-paid jobs in the United States
c. are jobs creating programs for computers and cell phones

B CITE EVIDENCE. Answer the questions. Where is the information? Write the line numbers.

Lines

1. The number of jobs in manufacturing today is _____ it was in the past. _____
   a. higher than   b. lower than   c. the same as
2. Personal care aides make about _____ on average. _____
   a. $2026 a month   b. $22,000 a year   c. $69,000 a year
3. By 2026, there will probably be _____ new jobs for software developers. _____
   a. about 100,000   b. more than 546,000   c. almost 300,000

C INTERPRET. Complete the sentences about the bar graph.

1. The bar graph shows _____. _____
   a. growing jobs in numbers   b. growing jobs in percentage   c. dying jobs in percentage
2. The growth in jobs for application software developers _____. _____
   a. is higher than for home health aides   b. is lower than for occupational therapy assistants   c. is the same as for physical therapist assistants

4 SUMMARIZE

Complete the summary with the words in the box.

| employment | health care | job market | software | technology |

The (1) _____ in the U.S. is changing. Two fields of (2) _____ are growing fast. There will be many new jobs in (3) _____, especially jobs for personal care aides. There will also be many new jobs in computer and information (4) _____, especially for (5) _____ developers.

Show what you know!

1. **THINK ABOUT IT.** What job do you want to have in five years? Why? What do you need to do to get that job?
2. **TALK ABOUT IT.** Talk about the jobs you want. Talk about how to get those jobs.
   In five years, I want to be a software developer. I need to learn about technology.
3. **WRITE ABOUT IT.** Now write about the job you want in five years.

I can predict the topic. ☐   I need more practice. ☐

To read more, go to MyEnglishLab.

Graphs and charts introduce students to information in a variety of formats, developing their visual literacy.

Academic tasks, such as summarizing, are introduced from the beginning and scaffolded to support low-level learners.

Informational readings containing level-appropriate complex text introduce academic language and build content knowledge.

Writing lessons follow a robust and scaffolded writing-process approach, engaging students in analyzing writing models, planning, and producing a final product.

A **Writing Skill** explains and models appropriate writing. Later in the lesson, students apply the skill to their own writing.

New **Soft Skills at Work** lessons engage students in real-life situations that develop the personal, social, and cultural skills critical for career success, and help students meet the WIOA requirements.

A brief scenario introduces a common workplace problem that can be solved using **critical thinking** and **soft skills**.

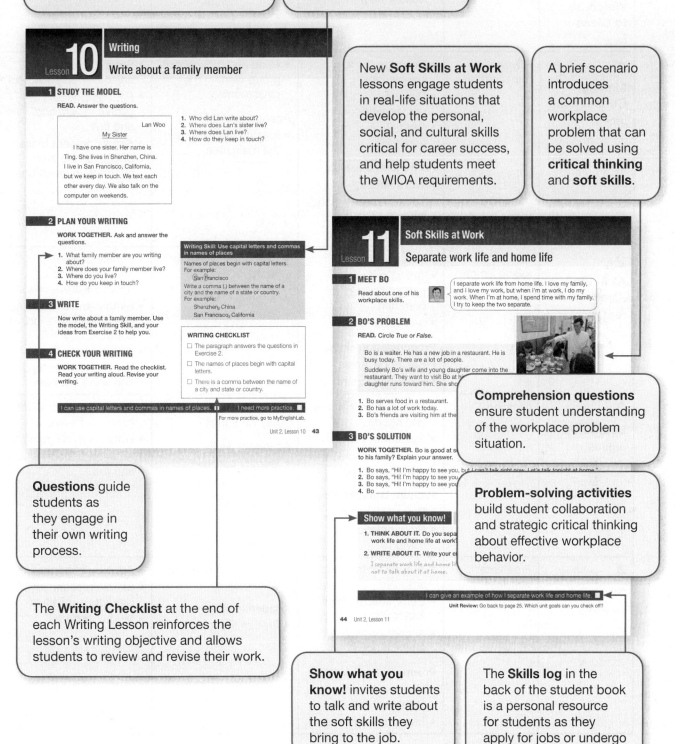

Questions guide students as they engage in their own writing process.

The **Writing Checklist** at the end of each Writing Lesson reinforces the lesson's writing objective and allows students to review and revise their work.

Comprehension questions ensure student understanding of the workplace problem situation.

Problem-solving activities build student collaboration and strategic critical thinking about effective workplace behavior.

Show what you know! invites students to talk and write about the soft skills they bring to the job.

The **Skills log** in the back of the student book is a personal resource for students as they apply for jobs or undergo performance reviews.

Unit	Vocabulary	Listening and Speaking	Reading	Grammar
Pre-Unit **Welcome to Class** *page 2*	Reasons for studying English	• Meet your classmates • Talk about your goals • Ask for help	• Locate information in your book	• Simple present: *be*
1 **Making Connections** *page 5*	Physical appearance	• Describe the way people look • Describe personalities • Get to know someone **Pronunciation skills:** • Word stress • Vowels in unstressed syllables • Sentence stress	• Read an article about group work in the classroom **Academic skill:** • Identify the topic and the main idea	• Simple present: *be* + adjective/*have* + object • *Be:* compound sentence with *and* and *but* • Simple present tense of *be: Yes/No* and information questions
2 **All in the Family** *page 25*	Family relationships	• Talk about family • Talk about what people have in common • Ask about people **Pronunciation skills:** • Sentence stress • Pronunciation of do	• Read an article about work/life balance **Academic skill:** • Retell information	• Simple present affirmative and negative: *live/work/have* • Simple present: *Yes/No* questions and short answers • Simple Present: Information questions and short answers
3 **Lots to Do** *page 45*	Clothing	• Describe your wants and needs • Talk about plans • Describe problems with purchases **Pronunciation skills:** • Pronunciation of *to* • Pronunciation of *going to*	• Read about ways to pay for things **Academic skill:** • Identify purpose	• Simple present: *Want/need* + infinitive • Future with *be going to* • Adverbs of degree: *very* and *too*
4 **Small Talk** *page 65*	Free-time activities	• Talk about free-time activities • Communicate likes and dislikes • Accept or decline an invitation **Pronunciation skills:** • Unpronounced syllables • *Have to* and *has to*	• Read about different writing styles **Academic skill:** • Predict the topic	• Adverbs of frequency • Simple present: *love/like/hate* + infinitive • Modal: *Have to*

Writing	Document Literacy Numeracy	Workplace, Life, and Community Skills	Soft Skills At Work
• Write questions to complete conversations	• Use unit and page numbers	• Introduce yourself • Greet people	
• Write about a study routine **Writing skill:** • Introduce and explain steps of a routine	• Read an application for an ID card • Interpret an ID card	• Read identification cards • Complete an application **Digital skill:** • Go online and search for an identification card application in your state	• Be inclusive
• Write about a family member **Writing skill:** • Use capital letters and commas in names of places	• Interpret a family tree • Complete a Venn Diagram • Interpret a chart	• Ask about mailing services **Digital skill:** • Go online and search for mailing services near you	• Separate work and home life
• Write about saving money **Writing skill:** • Use a topic sentence	• Compare cost • Calculate discount • Interpret an online order form • Understand a sales receipt • Compare ways to make big purchases	• Complete an online order and read a sales receipt **Digital skill:** • Go online and visit an online store.	• Listen actively
• Write about a free-time activity **Writing skill:** • Use details in your writing	• Complete a Venn Diagram • Interpret calendars • Interpret a bar graph • Understand emojis	• Understand a schedule of events **Digital skill:** • Go online and find a website of your local library. Add two events to a digital calendar. Invite a friend.	• Be professional

Text in purple refers to workplace and employability topics.

SCOPE AND SEQUENCE

Unit	Vocabulary	Listening and Speaking	Reading	Grammar
5 **At Home** *page 85*	Household problems	• Describe problems in your home • Ask about an apartment • Get directions **Pronunciation skills:** • Stress in two-word nouns • Voiced and voiceless *th*	• Read an article about renters and homeowners **Academic skill:** • Skimming	• Present continuous • *There is/There are* • Imperatives
6 **In the Past** *page 105*	Events	• Talk about past activities • Talk about milestones • Talk about something that happened **Pronunciation skills:** • Extra syllable for *-ed* endings • Statements as questions	• Read an article about President Barack Obama **Academic skill:** • Scan for information	• Simple past: Regular verbs • Simple past: Irregular verbs • Simple past: Information questions
7 **Health Watch** *page 125*	Health problems	• Make a doctor's appointment • Talk about an injury • Call in when you have to miss work **Pronunciation skills:** • Linking sounds • *t* between two vowel sounds • Using pauses	• Read an article about stress **Academic skill:** • Use formatting cues	• Prepositions of time • Simple past: More irregular verbs • Ways to express reasons: *because, for*
8 **Job Hunting** *page 145*	Job titles and duties	• Talk about your skills • Answer questions about work history • Answer questions about availability **Pronunciation skills:** • Pronunciation of *can* and *can't* • Intonation of questions with *or*	• Read an article about jobs in the U.S. **Academic skill:** • Predict the topic	• *Can* to express ability • Time expressions with *ago, last, in,* and *later* • Ways to express alternatives: *or, and*

Writing	Document Literacy Numeracy	Workplace, Life, and Community Skills	Soft Skills At Work
• Write about your home **Writing skill:** • Structure paragraphs and use indents	• Compare cost on rent and utilities • Interpret a utility bill • Interpret a bar graph • Follow directions on a map • Understand signs	• Read apartment ads • Read a utility bill **Digital skill:** • Go online and search for an apartment in your town or city	• Take initiative
• Write a biography **Writing skill:** • Use commas with dates	• Interpret a to-do list • Identify holidays on a calendar • Create a timeline	• Recognize U.S. holidays **Digital skill:** • Go online and search for other U.S. holidays	• Be dependable
• Write about treating a health problem **Writing skill:** • Give a reason	• Interpret appointment cards • Identify dosage on medicine labels	• Read medicine labels **Digital skill:** • Go online and search for an online pharmacy. Find information on a medicine.	• Respect others
• Write about your job history **Writing skill:** • Use the correct tense	• Interpret a timeline • Interpret a bar graph	• Read help wanted ads • Identify job requirements **Digital skill:** • Go online and search for a job posting website	• Be honest

Text in purple refers to workplace and employability topics.

SCOPE AND SEQUENCE

Unit	Vocabulary	Listening and Speaking	Reading	Grammar
9 **Parents and Children** *page 165*	School Subjects	• Make plans for school events • Talk about progress in school • Discuss your child's behavior in school **Pronunciation skills:** • Pronunciation of *will* • Extra syllables with *'s*	• Read an article about going to college **Academic skill:** • Use information in graphs and tables	• Future with *will* • Adverbs of manner • Object pronouns • Possessive nouns
10 **Let's Eat!** *page 185*	Food containers and quantities	• Ask for quantities of food • Make decisions when shopping for food • Order food in a restaurant **Pronunciation skills:** • Pronunciation of *to, the, a,* and *of*	• Read an article about the effects of coffee **Academic skill:** • Get meaning from context	• Count nouns/ Non-count nouns and *How much/ How many* • Comparative adjectives with *than* • Quantifiers with plural and non-count nouns
11 **Call 911!** *page 205*	Medical emergencies	• Call 911 to report a medical emergency • Describe an emergency • Respond to a police officer's instructions **Pronunciation skills:** • Stressed syllables • *H* sound	• Read an article about being safe at work **Academic skill:** • Identify supporting details	• Present continuous: Statements and questions • *There was/There were* • Compound imperatives
12 **The World of Work** *page 225*	Job Responsibilities	• Ask about policies at work • Ask a co-worker to cover your hours • Request a schedule change **Pronunciation skills:** • Intonation in *yes/no* questions • Intonation in information questions and statements	• Read an article about the Social Security program **Academic skill:** • Think about what you know	• Expressions of necessity and prohibition • Information questions with *Who/What/ Which/When/Where* • *Can/Could* to ask permission

Writing	Document Literacy Numeracy	Workplace, Life, and Community Skills	Soft Skills At Work
• Write about school **Writing skill:** • Use commas between words in a list	• Interpret a bar graph • Compare cost of tuition	• Leave a phone message • Leave a voice message **Digital skill:** • Go online and search how to set up a personal voicemail greeting message on your mobile phone	• Plan well
• Write about nutrients in a dish **Writing skill:** • Use *like* and *such as* to introduce examples	• Identify food containers and quantities • Understand nutritional information on food labels • Compare food price in ads • Interpret a bar graph • Read a menu	• Read food labels **Digital skill:** • Go online and search for ingredients in a food you like	• Ask for help
• Write about an emergency **Writing skill:** • Answer *wh-* questions to give information	• Interpret a fire escape plan • Interpret a bar graph	• Identify fire hazards • Understand fire safety procedures **Digital skill:** • Go online and search for workplace fire-escape plans or your own workplace's fire-escape plan	• Follow safety procedures
• Write about job responsibilities **Writing skill:** • Give details to support an idea	• Calculate earnings from a pay stub • Understand types of deduction • Calculate overtime pay • Interpret a work schedule	• Read a pay stub • Understand payroll deductions and overtime hours **Digital skill:** • Go online and search for other common deductions that can appear on a pay stub	• Be a team player

Text in purple refers to workplace and employability topics.

CORRELATIONS

Unit	CASAS Reading Standards (correlated to CASAS Reading Standards 2016)	CASAS Listening Standards (correlated to CASAS Listening Basic Skills Content Standards)
1	**L1:** RDG 1.1, 2.2, 2.3; **L2:** RDG 1.7, 2.2, 2.3; **L3:** RDG 1.7, 2.1, 2.2, 2.3; **L4:** RDG 1.7, 2.2; **L5:** RDG 1.7; **L6:** RDG 1.7, 2.9; **L7:** RDG 1.7, 1.8, 2.2, 2.3, 3.2, 3.7, 3.11, 4.2; **L8:** RDG 1.7; **L9:** RDG 1.7, 2.1, 2.2, 2.6; **L10:** RDG 1.7, 1.8; **L11:** RDG 1.7, 1.8, 3.2;	**L1:** 2.1, 2.3, 2.9; **L2:** 1.3, 1.4, 1.6, 2.1, 2.3, 4.1, 4.2; **L3:** 1.3, 2.1, 2.3, 3.1, 3.3, 3.5, 4.1, 4.2; **L4:** 2.1, 2.3, 4.1, 4.2; **L5:** 1.4, 1.6, 2.1, 2.3, 4.1, 4.2, 6.1; **L6:** 2.1, 2.3, 3.13, 4.1, 4.2; **L7:** 2.1, 2.3, 4.2, 5.8, 6.1; **L8:** 1.4, 2.1, 2.3, 4.1, 4.2, 6.5; **L10:** 2.1, 2.3; **L11:** 2.1, 2.3, 4.1, 4.2;
2	**L1:** RDG 1.1, 2.2, 2.3; **L2:** RDG 1.7, 2.2, 2.3; **L3:** RDG 1.7, 2.1, 2.9; **L4:** RDG 1.7, 1.8, 2.2, 2.3, 3.2, 3.7, 3.11; **L5:** RDG 1.7, 2.2, 2.3; **L6:** RDG 1.7, 2.9; **L7:** RDG 1.7, 1.8, 2.2, 2.3, 3.2, 4.2, 4.9; **L8:** RDG 1.7, 2.2, 2.3; **L9:** RDG 1.7, 2.9; **L10:** RDG 1.7, 1.8, 2.1; **L11:** RDG 1.7, 1.8, 3.2;	**L1:** 2.1, 2.3, 2.9; 4.1, 4.2; **L2:** 1.4, 2.1, 2.3, 4.1, 4.2, 6.5; **L3:** 1.3, 2.1, 2.3, 3.1, 3.3, 3.5, 4.1, 4.2; **L4:** 2.1, 2.3, 4.1, 4.2, 5.8, 6.1; **L5:** 1.4, 1.5, 2.1, 2.3, 4.1, 4.2, 5.8, 6.1; **L6:** 2.1, 2.3, 3.6, 3.13, 4.1, 4.2; **L7:** 2.1, 2.3, 4.2; **L8:** 2.1, 2.3, 4.1, 4.2, 6.1, 6.2; **L10:** 2.1, 2.3; **L11:** 2.1, 2.3, 4.1, 4.2;
3	**L1:** RDG 1.7, 2.2, 2.3; **L2:** RDG 1.7, 2.2, 2.3; **L3:** RDG 1.7, 2.9; **L4:** RDG 1.7, 1.8, 2.2, 2.3, 3.2, 3.6; **L5:** RDG 1.7, 2.2, 2.3; **L6:** RDG 1.7, 2.9; **L7:** RDG 1.7, 1.8, 2.2, 2.3, 3.2, 3.11, 3.14, 4.2, 4.9; **L8:** RDG 1.7, 2.2, 2.3; **L9:** RDG 1.7; **L10:** RDG 1.7, 1.8, 2.1; **L11:** RDG 1.7, 1.8, 3.2;	**L1:** 2.1, 2.3, 2.9, 4.1, 4.2; **L2:** 1.4, 2.1, 2.3, 4.1, 4.2, 6.1, 6.2, 6.5; **L3:** 1.3, 2.1, 2.3, 3.1, 4.1, 4.2; **L4:** 2.1, 2.3, 4.1, 4.2; **L5:** 1.5, 2.1, 2.3, 4.1, 4.2, 5.8, 6.1; **L6:** 2.1, 2.3, 3.1, 3.3, 3.6, 4.1, 4.2; **L7:** 2.1, 2.3, 4.2, 5.8, 6.1; **L8:** 2.1, 2.3, 4.1, 4.2, 6.1, 6.2; **L10:** 2.1, 2.3; **L11:** 2.1, 2.3, 4.1, 4.2;
4	**L1:** RDG 1.7, 2.2, 2.3; **L2:** RDG 1.7, 2.2, 2.3; **L3:** RDG 1.7, 2.9, 4.9; **L4:** RDG 1.7, 1.8, 2.2, 2.3, 3.2, 4.9; **L5:** RDG 1.7, 2.2, 2.3; **L6:** RDG 1.7, 2.9, 4.9; **L7:** RDG 1.7, 1.8, 2.2, 2.3, 3.2, 3.8, 3.11, 4.2, 4.9; **L8:** RDG 1.7, 2.2, 2.3; **L9:** RDG 1.7; **L10:** RDG 1.7, 1.8, 2.1; **L11:** RDG 1.7, 1.8, 3.2;	**L1:** 2.1, 2.3, 2.9, 4.1, 4.2; **L2:** 1.4, 2.01, 2.3, 4.1, 4.2, 6.1, 6.2; **L3:** 1.3, 2.1, 2.3, 3.1, 4.1, 4.2; **L4:** 2.1, 2.3, 4.1, 4.2; **L5:** 2.1, 2.3, 4.1, 4.2, 5.8, 6.1, 6.2, 6.5; **L6:** 2.1, 2.3, 3.1, 4.1, 4.2; **L7:** 2.1, 2.3, 4.2, 5.8, 6.1, 6.2; **L8:** 1.5, 2.1, 2.3, 4.1, 4.2, 6.1, 6.2, 6.5; **L9:** 3.1; **L10:** 2.1, 2.3; **L11:** 2.1, 2.3, 4.1, 4.2;
5	**L1:** RDG 1.7, 2.2, 2.3; **L2:** RDG 1.7, 2.2, 2.3; **L3:** RDG 1.7, 2.9, 4.9; **L4:** RDG 1.7, 1.8, 2.2, 2.3, 3.2, 3.6, 3.16, 4.9; **L5:** RDG 1.7, 2.2, 2.3; **L6:** RDG 1.7, 2.9; **L7:** RDG 1.7, 1.8, 2.3, 3.2, 3.4, 3.9, 3.11, 4.2, 4.9; **L8:** RDG 1.7, 2.2, 2.3, 3.4; **L9:** RDG 1.3, 1.7, 2.3, 3.6; **L10:** RDG 1.7, 1.8, 2.1; **L11:** RDG 1.7, 1.8, 3.2;	**L1:** 2.1, 2.3, 2.9, 4.2; **L2:** 2.1, 2.3, 4.1, 4.2, 6.1, 6.2, 6.5; **L3:** 1.3, 2.1, 2.3, 3.9, 4.1, 4.2; **L4:** 2.1, 2.3, 4.2; **L5:** 2.1, 2.3, 4.2, 6.1, 6.2; **L6:** 2.1, 2.3, 3.1, 4.2; **L7:** 2.1, 2.3, 4.2, 5.8, 6.1, 6.2; **L8:** 2.1, 2.3, 4.1, 4.2, 5.4, 5.5, 6.1, 6.2; **L9:** 3.1, 3.4; **L10:** 2.1, 2.3; **L11:** 2.1, 2.3, 4.1, 4.2;
6	**L1:** RDG 1.7, 2.3; **L2:** RDG 1.7, 2.2, 2.3; **L3:** RDG 1.7, 2.9, 4.9; **L4:** RDG 1.7, 1.8, 2.3, 3.2, 4.9; **L5:** RDG 1.7, 2.2, 2.3; **L6:** RDG 1.7, 2.9; **L7:** RDG 1.7, 1.8, 2.3, 3.2, 3.10, 3.11, 4.2; **L8:** RDG 1.7, 2.2, 2.3; **L9:** RDG 1.7, 2.3, 2.6; **L10:** RDG 1.7, 1.8, 2.1; **L11:** RDG 1.7, 1.81, 3.2;	**L1:** 2.1, 2.3, 2.9, 4.2; **L2:** 2.1, 2.3, 4.1, 4.2, 6.1, 6.2, 6.5; **L3:** 1.3, 2.1, 2.3, 3.9, 4.1, 4.2; **L4:** 2.1, 2.3, 4.2; **L5:** 1.4, 2.1, 2.3, 4.2, 6.1, 6.2, 6.5; **L6:** 2.1, 2.3, 3.6, 3.9, 4.2; **L7:** 2.1, 2.3, 4.2, 5.8, 6.1, 6.2; **L8:** 2.1, 2.3, 4.1, 4.2, 6.1, 6.2, 6.5; **L9:** 3.1, 3.9, 4.1, 4.2; **L10:** 2.1, 2.3; **L11:** 2.1, 2.3, 4.1, 4.2;
7	**L1:** RDG 1.7, 2.3; **L2:** RDG 1.7, 2.2, 2.3; **L3:** RDG 1.7, 2.9, 4.9; **L4:** RDG 1.7, 1.8, 2.3, 3.2, 3.6, 4.9; **L5:** RDG 1.7, 2.3; **L6:** RDG 1.7, 2.9; **L7:** RDG 1.7, 1.8, 2.3, 3.2, 3.10, 3.11, 4.2, 4.9; **L8:** RDG 1.7, 2.3; **L9:** RDG 1.7, 2.3; **L10:** RDG 1.7, 1.8, 2.1; **L11:** RDG 1.7, 1.8, 3.2;	**L1:** 2.1, 2.3, 2.9, 4.2; **L2:** 1.2, 2.1, 2.3, 4.2, 6.1, 6.2, 6.5; **L3:** 1.3, 2.1, 2.3, 4.1, 4.2; **L4:** 2.1, 2.3, 4.2, 5.4, 5.5; **L5:** 1.5, 2.1, 2.3, 4.2, 6.1, 6.2, 6.5; **L6:** 2.1, 2.3, 3.9, 4.2; **L7:** 2.1, 2.3, 4.2, 5.8, 6.1, 6.2; **L8:** 1.4, 2.1, 2.3, 4.1, 4.2, 6.1, 6.2, 6.5; **L9:** 4.1, 4.2; **L10:** 2.1, 2.3; **L11:** 2.1, 2.3, 4.1, 4.2;
8	**L1:** RDG 1.7, 2.3; **L2:** RDG 1.7, 2.3; **L3:** RDG 1.7, 3.1; **L4:** RDG 1.7, 1.8, 2.2, 2.3, 3.2; **L5:** RDG 1.7, 2.3; **L6:** RDG 1.7, 2.9; **L7:** RDG 1.7, 1.8, 2.3, 3.2, 3.8, 3.11, 4.2; **L8:** RDG 1.7, 2.3, 3.8; **L9:** RDG 1.7, 2.3; **L10:** RDG 1.7, 1.8; **L11:** RDG 1.7, 1.8, 3.2;	**L1:** 2.1, 2.3, 2.9, 4.2, 5.8; **L2:** 1.4, 2.1, 2.3, 4.2, 6.1, 6.2, 6.5; **L3:** 1.3. 2.1, 2.3. 4.1. 4.2; **L4:** 2.1, 2.3, 4.2, 5.4, 5.5; **L5:** 2.1, 2.3, 4.2, 6.1, 6.2, 6.5; **L6:** 2.1, 2.3, 3.11, 4.2; **L7:** 2.1, 2.3, 4.2, 5.8, 6.1, 6.2; **L8:** 1.4, 2.1, 2.3, 4.1, 4.2, 6.1, 6.2, 6.5; **L9:** 3.5, 4.1, 5.2; **L10:** 2.1, 2.3, 3.9; **L11:** 2.1, 2.3, 4.1, 4.2;
9	**L1:** RDG 1.7, 2.3; **L2:** RDG 1.7, 2.3; **L3:** RDG 1.7, 3.1; **L4:** RDG 1.7, 1.8, 2.3, 3.2; **L5:** RDG 1.7, 2.3; **L6:** RDG 1.7, 2.9; **L7:** RDG 1.7, 1.8, 2.3, 3.2, 3.4, 3.8, 3.11, 4.2; **L8:** RDG 1.7, 2.3; **L9:** RDG 1.7; **L10:** RDG 1.7, 1.8, 2.1; **L11:** RDG 1.7, 1.8, 3.2;	**L1:** 2.1, 2.3, 2.9, 4.2, 5.8; **L2:** 1.4, 2.1, 2.3, 4.2, 6.1, 6.2, 6.5; **L3:** 1.3, 2.1, 2.3, 3.3, 4.1, 4.2; **L4:** 2.1, 2.3, 4.2, 6.5; **L5:** 2.1, 2.3, 4.2, 6.1, 6.2, 6.5; **L6:** 2.1, 2.3, 3.2, 4.2; **L7:** 2.1, 2.3, 4.2, 5.8, 6.1, 6.2; **L8:** 1.2, 2.1, 2.3, 4.1, 4.2, 6.1, 6.2, 6.5; **L9:** 4.1, 4.2, 3.8; **L10:** 2.1, 2.3, 3.9; **L11:** 2.1, 2.3, 4.1, 4.2;
10	**L1:** RDG 1.7, 2.3; **L2:** RDG 1.7, 2.3; **L3:** RDG 1.7, 2.6; **L4:** RDG 1.7, 1.8, 2.3, 3.2; **L5:** RDG 1.7, 2.3; **L6:** RDG 1.7, 2.2, 2.6, 2.9; **L7:** RDG 1.7, 1.8, 2.3, 3.2, 3.11, 4.2, 4.9; **L8:** RDG 1.7, 2.3; **L9:** RDG 1.7; **L10:** RDG 1.7, 1.8, 2.1; **L11:** RDG 1.7, 1.8, 3.2;	**L1:** 2.1, 2.3, 2.9, 4.2; **L2:** 1.4, 2.1, 2.3, 4.2, 6.1, 6.2, 6.5; **L3:** 1.3, 2.1, 2.3, 3.3, 4.1, 4.2; **L4:** 2.1, 2.3, 4.2; **L5:** 2.1, 2.3, 4.21, 6.1, 6.2, 6.5; **L6:** 2.1. 2.3. 3.10. 4.2. 5.8; **L7:** 2.1, 2.3, 4.2, 5.8, 6.1, 6.2; **L8:** 1.4, 2.1, 2.3, 4.1, 4.2, 6.1, 6.2, 6.5; **L10:** 2.1, 2.3, 3.11; **L11:** 2.1, 2.3, 4.1, 4.2
11	**L1:** RDG 1.7, 2.3; **L2:** RDG 1.7, 2.3; **L3:** RDG 1.7, 2.6; **L4:** RDG 1.7, 1.8, 2.3, 3.2, 3.4, 3.6; **L5:** RDG 1.7, 2.3; **L6:** RDG 1.7, 2.9; **L7:** RDG 1.7, 1.8, 2.3, 3.2, 3.11, 4.2, 4.9; **L8:** RDG 1.7, 2.3; **L9:** RDG 1.7, 2.9; **L10:** RDG 1.7, 1.8, 2.1; **L11:** RDG 1.7, 1.8, 3.2;	**L1:** 2.1, 2.3, 2.9, 4.2; **L2:** 1.4, 2.1, 2.3, 4.2, 6.1, 6.2, 6.5; **L3:** 1.3, 2.1, 2.3, 3.3, 3.9, 4.1, 4.2; **L4:** 2.1, 2.3, 4.2; **L5:** 1.1, 2.1, 2.3, 4.2, 6.1, 6.2, 6.5; **L6:** 2.1, 2.3, 3.5, 4.2, 5.8; **L7:** 2.1, 2.3, 4.2, 5.8, 6.1, 6.2; **L8:** 1.4, 2.1, 2.3, 4.1, 4.2, 6.1, 6.2; **L9:** 3.4; **L10:** 2.1, 2.3, 3.6; **L11:** 2.1, 2.3, 4.1, 4.2;
12	**L1:** RDG 1.7, 2.3; **L2:** RDG 1.7, 2.3; **L3:** RDG 1.7, 1.8, 2.3, 3.2; **L4:** RDG 1.7, 1.8, 2.3, 3.2, 3.4; **L5:** RDG 1.7, 2.3; **L6:** RDG 1.7, 2.9, 3.4; **L7:** RDG 1.7, 1.8, 2.3, 3.2, 3.7, 3.11, 4.2; **L8:** RDG 1.7, 2.3; **L9:** RDG 1.7, 2.9; **L10:** RDG 1.7, 1.8, 3.2; **L11:** RDG 1.7, 1.8, 3.2;	**L1:** 2.1, 2.3, 2.9, 4.2; **L2:** 1.4, 2.1, 2.3, 4.2, 6.1, 6.2, 6.5; **L3:** 1.3, 2.1, 2.3, 3.9, 4.1, 4.2; **L4:** 2.1, 2.3, 4.2; **L5:** 1.4, 2.1, 2.3, 4.2, 6.1, 6.5; **L6:** 2.1, 2.3, 3.6; **L7:** 2.1, 2.3, 4.2, 5.8, 6.1, 6.2; **L8:** 1.4, 2.1, 2.3, 4.1, 4.2, 6.1, 6.2, 6.5; **L9:** 3.1; **L10:** 2.1, 2.3, 3.11; **L11:** 2.1, 2.3, 4.1, 4.2;

CASAS: Comprehensive Adult Student Assessment System
CCRS: College and Career Readiness Standards (R=Reading; W=Writing; SL=Speaking/Listening; L=Language)
ELPS: English Language Proficiency Standards

CASAS Competencies	CCRS Correlations, Level A	ELPS Correlations, Level 2
L1: 0.1.2, 0.1.5, 0.2.1, 7.4.1; **L2:** 0.1.2, 0.1.4, 0.1.5, 0.2.1; **L3:** 0.1.2, 0.1.4, 0.1.5, 0.1.6, 0.2.1; **L4:** 0.1.2, 0.1.5, 0.2.1, 4.1.1, 7.4.4, 7.7.3; **L5:** 0.1.2, 0.1.4, 0.1.5, 0.1.6, 0.2.1; **L6:** 0.1.2, 0.1.4, 0.1.5; **L7:** 0.1.2, 0.1.5, 4.8.1, 4.8.2; **L8:** 0.1.2, 0.1.4, 0.1.5, 0.1.6, 0.2.1; **L9:** 0.1.2, 0.1.4, 0.1.5, 0.1.6, 0.2.1; **L10:** 0.1.2, 0.1.5, 0.1.6, 0.2.1, 0.2.4, 7.4.1; **L11:** 0.1.2, 0.1.4, 0.1.5, 0.1.6, 0.2.1;	**L1:** SL.K.6, L.1.5a, L.1.5b, L.1.5c, L.1.6; **L3:** L.1.1c, L.1.1d, L.1.1e, L.1.1g; **L4:** W.1.7, W.1.8, SL.K.3; **L6:** L.1.1h; **L7:** RI.1.1, RI.1.2, RI.1.4, SL.K.2, SL.1.4; **L8:** SL.1.1, SL.K.6; **L9:** L.1.1e, L.1.1g; **L10:** W.1.2, W.1.5, L.1.1l;	ELPS 1-3, 5, 7-10
L1: 0.1.2, 0.1.5, 0.2.1, 7.4.1; **L2:** 0.1.2, 0.1.4, 0.1.5, 0.2.1; **L3:** 0.1.2, 0.1.4, 0.1.5; **L4:** 0.1.2, 0.1.5, 0.2.1; **L5:** 0.1.2, 0.1.4, 0.1.5, 0.2.1; **L6:** 0.1.2, 0.1.5, 0.1.6, 0.2.1; **L7:** 0.1.2, 0.1.5, 2.4.2, 2.4.3, 4.5.6, 7.4.4, 7.7.3; **L8:** 0.1.2, 0.1.4, 0.1.5, 0.1.6, 0.2.1; **L9:** 0.1.2, 0.1.5; **L10:** 0.1.2, 0.1.5, 0.1.6; **L11:** 0.1.2, 0.1.4, 0.1.5, 0.1.6, 0.2.1, 7.5.5; **L1:** SL.1.1, SL.K.6, L.1.5a, L.1.5b, L.1.5c, L.1.6;	**L3:** L.1.1c, L.1.1d, L.1.1e, L.1.1g; **L4:** RI/RL.1.1, RI.1.2, RI.1.4, SL.K.2, SL.1.4; **L5:** SL.K.3; **L6:** L.1.1e, L.1.1g; **L7:** W.1.7, W.1.8; **L8:** SL.1.1a, SL.1.1b, SL.1.1c, SL.K.6; **L9:** L.1.1c, L.1.1h, L.1.1k; **L10:** W.1.2, W.1.5, L.1.1l;	ELPS 1-3, 5-10
L1: 0.1.2, 0.1.5, 1.2.9, 7.4.1; **L2:** 0.1.2, 0.1.5, 0.2.1; **L3:** 0.1.2, 0.1.5; **L4:** 0.1.2, 0.1.5, 0.2.1, 1.6.4, 4.5.6, 7.4.4, 7.7.3; **L5:** 0.1.2, 0.1.5, 0.1.6, 0.2.1; **L6:** 0.1.2, 0.1.5, 0.1.6, 0.2.1; **L7:** 0.1.2, 0.1.5, 1.3.1; **L8:** 0.1.2, 0.1.4, 0.1.5, 0.1.6, 1.3.3; **L9:** 0.1.2; **L10:** 0.1.2, 0.1.5, 0.1.6; **L11:** 0.1.2, 0.1.4, 0.1.5, 0.1.6, 0.2.1, 4.8.3;	**L1:** SL.1.1a, SL.1.1b, SL.1.1c, SL.K.6, L.1.1l, L.1.2g, L.1.5a, L.1.5b, L.1.5c, L.1.6; **L3:** SL.1.4, L.1.1c, L.1.1d, L.1.1e, L.1.1g; **L4:** RI/RL.1.1, W.1.7, W.1.8; **L6:** L.1.1d, L.1.1e, L.1.1g; **L7:** RI/RL.1.1, RI.1.2, RI.1.4; **L8:** SL.1.1a, SL.1.1b, SL.1.1c, SL.K.6; **L10:** W.1.2, W.1.5, L.1.1l;	ELPS 1-3, 5, 7-10
L1: 0.1.2, 0.1.5, 0.2.1, 0.2.4, 7.4.1; **L2:** 0.1.2, 0.1.5, 0.2.1, 0.2.4; **L3:** 0.1.2, 0.1.5, 0.2.1, 0.2.4, 7.1.4; **L4:** 0.1.2, 0.1.5, 2.8.3, 4.5.6, 7.4.4, 7.7.3; **L5:** 0.1.2, 0.1.5, 0.1.6; **L6:** 0.1.2, 0.1.5, 0.1.6, 0.2.1, 0.2.4, 6.7.2; **L7:** 0.1.2, 0.1.5, 7.7.4; **L8:** 0.1.2, 0.1.4, 0.1.5, 0.1.6, 0.2.3; **L9:** 0.1.2; **L10:** 0.1.2, 0.1.5, 0.1.6, 0.2.4; **L11:** 0.1.2, 0.1.4, 0.1.5, 0.1.6, 0.2.1, 4.8.3, 4.8.4;	**L1:** SL.1.1a, SL.1.1b, SL.1.1c, SL.K.6, L.1.1l, L.1.5a, L.1.5b, L.1.5c, L.1.6; **L3:** L.1.1c, L.1.1d, L.1.1e, L.1.1g, L.1.1k; **L4:** RI.1.7, W.1.7, W.1.8, SL.K.3; **L5:** SL.1.4; **L7:** RI/RL.1.1, RI.1.2, RI.1.4, SL.K.2; **L8:** SL.1.1a, SL.1.1b, SL.1.1c, SL.K.6; **L10:** W.1.2, W.1.5, L.1.1l;	ELPS 1-3, 5-10
L1: 0.1.2, 0.1.5, 7.4.1, 8.2.6; **L2:** 0.1.2, 0.1.5, 4.1.8, 8.2.6; **L3:** 0.1.2, 0.1.5, 8.2.6; **L4:** 0.1.2, 0.1.5, 1.4.2, 1.5.3, 4.5.6, 7.4.4, 7.7.3; **L5:** 0.1.2, 0.1.5, 0.1.6, 1.4.2; **L6:** 0.1.2, 0.1.5, 0.1.6, 1.4.2; **L7:** 0.1.2, 0.1.5, 1.5.2, 6.7.2, 7.2.3; **L8:** 0.1.2, 0.1.5, 0.1.6, 2.2.1, 2.2.5; **L9:** 0.1.2, 1.9.1; **L10:** 0.1.2, 0.1.5, 0.1.6, 0.2.4, 1.4.1; **L11:** 0.1.2, 0.1.4, 0.1.5, 0.1.6, 0.2.1, 4.8.3, 4.8.4;	**L1:** SL.1.1a, SL.1.1b, SL.1.1c, SL.K.6, L.1.5a, L.1.5b, L.1.5c, L.1.6; **L3:** L.1.1c, L.1.1d, L.1.1e, L.1.1g, L.1.2h; **L4:** RI.1.9, W.1.7, W.1.8; **L5:** SL.K.3; **L6:** SL.1.1a, SL.1.1b, SL.1.1c, SL.K.6; **L7:** RI/RL.1.1, RI.1.2, RI.1.4, RI.1.5, SL.K.2, SL.1.4; **L10:** W.1.2, W.1.5, L.1.1l;	ELPS 1-5, 7-10
L1: 0.1.2, 0.1.5, 0.2.4, 7.4.1; **L2:** 0.1.2, 0.1.5, 0.2.4; **L3:** 0.1.2, 0.1.5, 0.2.4; **L4:** 0.1.2, 0.1.5, 2.7.1, 4.5.6, 7.7.3, 7.4.4; **L5:** 0.1.2, 0.1.5, 0.1.6, 0.2.1; **L6:** 0.1.2, 0.1.5, 0.1.6, 0.2.1; **L7:** 0.1.2, 0.1.5, 5.2.1; **L8:** 0.1.2, 0.1.5, 0.1.6, 0.1.8, 0.2.1; **L9:** 0.1.2, 0.1.5, 0.1.6, 0.2.1; **L10:** 0.1.2, 0.1.5, 0.1.6; **L11:** 0.1.2, 0.1.4, 0.1.5, 0.1.6, 0.2.1, 7.3.2;	**L1:** SL.1.1a, SL.1.1b, SL.1.1c, SL.K.6, L.1.1l, L.1.5a, L.1.6; **L3:** L.1.1c, L.1.1d, L.1.1e, L.1.1g; **L4:** RI/RL.1.1, RI.1.4, W.1.7, W.1.8; **L5:** SL.K.3, SL.1.4; **L6:** L.1.1c, L.1.1d, L.1.1e, L.1.1g; **L7:** RI/RL.1.1, RI.1.2, SL.K.2; **L8:** SL.1.1a, SL.1.1b, SL.1.1c, SL.K.6; **L9:** L.1.1c, L.1.1d, L.1.1e, L.1.1g, L.1.1k, L.1.1l; **L10:** W.1.2, W.1.5, L.1.1l;	ELPS 1-3, 5, 7-10
L1: 0.1.2, 0.1.5, 3.6.3, 7.4.1; **L2:** 0.1.2, 0.1.5, 3.1.2; **L3:** 0.1.2, 0.1.5, 0.2.1, 3.1.2; **L4:** 0.1.2, 0.1.5, 3.3.2, 3.4.1, 4.5.6, 7.7.3, 7.4.4; **L5:** 0.1.2, 0.1.5, 0.1.6, 0.2.1, 3.6.2; **L6:** 0.1.2, 0.1.5, 0.1.6; **L7:** 0.1.2, 0.1.5, 0.2.1, 7.5.4; **L8:** 0.1.2, 0.1.4, 0.1.5, 0.1.6, 0.1.8, 4.6.5; **L9:** 0.1.2; **L10:** 0.1.2, 0.1.5, 0.1.6, 3.6.3; **L11:** 0.1.2, 0.1.4, 0.1.5, 0.1.6, 0.2.1, 4.8.5, 7.3.2;	**L1:** SL.1.1a, SL.1.1b, SL.1.1c, SL.K.6, L.1.5a, L.1.5b, L.1.5c, L.1.6; **L2:** SL.K.3; **L3:** L.1.1j; **L4:** W.1.7, W.1.8; **L5:** SL.K.3; **L6:** L.1.1c, L.1.1d, L.1.1e, L.1.1g; **L7:** RI/RL.1.1, RI.1.2, RI.1.4, RI.1.5, SL.K.2, SL.1.4; **L8:** SL.1.1a, SL.1.1b, SL.1.1c, SL.K.6; **L9:** L.1.1h, L.1.1l; **L10:** W.1.2, W.1.5, L.1.1l;	ELPS 1-3, 5, 7-10
L1: 0.1.2, 0.1.5, 4.4.4, 7.1.1, 7.4.1; **L2:** 0.1.2, 0.1.5, 4.1.5; **L3:** 0.1.2, 0.1.5, 0.2.1, 3.1.2; **L4:** 0.1.2, 0.1.5, 4.1.3, 4.1.5, 4.5.6, 7.4.4, 7.7.3; **L5:** 0.1.2, 0.1.5, 0.1.6, 0.2.1; **L6:** 0.1.2, 0.1.5, 0.1.6, 0.2.1; **L7:** 0.1.2, 0.1.5, 0.2.1, 7.1.1; **L8:** 0.1.2, 0.1.4, 0.1.5, 0.1.6, 0.1.8, 0.2.1, 4.1.5, 4.6.5; **L9:** 0.1.2; **L10:** 0.1.2, 0.1.5, 0.1.6; **L11:** 0.1.2, 0.1.4, 0.1.5, 0.1.6, 0.2.1, 4.8.1, 4.8.5;	**L1:** SL.1.1a, SL.1.1b, SL.1.1c, SL.K.6, L.1.5a, L.1.5b, L.1.5c, L.1.6; **L2:** SL.K.3; **L4:** W.1.7, W.1.8; **L7:** RI/RL.1.1, RI.1.2, RI.1.4, SL.K.2; **L8:** RI.1.5, SL.1.1a, SL.1.1b, SL.1.1c, SL.K.3, SL.1.4, SL.K.6; **L9:** L.1.1h, L.1.1l; **L10:** W.1.2, W.1.5, L.1.1l;	ELPS 1-3, 5, 7-10
L1: 0.1.2, 0.1.5, 7.4.1; **L2:** 0.1.2, 0.1.5; **L3:** 0.1.2, 0.1.5, 0.2.1, 3.1.2; **L4:** 0.1.2, 0.1.5, 2.1.7, 4.5.6, 7.4.4, 7.7.3; **L5:** 0.1.2, 0.1.4, 0.1.5, 0.1.6, 2.8.6; **L6:** 0.1.2, 0.1.5, 0.1.6; **L7:** 0.1.2, 0.1.5, 0.2.1, 6.7.2, 7.1.1; **L8:** 0.1.2, 0.1.4, 0.1.5, 0.1.6, 2.8.6; **L9:** 0.1.2; **L10:** 0.1.2, 0.1.5, 0.1.6; **L11:** 0.1.2, 0.1.4, 0.1.5, 0.1.6, 0.2.1, 7.1.2;	**L1:** SL.1.1a, SL.1.1b, SL.1.1c, SL.1.4, SL.K.6, L.1.6; **L2:** SL.K.3; **L3:** L.1.1e, L.1.1g; **L4:** W.1.7, W.1.8; **L5:** SL.K.3; **L6:** L.1.1d, L.1.2h; **L7:** RI/RL.1.1, RI.1.2, RI.1.4, RI.1.7; **L8:** SL.1.1a, SL.1.1b, SL.1.1c, SL.K.3, SL.K.6, L.1.1b; **L9:** L.1.1b, L.1.1c, L.1.2h, L.1.2i; **L10:** W.1.2, W.1.5, L.1.1l, L.1.2e;	ELPS 1-3, 5, 7-10
L1: 0.1.2, 0.1.5, 1.2.8, 7.4.1; **L2:** 0.1.2, 0.1.5, 1.2.8; **L3:** 0.1.2, 0.1.5, 1.2.8, 2.6.3; **L4:** 0.1.2, 0.1.5, 1.2.8, 1.6.1, 3.5.1, 3.5.2, 4.5.6, 7.4.4, 7.7.3; **L5:** 0.1.2, 0.1.4, 0.1.5, 0.1.6, 1.2.8; **L6:** 0.1.2, 0.1.5, 0.1.6, 1.2.1; **L7:** 0.1.2, 0.1.5, 0.2.1; **L8:** 0.1.2, 0.1.5, 0.1.6, 2.6.4; **L9:** 0.1.2; **L10:** 0.1.2, 0.1.5, 0.1.6; **L11:** 0.1.2, 0.1.4, 0.1.5, 0.1.6, 0.2.1, 4.6.5, 4.8.3;	**L1:** SL.1.1a, SL.1.1b, SL.1.1c, SL.K.6, L.1.5a, L.1.5b, L.1.5c, L.1.6; **L2:** SL.K.3; **L3:** L.1.1c, L.1.1e, L.1.1f, L.1.1g, L.1.2h, L.1.2i; **L4:** W.1.7, W.1.8; **L5:** SL.K.3; **L6:** SL.1.4, L.1.1f, L.1.1l, L.1.2g, L.1.2i; **L7:** RI/RL.1.1, RI.1.2, RI.1.4, SL.K.2, L.1. 4; **L8:** SL.1.1a, SL.1.1b, SL.1.1c; **L9:** L.1.1c, L.1.1e, L.1.1g; **L10:** W.1.2, W.1.5, L.1.1l, L.1.2e;	ELPS 1-5, 7-10
L1: 0.1.2, 0.1.5, 2.1.2, 7.4.1; **L2:** 0.1.2, 0.1.5, 2.1.2; **L3:** 0.1.2, 0.1.5; **L4:** 0.1.2, 0.1.5, 1.4.8, 3.4.1, 3.4.2, 4.3.1, 4.5.6, 7.4.4, 7.7.3; **L5:** 0.1.2, 0.1.4, 0.1.5, 0.1.6; **L6:** 0.1.2, 0.1.5, 0.1.6; **L7:** 0.1.2, 0.1.5, 4.2.6, 4.3.1; **L8:** 0.1.2, 0.1.5, 0.1.6, 5.5.6; **L9:** 0.1.2; **L10:** 0.1.2, 0.1.5, 0.1.6; **L11:** 0.1.2, 0.1.5, 0.1.6, 0.2.1, 4.3.4;	**L1:** SL.1.1a, SL.1.1b, SL.1.1c, SL.K.6, L.1.5a, L.1.5b, L.1.5c, L.1.6; **L2:** SL.K.3; **L3:** L.1.1c, L.1.1e, L.1.2h; **L4:** W.1.7, W.1.8; **L5:** SL.K.3; **L6:** SL.1.4; **L7:** RI/RL.1.1, RI.1.2, RI.1.4, SL.K.2; **L8:** SL.1.1a, SL.1.1b, SL.1.1c, SL.K.3, SL.K.6; **L9:** L.1.1g, L.1.1h, L.1.1l; **L10:** W.1.2, W.1.5, L.1.1l;	ELPS 1-3, 5, 7-10
L1: 0.1.2, 0.1.5, 4.4.4, 7.4.1; **L2:** 0.1.2, 0.1.4, 0.1.5, 4.2.4; **L3:** 0.1.2, 0.1.5, 4.4.4; **L4:** 0.1.2, 0.1.5, 4.2.1, 4.5.6, 7.4.4, 7.7.3; **L5:** 0.1.2, 0.1.4, 0.1.5, 0.1.6, 4.1.6, 4.6.5; **L6:** 0.1.2, 0.1.5, 0.1.6; **L7:** 0.1.2, 0.1.5, 2.5.2; **L8:** 0.1.2, 0.1.4, 0.1.5, 0.1.6, 4.1.6, 4.6.5; **L9:** 0.1.2; **L10:** 0.1.2, 0.1.5, 0.1.6, 4.4.4; **L11:** 0.1.2, 0.1.5, 0.1.6, 0.2.1, 4.6.4, 4.6.5,	**L1:** SL.1.1a, SL.1.1b, SL.1.1c, SL.K.6, L.1.5a, L.1.5b, L.1.5c, L.1.6; **L2:** SL.K.3; **L4:** W.1.7, W.1.8; **L5:** SL.K.3; **L6:** L.1.1k, L.1.2a; **L7:** RI/RL.1.1, RI.1.2, RI.1.4; **L8:** SL.1.1a, SL.1.1b, SL.1.1c, SL.K.3, SL.K.6; **L9:** L.1.1l; **L10:** W.1.2, W.1.5, L.1.1l;	ELPS 1-3, 5, 7-10

All units of *Future* meet most of the **EFF Content Standards**. For details, as well as for correlations to other state standards, go to www.pearsoneltusa.com/future2e.

AUTHOR, SERIES CONSULTANT, AND LEARNING EXPERT

Sarah Lynn is an ESOL teacher, trainer, author, and curriculum design specialist. She has taught adult learners in the U.S. and abroad for decades, most recently at Harvard University's Center for Workforce Development. As a teacher-trainer and frequent conference presenter throughout the United States and Latin America, Ms. Lynn has led sessions and workshops on topics such as: fostering student agency and resilience, brain-based teaching techniques, literacy and learning, and teaching in a multilevel classroom. Collaborating with program leaders, teachers, and students, she has developed numerous curricula for college and career readiness, reading and writing skill development, and contextualized content for adult English language learners. Ms. Lynn has co-authored several Pearson ELT publications, including *Business Across Cultures, Future, Future U.S. Citizens,* and *Project Success.* She holds a master's degree in TESOL from Teachers College, Columbia University.

SERIES CONSULTANTS

Ronna Magy has worked as an ESOL classroom teacher, author, teacher-trainer, and curriculum development specialist. She served as the ESL Teacher Adviser in charge of professional development for the Division of Adult and Career Education of the Los Angeles Unified School District. She is a frequent conference presenter on the College and Career Readiness Standards (CCRS), the English Language Proficiency Standards (ELPS), and on the language, literacy, and soft skills needed for academic and workplace success. Ms. Magy has authored/ co-authored and trained teachers on modules for CALPRO, the California Adult Literacy Professional Development Project, including modules on integrating and contextualizing workforce skills in the ESOL classroom and evidence-based writing instruction. She is the author of adult ESL publications on English for the workplace, reading and writing, citizenship, and life skills and test preparation. Ms. Magy holds a master's degree in social welfare from the University of California at Berkeley.

Federico Salas-Isnardi has worked in adult education as a teacher, administrator, professional developer, materials writer, and consultant. He contributed to a number of state projects in Texas including the adoption of adult education content standards and the design of statewide professional development and accountability systems.

Over nearly 30 years he has conducted professional development seminars for thousands of teachers, law enforcement officers, social workers, and business people in the United States and abroad. His areas of concentration have been educational leadership, communicative competence, literacy, intercultural communication, citizenship, and diversity education. He has taught customized workplace ESOL and Spanish programs as well as high-school equivalence classes, citizenship and civics, labor market information seminars, and middle-school mathematics. Mr. Salas-Isnardi has been a contributing writer or series consultant for a number of ESL publications, and he has co-authored curriculum for site-based workforce ESL and Spanish classes.

Mr. Salas-Isnardi is a certified diversity trainer. He has a Masters Degree in Applied Linguistics and doctoral level coursework in adult education.

AUTHOR

Wendy Pratt Long has previously worked as an EFL teacher and administrator. She has taught English to children, adolescents, and adults at all language levels in Mexico and Canada. She earned a master's degree in applied linguistics from the Universidad de las Americas, in Puebla, Mexico. Now working in the field of educational publishing, she has authored and co-authored ancillary materials including *Center Stage 2 Teacher's Edition, Summit 2 Workbook, Top Notch 2 Workbook, Top Notch Copy & Go* (Fundamentals and Level 3), and *Top Notch Assessment Packages* (Fundamentals and Levels 2 and 3). She has collaborated with Pearson on numerous other projects, including the assessment programs for *Center Stage 2* and *Summit 2* and CD-ROMs for multiple levels of the *WorldView* and *Trends* series.

ACKNOWLEDGMENTS

The Publisher would like to acknowledge the teachers, students, and survey and focus-group participants for their valuable input. Thank you to the following reviewers and consultants who made suggestions, contributed to this *Future* revision, and helped make *Future: English for Work, Life, and Academic Success* even better in this second edition. There are many more who also shared their comments and experiences using *Future*—a big thank you to all.

Fuad Al-Daraweesh The University of Toledo, Toledo, OH

Denise Alexander Bucks County Community College, Newtown, PA

Isabel Alonso Bergen Community College, Hackensack, NJ

Veronica Avitia LeBarron Park, El Paso, TX

Maria Bazan-Myrick Houston Community College, Houston, TX

Sara M. Bulnes Miami Dade College, Miami, FL

Alexander Chakshiri Santa Maria High School, Santa Maria, CA

Scott C. Cohen, M.A.Ed. Bergen Community College, Paramus, NJ

Judit Criado Fiuza Mercy Center, Bronx, NY

Megan Ernst Glendale Community College, Glendale, CA

Rebecca Feit-Klein Essex County College Adult Learning Center, West Caldwell, NJ

Caitlin Floyd Nationalities Service Center, Philadelphia, PA

Becky Gould International Community High School, Bronx, NY

Ingrid Greenberg San Diego Continuing Education, San Diego Community College District, San Diego, CA

Steve Gwynne San Diego Continuing Education, San Diego, CA

Robin Hatfield, M.Ed. Learning Institute of Texas, Houston,TX

Coral Horton Miami Dade College, Kendall Campus, Miami, FL

Roxana Hurtado Miami-Dade County Public Schools, Miami, FL

Lisa Johnson City College of San Francisco, San Francisco, CA

Kristine R. Kelly ATLAS @ Hamline University, St. Paul, MN

Jennifer King Austin Community College, Austin, TX

Lia Lerner, Ed.D. Burbank Adult School, Burbank, CA

Ting Li The University of Toledo, Ottawa Hills, OH

Nichole M. Lucas University of Dayton, Dayton, OH

Ruth Luman Modesto Junior College, Modesto, CA

Josephine Majul El Monte-Rosemead adult School, El Monte, CA

Dr. June Ohrnberger Suffolk County Community College, Selden, NY

Sue Park The Learning Institute of Texas, Houston, TX

Dr. Sergei Paromchik Adult Education Department, Hillsborough County Public Schools, Tampa, FL

Patricia Patton Uniontown ESL, Uniontown, PA

Matthew Piech Amarillo College, Amarillo, TX

Guillermo Rocha Essex County College, NJ

Audrene Rowe Essex County School, Newark, NJ

Naomi Sato Glendale Community College, Glendale, CA

Alejandra Solis Lone Star College, Houston, TX

Geneva Tesh Houston Community College, Houston, TX

Karyna Tytar Lake Washington Institute of Technology, Kirkland, WA

Miguel Veloso Miami Springs Adult, Miami, FL

Minah Woo Howard Community College, Columbia, MD

1 MEET YOUR CLASSMATES

A ▶ Read and listen to the conversation.

Ayida:	Hi. My name is Ayida.
Carmen:	Hello, Ayida. I'm Carmen.
Ayida:	Nice to meet you, Carmen.
Carmen:	Nice to meet you, too.
Ayida:	Where are you from?
Carmen:	Peru. How about you?
Ayida:	I'm from Haiti.

B **WORK TOGETHER.** Practice the conversation. Use your own names and information.

2 TALK ABOUT YOUR GOALS

A Why are you studying English? Check the boxes.

☐ to get a job or a better job

☐ to get United States citizenship

☐ to continue my education

☐ to help my children with schoolwork

☐ to get into a career program

☐ other goal: _____

B **DISCUSS.** Talk about your goals. Do you have any of the same goals?

3 ASK FOR HELP

A Look at the pictures. Complete the conversations.

~~Can you speak more slowly?~~	Can you repeat that?
How do you pronounce this?	How do you spell that?
What does this word mean?	What's this called in English?

1.

Where are you from?

I'm sorry. *Can you speak more slowly?*

Oh, sorry. Where are you from?

I'm from Korea.

2.

_____

It's a pencil sharpener.

Thank you.

3.

Excuse me. _____

Registration.

New Student Registration

Registration?

Yes. That's right.

4.

Can you help me?

Sure.

_____

Occupation? It means a job or career.

5.

Please turn to page 45.

I'm sorry. _____

Sure. Please turn to page 45.

6.

My name is Chiao.

Chiao? _____

C-H-I-A-O.

Thanks.

B ▶ **SELF-ASSESS.** Listen and check your answers.

C **ROLE-PLAY.** Choose one conversation from Exercise A. Make your own conversation. Use different information.

Welcome to Class

4 LEARN ABOUT *FUTURE*

A EXPLORE. Turn to page iii. Answer the questions.

1. What information is on this page? _____

2. How many units are in this book? _____

3. Which unit is about food? _____

4. Which two units are about work? _____

B Sometimes you will need to go to the back of the book to do activities. Look at the chart. Find the pages in the book and complete the chart.

Page	
245	My Soft Skills Log
247	

C There is additional information for you in the back of the book. Find each section. Write the page number.

Grammar Reference _____   Map of the U.S. and Canada _____

Audio Script _____   Map of the World _____

Word List _____   Index _____

D Look at the inside front cover. How will you get the Pearson Practice English app with audio? _____

1 Making Connections

PREVIEW

Look at the picture. What do you see?
Where are the people? What are they doing?

UNIT GOALS

- ☐ Describe physical appearance
- ☐ Describe the way people look
- ☐ Complete an application
- ☐ Read identification cards
- ☐ Describe personalities
- ☐ Get to know someone

- ☐ **Academic skill:** Identify the topic and the main idea
- ☐ **Writing skill:** Introduce and explain steps of a routine
- ☐ **Workplace soft skill:** Show how you are inclusive

5

Vocabulary

Words to describe physical appearance

A **PREDICT.** Look at the pictures. What words describe the people?

Taha: short, thin

B ▶ **LISTEN AND POINT.** Then listen and repeat.

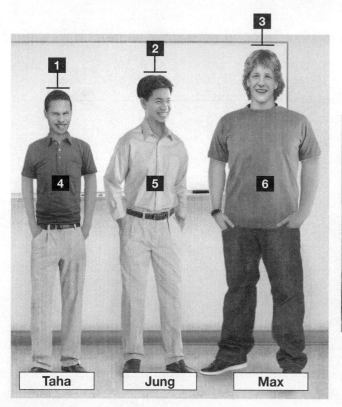

Taha   Jung   Max

Felix   Sara   Ana   Mai

Kwami   Yusef   David

Vocabulary

Words to describe physical appearance

A. height
1. short
2. average height
3. tall

B. weight
4. thin/slim
5. average weight
6. heavy

C. hair type
7. bald
8. curly
9. wavy
10. straight

D. hair length
11. short
12. medium-length
13. long

E. facial hair
14. a beard
15. a mustache
16. a goatee

C **WORK TOGETHER.** Look at the pictures. Student A, point to a picture. Describe the person. Student B, name the person.

Student A points to picture 1.
A: Short. Thin.
B: Taha?
A: Yes!

D **COMPLETE.** Look at the people in the pictures. Complete the sentences.

	Length	Type
1. Taha has	short	curly	hair.
2. Ana has	_____	_____	hair.
3. Mai has	_____	_____	hair.
4. David has	_____	_____	hair.

Study Tip

Make connections

Think of a friend. Write four words to describe your friend.

Show what you know!

1. **WRITE ABOUT IT.** Look at the words to describe weight, height, and hair. Which words describe you? Write four words on a piece of paper. Put your paper in a box.

   thin, short, long wavy hair

2. **TALK ABOUT IT.** Take a piece of paper from the box. Read the words to the class. Ask the class, "Who is it?"

I can describe people's height, weight, and hair. ■   I need more practice. ■

Listening and Speaking

Describe the way people look

1 BEFORE YOU LISTEN

CATEGORIZE. Read the words. Complete the chart.

| attractive | good-looking | ugly |
| beautiful | handsome | unattractive |

Positive	Negative
attractive	

2 LISTEN

A ▶ **LISTEN FOR MAIN IDEA.** Look at the picture of two co-workers. Listen to the conversation. What does Min ask about?

Min   Eva

a. a party
b. Eva's friend
c. a supervisor

B ▶ **LISTEN FOR DETAILS.** Answer the questions.

1. Where is Min going tonight?

    a. to her class   b. to her job   c. to a party

2. What does Min say about Eva's friend?

    a. "He's unattractive."   b. "He's good-looking."   c. "He's handsome."

3. What does Eva's friend look like?

    a.    b.    c.

C ▶ **EXPAND.** Listen to the whole conversation. Complete the sentence.

Victor is Eva's _____.

    a. friend   b. brother

Listening and Speaking

3 PRONUNCIATION

A ▶ **PRACTICE.** Listen. Then listen again and repeat.

par·ty   to·**night**   **beau**·ti·ful   at·**trac**·tive

B ▶ **APPLY.** Listen. Mark (•) the stressed syllable.

1. hand·some
2. in·vit·ing
3. ug·ly
4. in·tro·duce

4 CONVERSATION

A ▶ **LISTEN AND READ.** Then listen and repeat.

A: Hi, Eva.
B: Hi, Min. Are you coming to my party tonight?
A: Of course. Are you inviting your friend?
B: Which friend?
A: You know—he's handsome and he has short, black hair.

B **WORK TOGETHER.** Practice the conversation in Exercise A.

C **CREATE.** Make new conversations. Use the words in the boxes.

A: Hi, _____.
B: Hi, _____. Are you coming to my party tonight?
A: Of course. Are you inviting your friend?
B: Which friend?
A: You know—he's ▓▓▓▓▓▓▓▓▓▓ and he has ▓▓▓▓▓▓▓▓, ▓▓▓▓▓▓▓▓ hair.

thin
average height
average weight

wavy
long
curly

red
brown
black

D **ROLE-PLAY.** Make your own conversations. Use different words to describe the friend.

I can describe the way people look. ▢   I need more practice. ▢

Lesson 3

Simple present: *be* + adjective / *have* + object

Simple present: *be* + adjective

Affirmative			Negative			
I	am		I	am		
They	are	tall.	They	are	not	short.
He	is		He	is		

Simple present: *have* + object

Affirmative			Negative				
I			I				
	have			do			
They		black hair.	They		not	have	red hair.
He	has		He	does			

Grammar Watch

Contractions are short forms. Here are some examples:

- *he is not* = **he isn't**
- *he does not* = **he doesn't**
- *they are* = **they're**
- *they are not* = **they aren't**
- *they do not* = **they don't**

For more contractions, see page 258.

A **IDENTIFY.** Cross out the incorrect words.

My sister and brother ~~is~~ / **are** very good-looking, but they don't look alike. My sister **is** / **has** brown eyes, but my brother **has** / **isn't** blue eyes. My sister **has** / **have** long hair. It **has** / **is** curly. My brother's hair **are** / **is** short. And it **isn't** / **is** curly—it's straight. Also, my sister **has** / **is** tall, and my brother **has** / **is** average height. But my sister and brother **is** / **are** alike in one way: They **are** / **have** both slim.

B **CHOOSE.** Write the correct forms of *be* or *have*. Use contractions for the negative sentences.

1. Omar _____*has*_____ brown hair.
2. Na (not) _____*isn't*_____ thin.
3. Her co-workers _____ blond hair.
4. Josh and Jen _____ tall.
5. Amy's hair (not) _____ curly.
6. My supervisor's eyes _____ green.
7. Mike and Olga _____ very attractive.
8. Steve (not) _____ a beard.

Grammar

C **DESCRIBE.** Look at the picture. Describe the people. Talk about their height, weight, and hair. There is more than one correct answer.

Shakira has long, wavy blond hair. She's short and thin.

D **WRITE.** Write two sentences to describe each person.

Zhou Qi   Simone Biles   Daddy Yankee   Shakira   Zhang Ziyi   Cristiano Ronaldo

Show what you know!

1. THINK ABOUT IT. Describe someone in the class. Write three sentences.

This person is tall and slim.

2. TALK ABOUT IT. Student A, read your sentences. Student B, guess the person. Take turns.

A: This person is tall and slim.
B: Is it Bela?
A: No, it isn't. This person has straight, blond hair.
B: Is it Sofia?
A: Yes!

3. WRITE ABOUT IT. Now write about three people in your class.

Sofia is tall and slim and has straight, blond hair.

_____

_____

_____

I can use the simple present with *be* + adjective and *have* + object. ■

I need more practice. ■

Workplace, Life, and Community Skills

ID cards

1 READ AN APPLICATION

A **INTERPRET.** Read the application for a state identification card. Answer the questions.

APPLICANT INFORMATION:

Last Name	First Name	Middle Name	Suffix
Jaylen	Isaiah	Caleb	Jr.

Address	Apt/Unit	City and State	Zip Code
3602 College Avenue	4B	Clarkston, Georgia	30021

Date of Birth	Social Security Number	U.S. Citizen	Gender
12 / 03 / 1990 MM DD YYYY	555 / 33 / 4444	○ Yes ● No	● Male ○ Female ○ Unspecified

Weight	Height	Eye Color	Hair Color
LBS. 178	FT. 5 IN. 10	green	brown

Telephone Number	E-mail Address	Do you need assistance in another language? Which One?
404-666-3333	icaleb@medinc.com	/

1. What is the applicant's full name? _____

2. When was he born? _____

3. What is his Social Security number? _____

4. How tall is he? _____

5. How much does he weigh? _____

6. What color are his eyes? _____

7. What is his address? _____

8. What is his e-mail address? _____

B **MATCH.** Look at the identification card. Match the abbreviations and the words.

1. ____ F   **a.** brown
2. ____ DOB   **b.** weight
3. ____ BRN   **c.** height
4. ____ Ht.   **d.** date of birth
5. ____ Wt.   **e.** female
6. ____ BLK   **f.** black

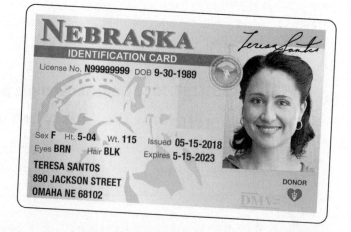

I can read identification cards. ■   I need more practice. ■

Workplace, Life, and Community Skills

2 COMPLETE AN APPLICATION

A **INTERPRET.** Read the ID card. Use the information to complete the application. What information is missing?

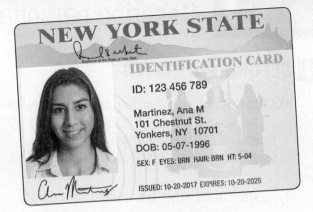

NEW YORK STATE
Governor of the State of New York
IDENTIFICATION CARD

ID: 123 456 789

Martinez, Ana M
101 Chestnut St.
Yonkers, NY 10701
DOB: 05-07-1996
SEX: F EYES: BRN HAIR: BRN HT: 5-04

ISSUED: 10-20-2017 EXPIRES: 10-20-2025

APPLICANT INFORMATION:

Last Name	First Name	Middle Name	Suffix

Address	Apt/Unit	City and State	Zip Code

Date of Birth	Social Security Number	U.S. Citizen	Gender
___ / ___ / ___ MM DD YYYY	___ / ___ / ___	○ Yes ○ No	○ Male ○ Female ○ Unspecified

Weight	Height	Eye Color	Hair Color
LBS. ___	FT. ___ IN. ___		

B **WORK TOGETHER.** Ask and answer questions about the identification card.

A: What's his last name?
B: Smith. What's his first name?
A: Joseph.

Illinois
NUMBER   ISSUED   EXPIRES: **ID CARD**
P142-5045 01-12-2018 02-14-2022

Jesse White - Secretary of State

Joseph C. Smith
36 Almond Drive Apt # 4E
Chicago, IL 60604

DOB: 02-14-1980   SEX: Male
HT: 6-01   EYES: BRN
HAIR: BLK

DONOR

C **GO ONLINE.** Search for an identification card application in your state. Check the information it asks for.

☐ Social Security Number
☐ last name
☐ first name
☐ middle name
☐ height

☐ weight
☐ eye color
☐ address
☐ mobile phone number
☐ e-mail address

I can complete an application. ■   I need more practice. ■

5 Lesson

Listening and Speaking

Describe personalities

1 BEFORE YOU LISTEN

MATCH. Write the words next to the definitions.

bossy	demanding	moody	shy	talkative
cheerful	laid-back	outgoing	supportive	

1. always tells other people what to do _____ *bossy* _____

2. is nervous when speaking to other people _____

3. likes to talk a lot _____

4. changes feelings quickly and often _____

5. is relaxed and not worried _____

6. is happy and positive _____

7. is helpful, caring, and giving _____

8. enjoys meeting new people _____

9. expects good work _____

2 LISTEN

A ► **LISTEN FOR MAIN IDEA.** Listen to two co-workers. What are they talking about?

a. work   **b.** a friend   **c.** a supervisor

B ► **LISTEN FOR DETAILS.** What is the new supervisor like? Check the words.

☐ outgoing   ☐ laid-back   ☐ bossy
☐ cheerful   ☐ demanding   ☐ supportive

C ► **EXPAND.** Listen to the whole conversation.

Kay is _____.
a. quiet   **b.** loud   **c.** bossy

Listening and Speaking

3 PRONUNCIATION

A ▶ **PRACTICE. Listen. Then listen again and repeat.**

| about | quiet | talkative | beautiful | attractive |

B ▶ **APPLY. Listen. Circle the unstressed syllables.**

1. cheer·ful
2. sup·por·tive
3. de·mand·ing
4. pro·blem

> **Vowels in unstressed syllables**
>
> The vowel sound in a stressed syllable is long and clear. Vowels in unstressed syllables often have a very short, quiet sound. For example, ab**out**.

4 CONVERSATION

A ▶ **LISTEN AND READ. Then listen and repeat.**

A: Kay, tell me about your new supervisor. What's she like?
B: Well, she's outgoing and she's cheerful.
A: Yeah? What else?
B: She's demanding but she's supportive, too.

B **WORK TOGETHER. Practice the conversation in Exercise A.**

C **CREATE. Make new conversations. Use the words in the boxes.**

A: Tell me about ⬚⬚⬚⬚⬚⬚. What's he like?
B: Well, he's ⬚⬚⬚⬚⬚ and he's ⬚⬚⬚⬚⬚.
A: Yeah? What else?
B: He's ⬚⬚⬚⬚⬚.

D **MAKE CONNECTIONS. Talk about the personalities of friends, family members, or co-workers.**

| your new co-worker |
| your supervisor |
| a good friend |

| talkative |
| friendly |
| cheerful |

| funny |
| outgoing |
| interesting |

| talkative but moody |
| laid-back but supportive |
| cheerful but demanding |

I can describe personalities. ☐   I need more practice. ☐

Be: compound sentence with *and* and *but*

Be: compound sentence with *and* and *but*		
She's outgoing	and	she's cheerful.
She's demanding	but	she's supportive.

Grammar Watch

- Use *and* to join two sentences with similar ideas.
- Use *but* to join two sentences with opposite ideas.
- Use *but* when the second idea is surprising or unexpected.

A **IDENTIFY.** Cross out the incorrect word.

1. Karim is bald ~~and~~ / **but** Mac's hair is long.
2. Sara is my friend. She's funny **and** / **but** she's nice.
3. Amy isn't a supervisor **but** / **and** she is bossy.
4. I'm shy **and** / **but** my brother is outgoing. We're different.
5. Brad is happy at his job **but** / **and** he is a good worker.

Karim   Mac

B **CHOOSE.** Write *and* or *but*.

1. We have a nice breakroom at work. It isn't big ___*but*___ it is comfortable. We have a refrigerator _____ we have a microwave. We have a TV, too, _____ we don't have time to watch it.
2. Jim is a customer service representative _____ he is good at his job. He is outgoing _____ he is kind to customers. His co-workers like him. He is helpful _____ he is supportive.
3. I have a job in a medical office. A lot of people work there, _____ it's really busy. My supervisor is OK. She has good ideas _____ she is very bossy.

Grammar

C APPLY. Make sentences. Use the words and the correct form of *be*. Use *and* or *but*.

1. (Nan / cheerful / she / laid-back) _Nan is cheerful and she is laid-back._
2. (Ken / outgoing / he / moody) _____
3. The cafeteria at my office is great. (The food / delicious / the workers / friendly)

   _____
4. I have a good job. (My department head / interesting / my co-workers / funny)

   _____
5. (Tina / shy / her sister / talkative) _____

D WRITE. Now write two sentences about a person you work or live with. Then write a new sentence with *and* or *but*.

My supervisor is cheerful. She is supportive.
My supervisor is cheerful and she is supportive.

_____

_____

_____

_____

Show what you know!

1. **THINK ABOUT IT.** Write four sentences about the way you look or your personality. Use a form of *be*. Write two sentences with *and*. Write two sentences with *but*.

   I am shy and I am quiet.
   I am slim but I am not tall.

2. **TALK ABOUT IT.** Share your sentences. Are you and your classmates similar? Make sentences with *and* or *but*.

3. **WRITE ABOUT IT.** Write four sentences about the way your classmates are similar or different. Write two sentences with *and*. Write two sentences with *but*.

   I am short but Dan is tall.
   Liz has blue eyes and so does Ian.

I can make compound sentences with *and* / *but*. ■   I need more practice. ■

Lesson 7 Reading

Read about group work in the classroom

1 BEFORE YOU READ

A **DECIDE.** Complete the sentences with the words in the box.

> communication   discussion   participate   practice

1. I'm learning to play the guitar. I need to _____ every day.
2. We need to talk about the problem. Let's sit down and have a _____.
3. All the children can join in the game. They can all _____.
4. Anna is a good speaker and a good listener. She has good _____ skills.

B **MAKE CONNECTIONS.** What's happening in the picture? Do you ever do this?

> **Academic Skill:**
> **Identify the Topic and the Main Idea**
>
> After you read, ask yourself, "What's the article about?" The answer is the topic of the article.
>
> Then ask, "What does the writer say about the topic?" The answer is the main idea.

2 READ

▶ Listen and read.

Group Work in English Classes

1 English language teachers often ask students to work in small groups. The groups usually have three or four students. Working in small groups is good for language learning. Why? Here are a few reasons.

5 **1.** If someone wants to learn a new language, they have to practice it. In a small group, learners can get more practice speaking. They get practice listening to different speakers, too. Listening and speaking
10 improves communication skills.

2. Speaking in a small group is easier for many students. In the classroom, outgoing and talkative students often speak. Shy students
15 often don't. Small groups help shy students relax and participate more.

3. In small groups, students can help each other. When Student A helps Student B, Student A learns to explain something clearly. That's not easy. It's a
20 good skill to have.

What ideas from the article do you see in this picture?

Student B learns to ask questions. To ask a question, you have to think about what you know and what you don't. Both students are more active in their learning. Active learners learn and
25 remember more.

4. Small-group work helps students improve their interpersonal skills. Everyone needs to help the group to work well. Talkative students
30 have to listen. Quiet students can't be too laid-back. They have to share their ideas. Bossy students have to respect the other members of the group.

35 **5.** In many jobs, people have to work in teams. Employers want workers with good communication and interpersonal skills.

For these reasons, English language classes often have small-group work. It's an important part of
40 education in the United States.

Reading

3 CLOSE READING

A IDENTIFY. Answer the questions.

1. What is the article about?
   - **a.** teachers of English
   - **b.** group work in ESL classes
   - **c.** education in the U.S.

2. What is the main idea?
   - **a.** Employers want workers with good communication and interpersonal skills.
   - **b.** Small-group work in class is good for English language learners.
   - **c.** Small-group work is often part of education in the United States.

B CITE EVIDENCE. Answer the questions. Where is the information? Write the line numbers.

Lines

1. What is an example of a communication skill?
   - **a.** working
   - **b.** reading
   - **c.** speaking

   _____

2. Why are small groups good for shy students?
   - **a.** They can just sit and listen.
   - **b.** They can relax.
   - **c.** They can be bossy.

   _____

3. Which statement is true about active learners?
   - **a.** They talk too much in class.
   - **b.** It's hard for them to sit for a long time.
   - **c.** They do more thinking and learning.

   _____

4. When do people need to use interpersonal skills?
   - **a.** to work well with other people
   - **b.** to understand their own feelings
   - **c.** to remember what they learn

   _____

4 SUMMARIZE

Complete the summary with the words in the box.

active	communication	practice	skills

Small-group work is important in English language classes. It helps students be more
(1) _____ learners. They get more (2) _____ speaking. They can develop
other (3) _____ skills, too. They can also develop interpersonal (4) _____.
These are important in school and at work.

Show what you know!

1. **WRITE ABOUT IT.** Write about how small-group work helps you learn English.

   Small group work helps me learn English because _____.

2. **PRESENT IT.** Make a short presentation. How does small-group work help people learn English? How does it help shy students, talkative students, bossy students, students with strong skills, or students who have questions?

I can identify the topic and main idea. ■   I need more practice. ■

Lesson 8

Get to know someone

1 BEFORE YOU LISTEN

MAKE CONNECTIONS. In the U.S., which questions are OK to ask when you meet someone at work? Check the questions.

☐ What do you do?   ☐ Where are you from?

☐ Are you married?   ☐ Do you like your supervisor?

☐ How old are you?

2 LISTEN

A **PREDICT.** Look at the picture. Where are they?

B ► **LISTEN FOR MAIN IDEA.** Listen to the conversation. Answer the questions.

1. What's happening?
   a. Ron is asking Pia's name.
   b. Ron and Pia are meeting for the first time.
   c. Pia and Ron are saying good-bye.

2. Where does Ron work?
   a. At a hospital.
   b. At a restaurant.
   c. At a school.

C ► **LISTEN FOR DETAILS.** Listen again. Read the sentences. Circle *True* or *False*.

1. Ron is Kara's friend.	True	False
2. Kara is a nurse.	True	False
3. Ron is a cook.	True	False

D ► **EXPAND.** Listen to the whole conversation. Read the sentences. Circle *True* or *False*.

1. Pia works at a hospital.	True	False
2. Pia is a nurse.	True	False

Listening and Speaking

3 PRONUNCIATION

A ▶ **PRACTICE. Listen. Then listen again and repeat.**

Are **you** a **nurse**?

No, I'm **not**.

I **work** in the **cafeteria**.

I'm a **cook**.

Sentence stress

In English, the important words in a sentence are stressed. They are usually long and loud. Some important words have more than one syllable. Only one of the syllables is stressed.

B ▶ **APPLY. Listen. Mark (•) the stressed words.**

1. Nice to meet you.
2. I'm a medical assistant.
3. How about you?

4 CONVERSATION

A ▶ **LISTEN AND READ. Then listen and repeat.**

A: Pia, I want to introduce you to my friend. Pia, this is Ron. Ron, this is Pia.
B: Nice to meet you, Ron.
C: Nice to meet you, too.
B: So, are you a nurse, like Kara?
C: No, I'm not. I work at the hospital, but I'm a cook in the cafeteria. How about you?

B **WORK TOGETHER. Practice the conversation in Exercise A.**

C **ROLE-PLAY. Make your own conversations. Introduce your classmates and continue the conversation.**

A: I want to introduce you to my classmate. _____, this is _____.
_____, this is _____.
B: Nice to meet you.
C: Nice to meet you, too.
B: So, _____ . . .

I can get to know someone. ■   I need more practice. ■

9

Simple present tense of *be*: *Yes / No* and information questions

Yes/no questions with *be*
Are   you   a nurse?

Short answers
Yes, I am. No, I am not.

Information questions with *be*
How is it?

Short answers
Good.

Grammar Watch

- You can use contractions in negative short answers to *Yes / No* questions.

  I am not. = **I'm not.**

  You are not. = **You're not.**
  You aren't.

- You can't use contractions in affirmative short answers.

- For more contractions, see page 258.

A MATCH. Choose the correct answers to the questions.

1. __d__ Is she talkative?
2. ____ Who is your manager?
3. ____ Am I bossy?
4. ____ Where is your family from?
5. ____ Are you from China?
6. ____ Is he your co-worker?
7. ____ What is your country like?
8. ____ How old is your daughter?

a. She's four.
b. Brazil.
c. No, I'm not.
d. Yes, she is.
e. No, you're not.
f. Yes, he is.
g. Mr. Gómez.
h. It's beautiful.

B WRITE. Read the answers. Write questions about the underlined information.

1. **A:** *What is your last name?*
   B: My last name is <u>Chow</u>.

2. **A:** _____
   B: No, they aren't. <u>His sisters</u> are tall.

3. **A:** _____
   B: They're from <u>Cuba</u>.

4. **A:** _____
   B: My son is <u>five years old</u>.

5. **A:** _____
   B: My office is on <u>Fifth Street</u>.

6. **A:** _____
   B: No, he isn't. <u>He's not outgoing</u>. He's really shy!

7. **A:** _____
   B: Her name is <u>May</u>.

8. **A:** _____
   B: Yes, they are. <u>Ted and Chris</u> are co-workers.

I can use the simple present tense of *be* with *Yes / No* and information questions. ■   I need more practice. ■

Writing

Write about a study routine

1 STUDY THE MODEL

READ. Answer the questions.

> Mona Jibril
>
> My Study Routine
>
> This is my routine to practice new words in English. First, I silently read a word from my list of new words. Then, I say the word aloud. After that, I close my notebook and write the word on a piece of paper.

1. What is Mona's routine for?
2. What is the first step of her routine?
3. What does she do next?
4. What does she do after that?

2 PLAN YOUR WRITING

WORK TOGETHER. Ask and answer the questions.

1. What's one of your study routines?
2. What's the first step of your routine?
3. What do you do next?
4. What do you do after that?

3 WRITE

Now write about your study routine. Use the model, the Writing Skill, and your ideas from Exercise 2 to help you.

Writing Skill: Introduce and explain steps of a routine

When you write about how to do something, explain each step. For each step, use words like *first, then,* and *after that.*

For example: First, I silently read a word from my list of new words. Then, I say the word aloud. After that, I close my notebook and write the word on a piece of paper.

4 CHECK YOUR WRITING

WORK TOGETHER. Read the checklist. Read your writing aloud. Revise your writing.

WRITING CHECKLIST

☐ The paragraph answers the questions in Exercise 2.

☐ The paragraph uses the words *first, then,* and *after that.*

I can introduce and explains steps of a routine. ■   I need more practice. ■

1 MEET MEG

Read about one of her workplace skills.

> I am inclusive. I work with many different people, and I am friendly to everyone. At work, everyone is included because we are all on the same team.

2 MEG'S PROBLEM

READ. Circle *True* or *False*.

Meg has a 15-minute break at work. She walks into the break room. She sees some of her friends. They are sitting at one table. They're telling stories and laughing. A new co-worker, Jana, is sitting at the table alone. She looks shy and a little lonely.

1. Meg and her co-workers are on a break.   True   False
2. Jana is talking to Meg's friends.   True   False
3. Jana is outgoing.   True   False

3 MEG'S SOLUTION

WORK TOGETHER. Meg is inclusive at work. What does she do next? Explain your answer.

1. Meg sits down with her friends and starts talking to them.
2. Meg says, "Hi, Jana," and then sits down with her friends.
3. Meg says, "Hi, Jana. Come sit with us over here."
4. Meg _____.

Show what you know!

1. **THINK ABOUT IT.** Are you inclusive and friendly to everyone? What ways are you inclusive to people in class? At work? At home? Give examples.

2. **WRITE ABOUT IT.** Write an example in your Skills Log.

I am inclusive and friendly to everyone. For example, sometimes a new student joins the class. I always say hi and invite him or her to be my partner in pair work.

I can give an example of how I am inclusive. ■

Unit Review: Go back to page 5. Which unit goals can you check off?

2 All in the Family

PREVIEW

Look at the picture. What do you see?
Who are these people?

UNIT GOALS

- ☐ Identify family relationships
- ☐ Talk about family
- ☐ Talk about what people have in common
- ☐ Ask about mailing services
- ☐ Ask about people

- ☐ **Academic skill:** Retell information
- ☐ **Writing skill:** Use capital letters and commas in names of places
- ☐ **Workplace soft skill:** Separate work and home life

Vocabulary

Family relationships

A **PREDICT.** Look at the pictures. Find Marta in each picture. Who are the other people in the pictures? What is their family relationship to Marta?

I think Paco is Marta's brother.

B ▶ **LISTEN AND POINT.** Then listen and repeat.

Paco   Tina   Manuel   Ella   Marta   Lina   Tony   Delmar

Ben   Marta   Tina   Eva   Felix

Marta   Ben   Sandra   Tom   Ann

Tommy   Liz   Marta   Ben

Liz   Marta   Ben   Mary   Tommy   Sue   Benny

Vocabulary

Family relationships

1. brother	6. cousin	11. nephew	16. sister-in-law	21. grandmother
2. sister	7. uncle	12. wife	17. son	22. grandfather
3. father	8. fiancé	13. husband	18. daughter	23. granddaughter
4. mother	9. fiancée	14. mother-in-law	19. children	24. grandson
5. aunt	10. niece	15. father-in-law	20. parents	25. grandchildren

C **WORK TOGETHER.** Look at the pictures. Student A, ask a question about Marta's family. Student B, answer.

A: Who is Marta's sister?
B: Tina. Who are Marta's grandchildren?

D **CATEGORIZE.** Which family words are for females? Which are for males? Which are for both? Complete the chart.

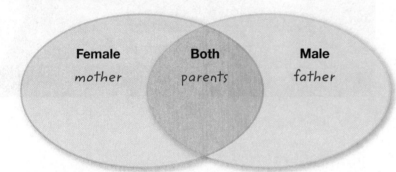

Study Tip

Make connections

Write the names of five people in your family and their relationship to you.

Marie: niece
Pete: nephew

Show what you know!

1. THINK ABOUT IT. Make a list of your family members. Where do they live?

husband – New York   son – New York   parents – China
daughter – New York   brother – San Francisco

2. TALK ABOUT IT. Talk about your family.

A: Is your family here?
B: My son and daughter are here. My mother and father are in China.

3. WRITE ABOUT IT. Write about your family.

My children are in New York. My parents are in China.

I can identify family relationships. ■	I need more practice. ■

Lesson 2

Talk about family

1 BEFORE YOU LISTEN

MAKE CONNECTIONS. How many family members live with you? Who are they?

2 LISTEN

A **PREDICT.** Look at the picture of two new co-workers. What are they talking about? What do people talk about when they meet for the first time?

B ▶ **LISTEN FOR MAIN IDEA.** Choose the correct word.

Amy and Sam are talking about _____.

a. work   **b.** families   **c.** cars

C ▶ **LISTEN FOR DETAILS.** Choose the correct word.

1. Sam doesn't have a _____ family.
   a. big
   b. small

2. Sam has _____.
   a. one brother
   b. two brothers

3. Sam's _____ live in Senegal.
   a. brothers
   b. sisters

D ▶ **EXPAND.** Listen to the whole conversation. Choose the correct word.

Sam's brother lives _____ Sam.
a. far from   **b.** with   **c.** near

Listening and Speaking

3 PRONUNCIATION

A ▶ **PRACTICE.** Listen. Then listen again and repeat.

I have a brother and two sisters.

We live in the same apartment.

He works in a hospital.

B ▶ **APPLY.** Listen. Circle the words that are not stressed.

1. I don't have a very big family.
2. My sisters live in Senegal.
3. He's a medical assistant.

4 CONVERSATION

A ▶ **LISTEN AND READ.** Then listen and repeat.

A: Tell me about your family.
B: Well, I don't have a very big family. I have a brother and two sisters.
A: Do they live here?
B: My sisters live in Senegal, but my brother lives here.

B **WORK TOGETHER.** Practice the conversation in Exercise A.

C **MAKE CONNECTIONS.**
Talk about your own family.

A: Tell me about your family.
B: I have a very big family.
   I have ...

I can talk about family. ☐   I need more practice. ☐

Grammar

Simple present affirmative and negative: *live / work / have*

Simple present affirmative and negative: *live / work / have*					
Affirmative			**Negative**		
I			I		
You	**live /**		You	**don't**	
We	**work**		We		**live /**
They		in the U.S.	They		**work**	in Senegal.
He	**lives /**		He	**doesn't**	
She	**works**		She		
I			I		
You	**have**		You	**don't**	
We			We		
They		a small family.	They		**have**	a big family.
He	**has**		He	**doesn't**	
She			She		

Grammar Watch

- With *he, she,* or *it,* the simple present verb ends in -*s.*
- *Have* is an irregular verb. With *he, she,* or *it,* use *has.*
- Use *don't* or *doesn't* to make a verb negative. Use the base form of the verb after *don't* and *doesn't.*

For contractions, see page 258.

A IDENTIFY. Cross out the incorrect words.

1. My cousin **has / ~~have~~** a wife and two children.
2. They **doesn't / don't** have children.
3. Her brother **work / works** in a theater.
4. My mother-in-law **lives / live** on South Street.
5. Our grandparents **doesn't / don't** live here.
6. We **don't / doesn't** work on weekends.
7. Pam and Ben **have / has** two boys.

B COMPLETE. Write the simple present form of the verbs.

1. Mary (work) _____*works*_____ at a hair salon.
2. His sister-in-law (not have) ___*doesn't have*___ a job.
3. Nina's fiancé (live) _____ near the city.
4. Her husband (work) _____ with her brother.
5. I (not live) _____ with my parents.
6. Our family (live) _____ in Colombia.
7. They (not work) _____ in a big office.
8. Tom (not have) _____ any cousins.

Grammar

C **INTERPRET.** Look at the family tree. Complete the sentences with the simple present.

The Méndez Family

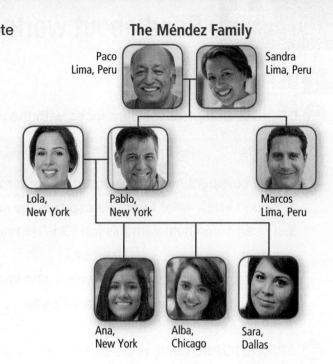

1. Alba ___doesn't live___ in Los Angeles.
   (live)

2. Marcos _____ in Lima.
   (live)

3. Lola _____ a son.
   (have)

4. Marcos _____ a brother.
   (have)

5. Lola and Pablo _____ in New York.
   (live)

6. Sandra _____ three grandchildren.
   (have)

7. Pablo and Marcos _____ a sister.
   (have)

8. Sandra and Paco _____ in Dallas.
   (live)

D **WRITE.** Now write three new sentences about the Méndez family.

Sara doesn't live in New York. She lives in Dallas.
She has two sisters.

Show what you know!

1. **THINK ABOUT IT.** Write two true sentences and one false sentence about your family and life.

   I have _____.
   I live in _____
   I work in _____.

2. **TALK ABOUT IT.** Play a guessing game with three students. Read your sentences. Guess the false sentence.

   A: I have four sisters. I live in Oak Park. I work in a hotel.
   B: I think the first sentence is false. I don't think you have four sisters.
   A: That's right. I don't have four sisters. I have one sister.

3. **WRITE ABOUT IT.** Write three sentences about someone in your group.

   _____
   _____
   _____

I can use the simple present. ■   I need more practice. ■

Lesson 4

Read about work / life balance

1 BEFORE YOU READ

A DECIDE. Complete the sentences with the words from the box.

> advice   expert   handle   responsibilities

1. The president has an important job with many _____.
2. I don't know what to do! Please give me some _____.
3. I need some help with this job. One person cannot _____ it all.
4. An _____ is a person who knows a lot about a topic or has special skills.

B BRAINSTORM. Look at the picture. What do you think it means?

2 READ

▶ Listen and read.

Academic Skill: Retell information

Retell means to say in your own words what you read or hear. The words are different, but the meaning is the same.

Work / Life Balance

1 Today, it is hard for many adults in the United States to find enough time for both their work and their personal lives. Men and women have many responsibilities. Some are things they have
5 to do for their jobs. For example, they might have to travel for work, or they might have to work extra hours to finish a task. Others are things they need to do for themselves and their families. For example, they have to cook, clean,
10 and pay bills. People with children have to take care of them. How can busy adults handle all these responsibilities? Experts on work/life balance give this advice:

1. Prioritize. Ask yourself, "What is most
15 important?" You can't do everything. So write a list each day. Put a star ★ next to the most important thing to do. Only do the important things on your list.

2. Say no. You already have many responsibilities.
20 When people ask you to do something extra, tell them you can't. Say, "I'm sorry, but I don't have the time right now."

3. Take some time for yourself. Make sure you get a little time every day to do something you
25 like. Watch a TV program, take a bath, get some exercise, or read. Take care of yourself so you will have the energy to take care of your biggest responsibilities.

Reading

3 CLOSE READING

A **IDENTIFY. What is the main idea?**

To have a good work/life balance, you need to _____.

a. have a job, be married, and have children
b. find time for both your responsibilities and the things you enjoy
c. always say no when people ask for your help

B **CITE EVIDENCE. Complete the sentences. Where is the information? Write the line numbers.**

1. It's hard for many adults to find a good work/life balance because they _____.   **Lines**
   a. don't know how to work hard
   b. spend too much time watching TV
   c. have a lot of responsibilities   _____

2. Experts say to write a to-do list and _____.
   a. put the things you like to do on it
   b. do the most important things on it
   c. finish everything on it every day   _____

3. The experts explain how to _____ when people ask you to do something extra.
   a. say no
   b. write a list
   c. get enough sleep   _____

4. Taking a bath is an example of _____.
   a. a way to take care of yourself
   b. a responsibility
   c. a way to get exercise   _____

5. The experts say that _____ will give you more energy.
   a. spending time with children
   b. handling responsibilities
   c. taking care of yourself   _____

4 SUMMARIZE

Complete the summary with the words in the box.

| advice | responsibilities |
| balance | take care of |

When you have a lot of (1) _____, both at work and at home, it's hard to have a good work/life (2) _____. Experts give this (3) _____: Write a to-do list every day, say no when people ask you to do extra things at work or at home, and (4) _____ yourself.

Show what you know!

1. **THINK ABOUT IT.** What are your family, school, and work responsibilities? Make a list. Put a star next to the most important responsibilities.

2. **WRITE ABOUT IT.** Write sentences about your everyday responsibilities. Prioritize them.

   At work, I am responsible for sending and delivering mail.

3. **PRESENT IT.** Give a short presentation about your responsibilities at home, at work, and at school. What do you think about the experts' advice? What do you need to do to have a good work/life balance?

I can retell information. ■   I need more practice. ■

Listening and Speaking

Lesson 5

Talk about what people have in common

1 BEFORE YOU LISTEN

DESCRIBE. Look at the picture of three brothers. How are they alike? What are some things that family members have in common?

2 LISTEN

A PREDICT. Look at the picture of two co-workers. What are they talking about?

- **a.** a problem at work
- **b.** their families
- **c.** the latest smartphone

B ▶ LISTEN FOR MAIN IDEA. Listen to the conversation. Complete the sentence.

Tina and Lili _____.

- **a.** don't have a lot in common
- **b.** have a little in common
- **c.** have a lot in common

Tina   Ming

C ▶ LISTEN FOR DETAILS. Listen again. Choose the answer.

1. Lili is Tina's _____.
   - **a.** sister   **b.** mother   **c.** grandmother

2. Tina looks like her _____.
   - **a.** father   **b.** sister   **c.** mother

3. Tina works in a _____.
   - **a.** hospital   **b.** store   **c.** bank

D ▶ EXPAND. Listen to the whole conversation. Answer the questions.

1. Does Tina have any sisters? _____
2. Does Ming have any brothers? _____

Listening and Speaking

3 PRONUNCIATION

A ▶ **PRACTICE. Listen. Then listen and repeat.**

Do you have a lot in common?
Do you have brothers or sisters?
Do you work in a bank?

Pronunciation of do

Do often has a short, weak pronunciation before *you*. *Do you* often sounds like "d'ya."

B ▶ **APPLY. Listen. Circle *do* with a short, weak pronunciation.**

1. Do you have any brothers?
   Yes, I do.

2. Do we look alike?
   Yes, you do.

3. Do you look like your sister?
   Yes, I do.

4 CONVERSATION

A ▶ **LISTEN AND READ. Then listen and repeat.**

A: Tina, is that your sister?
B: Yes, it is. That's my sister, Lili. Do we look alike?
A: Yes, you do. You look a lot alike. Do you have a lot in common?
B: Actually, we do. She works in a bank, and I work in a bank, too.
She's really talkative, and I'm really talkative.

B **WORK TOGETHER. Practice the conversation in Exercise A.**

C **CREATE. Make new conversations. Use the words in the boxes.**

A: Tina, is that your [   ]?

B: Yes, it is. That's my [   ]. Do we look alike?

A: Yes, you do. You look a lot alike. Do you have a lot in common?

B: Actually, we do. She works in a [   ], and I work
in a [   ], too. She's really [   ],
and I'm really [   ].

niece
aunt
cousin

restaurant
clothing store
hospital

outgoing
shy
laid-back

D **MAKE CONNECTIONS. Talk about your family.**
Do you have a lot in common?

A: Do you have any brothers or sisters?
B: Yes, I do. I have two brothers.
A: Do you have a lot in common?

I can talk about what people have in common. ■	I need more practice. ■

Lesson 6

Simple Present: *Yes / No* questions and short answers

Simple present: *Yes / No* questions and short answers

Do	you			I		do.		I		don't.
	they	**have** a lot in common?	**Yes,**	they			**No,**	they		
	she			she		does.		she		doesn't.
Does	he			he				he		

A **MATCH.** Choose the correct answers to the questions.

1. __c__ Do you have a big family?
2. ____ Do they work in a bank?
3. ____ Does he work in an office?
4. ____ Do I work more than Dan?
5. ____ Does she have a lot in common with you?
6. ____ Do we look alike?

    a. Yes, they do.
    b. Yes, we do.
    c. No, I don't.
    d. Yes, she does.
    e. No, you don't.
    f. Yes, he does.

Grammar Watch

- Use *do / does* + subject + the base form of the verb in questions.
- Use *do / does* or *don't / doesn't* in short answers. Don't use the main verb.

B **IDENTIFY.** Cross out the incorrect words.

1. **A: Do / Does** you have any sisters?
   B: Yes, I **do / does**.

2. **A: Do / Does** he visit his family often?
   B: No, he **does / doesn't**.

3. **A: Do / Does** they work for a big company?
   B: No, they **do / don't**. It's a small business.

4. **A: Do / Does** your parents work?
   B: Yes, they **do / does**.

5. **A: Do / Does** your niece have children?
   B: Yes, she **does / doesn't**.

6. **A: Do / Does** your son live in Dallas?
   B: Yes, he **does / doesn't**.

Grammar

C **APPLY.** Write the questions. Then look at the picture and write short answers.

1. A: _____Do_____ Sarah and Brad _____have_____ a daughter? (have)

   B: _Yes, they do._

2. A: _____ Meg _____ in Tampa? (live)

   B: _____

3. A: _____ Brian and Katie _____ two sons? (have)

   B: _____

4. A: _____ Emily _____ brown hair? (have)

   B: _____

5. A: _____ Brian and Todd _____ glasses? (have)

   B: _____

6. A: _____ James _____ a brother? (have)

   B: _____

7. A: _____ Emily and Todd _____ in Seattle? (live)

   B: _____

8. A: _____ Sarah _____ blond hair? (have)

   B: _____

Brian · Katie · Emily · Todd · Sarah · Brad · Grace · Meg · James

Tampa — Vancouver — Seattle

Show what you know!

1. **THINK ABOUT IT.** Complete the questions to ask a partner.

   Do you have any family in _____?

   Do you live in _____? Do you work in _____?

2. **TALK ABOUT IT.** Student A, read your questions. Student B, answer the questions. Take turns.

   A: Do you have any family in Chicago?
   B: Yes, I do. My brother lives in Chicago.
   A: Do you live in Chicago?
   B: No, I don't.

3. **WRITE ABOUT IT.** Now write about your partner.

   Jan has a brother. He lives in Chicago. Jan doesn't live in Chicago. She lives . . .

I can ask and answer *Yes / No* questions in simple present. ■   I need more practice. ■

A **MATCH.** Label the pictures with the words from the box.

book of stamps	letter	tracking receipt
large envelope	package	

1. _____   4. _____

2. _____   5. _____

3. _____

B **INTERPRET.** Read the chart. Circle *True* or *False*.

Service	Package or letter	Speed	Service	Package or letter	Speed
Priority Mail Express	70 pounds or less	1 day	First-Class Mail	3.5 ounces or less for standard-sized envelopes 13 ounces or less for large envelopes and small packages	1-3 business days
Priority Mail	70 pounds or less	1–3 business days	Retail Ground	70 pounds or less	2-8 business days

1. It takes three days for a Priority Mail Express package to arrive.   True   False
2. You can send a 30-pound package by First-Class Mail.   True   False
3. You can send a letter by Priority Mail Express.   True   False
4. You can send a 2-pound package by Priority Mail.   True   False
5. It takes 1-3 days for a Retail Ground package to arrive.   True   False
6. Retail Ground is the fastest way to mail a package.   True   False

Workplace, Life, and Community Skills

C **DECIDE.** Look at the list of mailing services. Then read what each customer wants. Which mailing service is best for each customer?

Extra Mailing Services

Certificate of Mailing
You get a receipt to show you mailed the item on a certain date.

Delivery Confirmation
You can find out when your package is delivered.

Certified Mail
You get a receipt to show you mailed the item. You can find out when the item is delivered and who signed for it.

Insurance
If your package is lost or damaged, you get money back.

Registered Mail
You get a receipt to show you mailed the item. Your item is both certified and insured.

COD (Collect on Delivery)
The person who receives the item pays for the cost of mailing.

I need to show my manager a receipt that says I mailed this letter today. I want to know when it arrives, but I don't need insurance.

I'm sending a gift to my brother. I want my money back if the package gets lost. I don't need the package certified.

D **LISTEN.** Write the missing words.

Customer: Hello. I'd like to mail this _____.
Clerk: How do you want to send it?
Customer: How long does _____ take?
Clerk: Two to eight days.
Customer: Okay. I'll send it _____.
Clerk: Do you want _____ or insurance?
Customer: Yes. _____, please.
Clerk: Does it contain any hazardous materials?
Customer: No.

E **ROLE-PLAY.** Create another conversation about mailing services.

F **GO ONLINE.** Search for mailing services near you. Write the address of the mailing service nearest you. What kind of packages can you send with this service?

I can ask about mailing services. ■   I need more practice. ■

1 BEFORE YOU LISTEN

MAKE CONNECTIONS. What are game shows? Do you watch or listen to game shows on TV or on podcasts? Which shows do you watch?

2 LISTEN

A PREDICT. Look at the picture. What is the podcast about?

a. a person's job
b. a person's family

B ▶ LISTEN FOR MAIN IDEA. Complete the sentence.

The name of the podcast is _____.
a. Oliver Marley and Family
b. The Rules of the Game
c. They're Your Family Now!

C ▶ LISTEN FOR DETAILS. Who are the questions about?

a. Trevor's wife   b. Trevor's in-laws   c. Marley's family

D ▶ EXPAND. Listen to the whole conversation. Answer the questions.

1. Where do Trevor's wife's grandparents live?
   a. with Trevor   b. in San Antonio   c. in a big house

2. How many sisters does Trevor's mother-in-law have?
   a. two   b. three   c. five

3. What does Trevor's brother-in-law do?
   a. He's an artist.   b. He's an engineer.   c. He's an accountant.

4. When does Ella work?
   a. at night   b. during the day   c. on weekends

Listening and Speaking

3 CONVERSATION

A ▶ **LISTEN AND READ.** Then listen and repeat.

A: Where does your son live?
B: He lives in San Antonio.
A: How many children does he have?
B: Well, he has two sons and two daughters.
A: Really? What does he do?
B: He works in an office. He's an engineer.

B **WORK TOGETHER.** Practice the conversation in Exercise A.

C **CREATE.** Make new conversations. Use the words in the boxes.

A: Where does your ▭ live?
B: He lives in San Antonio.
A: How many ▭ does he have?
B: Well, he has two ▭ and
   two ▭.
A: Really? What does he do?
B: He works in ▭.
   He's ▭.

| cousin |
| father-in-law |
| son-in-law |

| sons |
| daughters |
| brothers |
| sisters |

| an office, an accountant |
| a hospital, a technician |
| a school, a security guard |

D **MAKE CONNECTIONS.** Talk about your family. What do they do? Where do they live?

I have a little brother. He is in school. He lives with my parents in Oklahoma.

I can ask about people. ■   I need more practice. ■

Grammar

Lesson 9
Simple Present: Information questions and short answers

Simple present: Information questions and answers					Grammar Watch

When	do	you	work?	At night.
		they		
	does	he		
		she		

Where	do	you	live?	In San Antonio.
		they		
	does	he		
		she		

How many brothers	do	you	have?	Two.
		they		
	does	he		
		she		

Grammar Watch

Other question words:
What does she do?
How often do you
see them?

A **IDENTIFY. Cross out the incorrect words. Then match the questions and answers.**

1. __b__ How many days **do / ~~does~~** you work?
2. ____ What **do / does** your husband do?
3. ____ When **do / does** they work?
4. ____ How many grandchildren **do / does** they have?
5. ____ Where **do / does** your parents live?
6. ____ What **do / does** his co-workers have in common?

a. On Green Street.
b. I work six days a week.
c. Two.
d. On Monday, Thursday, and Friday.
e. He is an electrician.
f. They're cheerful.

B **COMPLETE. Write the questions.**

1. What _____do_____ your brothers _____do_____? (do)
2. How often _____ your cousins _____? (visit)
3. When _____ your husband _____ to work? (go)
4. Where _____ he _____? (live)
5. How many children _____ she _____? (have)

I can use simple present information questions and answers. ■   I need more practice. ■

42 Unit 2, Lesson 9

Write about a family member

1 STUDY THE MODEL

READ. Answer the questions.

> Lan Woo
>
> ### My Sister
>
> I have one sister. Her name is Ting. She lives in Shenzhen, China. I live in San Francisco, California, but we keep in touch. We text each other every day. We also talk on the computer on weekends.

1. Who did Lan write about?
2. Where does Lan's sister live?
3. Where does Lan live?
4. How do they keep in touch?

2 PLAN YOUR WRITING

WORK TOGETHER. Ask and answer the questions.

1. What family member are you writing about?
2. Where does your family member live?
3. Where do you live?
4. How do you keep in touch?

Writing Skill: Use capital letters and commas in names of places

Names of places begin with capital letters. For example:

San Francisco

Write a comma (,) between the name of a city and the name of a state or country. For example:

Shenzhen, China
San Francisco, California

3 WRITE

Now write about a family member. Use the model, the Writing Skill, and your ideas from Exercise 2 to help you.

4 CHECK YOUR WRITING

WORK TOGETHER. Read the checklist. Read your writing aloud. Revise your writing.

WRITING CHECKLIST

☐ The paragraph answers the questions in Exercise 2.

☐ The names of places begin with capital letters.

☐ There is a comma between the name of a city and state or country.

I can use capital letters and commas in names of places. ■   I need more practice. ■

Separate work life and home life

1 MEET BO

Read about one of his workplace skills.

I separate work life from home life. I love my family, and I love my work, but when I'm at work, I do my work. When I'm at home, I spend time with my family. I try to keep the two separate.

2 BO'S PROBLEM

READ. Circle *True* or *False*.

Bo is a waiter. He has a new job in a restaurant. He is busy today. There are a lot of people.

Suddenly Bo's wife and young daughter come into the restaurant. They want to visit Bo at his new job. Bo's daughter runs toward him. She shouts, "Hi, Daddy!"

1. Bo serves food in a restaurant.	True	False
2. Bo has a lot of work today.	True	False
3. Bo's friends are visiting him at the restaurant.	True	False

3 BO'S SOLUTION

WORK TOGETHER. Bo is good at separating work life and home life. What does he say to his family? Explain your answer.

1. Bo says, "Hi! I'm happy to see you, but I can't talk right now. Let's talk tonight at home."
2. Bo says, "Hi! I'm happy to see you. Come see the kitchen! I'll get you something to eat!"
3. Bo says, "Hi! I'm happy to see you. I'll talk to you after I help these customers."
4. Bo _____.

Show what you know!

1. **THINK ABOUT IT.** Do you separate work life and home life? How do you separate work life and home life at work? At home? Give examples.

2. **WRITE ABOUT IT.** Write your example in your Skills Log.

I separate work life and home life. Sometimes I have a hard day at work, but I try not to talk about it at home.

I can give an example of how I separate work life and home life. ☐

Unit Review: Go back to page 25. Which unit goals can you check off?

3 Lots to Do

PREVIEW

Look at the picture. What do you see? Where are the people? What are they doing?

UNIT GOALS

- ☐ Identify clothing
- ☐ Describe wants and needs
- ☐ Complete an online order and read store ads and sales receipts
- ☐ Talk about plans

- ☐ Describe problems with purchases
- ☐ **Academic skill:** Identify purpose
- ☐ **Writing skill:** Use a topic sentence
- ☐ **Workplace soft skills:** Show how you listen actively

Vocabulary

Clothing

Ⓐ **PREDICT.** Look at the pictures. What do you see? What words for clothing do you know?

Ⓑ ▶ **LISTEN AND POINT.** Listen again and repeat.

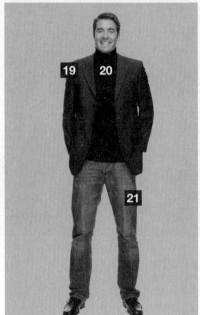

Vocabulary

Clothing

1. a coat	6. a suit	11. sweatpants	16. a raincoat	19. jacket
2. a hat	7. a tie	12. a cap	17. an umbrella	20. sweater
3. a scarf	8. high heels	13. sneakers	18. boots	21. jeans
4. gloves	9. dress	14. a uniform		
5. a shirt	10. a sweatshirt	15. a helmet		

C **WORK TOGETHER.** Look at the pictures. Student A, point to a picture. Student B, name the clothing in the picture.

Student A points to a picture.
B: A uniform, a helmet.
A: Right!

D **CATEGORIZE.** What do you wear for work, for cold weather, for a party? Write the words in the chart.

Clothing for Work	Clothing for Cold Weather	Clothing for a Party
uniform	coat	dress

Study Tip

Test your spelling

Read a word in the word list. Close your book. Write the word. Open your book and check your spelling. Continue with all the words in the list.

Show what you know!

1. **THINK ABOUT IT.** Look at the clothing words. On a piece of paper, write the name of 4 pieces of clothing you have on today. Put your paper in a box.

   sweater   jeans
   shirt   boots

2. **TALK ABOUT IT.** Take a piece of paper from the box. Read it to the class. Who has that clothing on today?

3. **WRITE ABOUT IT.** Now write a sentence about your clothing today.

   I have on a _____

I can identify clothing. ■	I need more practice. ■

Describe your wants and needs

1 BEFORE YOU LISTEN

A **LABEL.** Write the words under the pictures.

| clearance sale | pair of pants | receipt | shoppers |

1. _____

2. _____

3. _____

4. _____

B **DISCUSS.** Do you look for sales when you shop? Do you shop in stores, online, or both?

2 LISTEN

A **PREDICT.** Look at the picture. What is the woman doing? What is she listening to?

B ▶ **LISTEN FOR MAIN IDEA.** Listen to the podcast. Who is Lucy talking to?

a. people shopping at a clothing store
b. workers at a clothing store

C ▶ **EXPAND.** Listen to the whole conversation. What do the people talk about? Match.

1. _____ Erica **a.**  **b.**   **c.**

2. _____ Karen

3. _____ Nick

D ▶ **LISTEN FOR DETAILS.** Check (✓) the reason each person shops at Big Deals.

	Erica	Karen	Nick
It's convenient.			
They have great prices.			
It's easy to return things.			

Listening and Speaking

3 PRONUNCIATION

A ▶ **PRACTICE.** Listen. Then listen again and repeat.

need to	I need to buy a new uniform.
like to	I don't like to shop.
want to	I want to buy some jeans.

> **Pronunciation of *to***
>
> The word *to* often has a short, weak pronunciation. It sounds like *ta.* In informal conversation, *want to* sounds like "wanna."

B ▶ **APPLY.** Listen. Circle *to* with a short, weak pronunciation.

1. I don't need to buy a suit.
2. I like to shop.
3. I want to get a new tie.
4. I need to buy a suit.

4 CONVERSATION

A ▶ **LISTEN AND READ.** Then listen and repeat.

A: What do you need to buy today?
B: Well, I don't need to buy anything, but I want to buy a new pair of pants for work.
C: And I want to look for a raincoat while I'm here.

B **WORK TOGETHER.** Practice the conversation in Exercise A.

C **CREATE.** Make new conversations. Use the words in the boxes.

A: What do you _____ buy today?
B: Well, I don't need to buy anything, but I want to buy _____.
A: And I want to look for _____ while I'm here.

need to	boots	a sweatshirt
want to	gloves	a scarf
have to	sweatpants	a jacket

D **MAKE CONNECTIONS.** Talk about the clothes that you need or want for work, for school, or for your free time.

A: What do you need?
B: I need a new uniform for work. How about you?

I can describe my wants and needs. ◻   I need more practice. ◻

Simple present: *want / need* + infinitive				
Affirmative			**Negative**	
I			I	
You	**want**		You	**don't**
We		**to buy** a new pair of pants.	We	**need to** buy anything.
They			They	
He	**wants**		He	**doesn't**
She			She	

A COMPLETE. Write the correct form of the verbs.

1. **A:** I want ____to buy____ a few things after work today.
   (buy)

   Do you want _____ to Shop Mart with me?
   (go)

   B: Sure. I need _____ a cap there.
   (return)

   A: OK. What time do you want _____ here?
   (leave)

2. **A:** Do you want _____ shopping during lunch
   (go)

   today?

   B: Maybe. I need _____ a present for my co-worker. But I don't want
   (get)

   _____ a lot of money. I need _____ the sales online.
   (spend)   (check)

   A: I understand. I need _____ careful with my money, too.
   (be)

3. **A:** All my uniforms for work are old. I need _____ some new ones.
   (buy)

   B: Oh, really? I don't need _____ a uniform to work—regular clothes like
   (wear)

   jeans are OK.

B ▶ SELF-ASSESS. Listen and check your answers.

Grammar Watch

- Use *want* and *need* + an infinitive.
- An infinitive = *to* + the base form of the verb.
- You can also use *want / need* + a noun. *I want a denim jacket. He needs sweatpants.*

50 Unit 3, Lesson 3

Grammar

C APPLY. Look at the pictures. Complete the sentences. Use the correct form of the verbs.

Mary   Jim

1. Mary ___needs to go to the shoe store___.
                    (need + go)

2. Jim _____.
                    (want + go)

Larry   Ray

3. Larry _____.
                    (need + buy)

4. Ray _____.
                    (want + get)

RETURNS

Hector   Mariko

5. Hector _____.
                    (need + return)

6. Mariko _____.
                    (want + exchange)

D WORK TOGETHER. Compare your answers.

Show what you know!

1. **THINK ABOUT IT.** Make a list of three things you want and three things you need to buy, exchange, or return.

2. **TALK ABOUT IT.** Play the memory game. Use your lists.

   Ravi: I want to buy new gloves.
   Marc: Ravi wants to buy new gloves. I need to return a wool sweater.
   Silvia: Ravi wants to buy new gloves. Marc needs to return a wool sweater. I need to get a new umbrella.

3. **WRITE ABOUT IT.** Now write three sentences about your needs and wants. Then write three sentences about your classmates.

   I want to return . . .
   I need to exchange . . .
   They want to buy . . .

Lesson 4 — Store Ads, Online Orders, and Sales Receipts

1 READ A STORE AD

WORK TOGETHER. Talk about the online ad. Answer the questions.

ZIP⚡ Superstore

WOMEN | MEN | HOME | BED & BATH | SHOES | BEAUTY | KIDS | JUNIORS | JEWELRY | WATCHES | ACTIVE 🔍 Search

DAILY DEALS for Tuesday, April 22nd

Designer raincoats
regular price: $89.00
daily deal: $24.98
You save over 70%

Men's gloves
$36.55
daily deal: $18.55
You save over 40%

Women's leather boots
regular price: $99.00
daily deal: $45.00
You save over 50%

Men's wool scarves
regular price: $30.00
Daily Deal
Discount 50%

1. What's on sale?
2. How much is the discount on each item?
3. Which item saves the most money?
4. Which item do you want to buy? Why?
5. What is the sale price of wool scarves?

2 COMPLETE AN ONLINE ORDER

A **INTERPRET.** Read the online order form. Circle *True* or *False*.

🛒 **Items in Your Cart**

		Quantity	Price
Item 1:	Designer Raincoat	1	$24.98
Item 2:	Women's Leather Boots	1	$45.00

Subtotal: $69.98
Shipping: FREE
Tax: $4.19
Total $74.17

Payment Method
Secure credit card payment

*Credit card number   *Expiration date   *Security code
11122233355668899   01 / 22   001

I can read a store ad. ■   I need more practice. ■

Workplace, Life, and Community Skills

1. The shopper orders two items.   True   False
2. Shipping costs $4.37.   True   False
3. The shopper pays with a credit card.   True   False
4. The site is a safe site to enter your credit card. True   False
5. The shopper's credit card expires in February.   True   False
6. The shopper doesn't need to pay sales tax.   True   False

3 READ A SALES RECEIPT

A INTERPRET. Read the sales receipt. Answer the questions.

1. What is the date of purchase?
2. What is the discount on the swimsuit?
3. How much does the swimsuit cost before tax?
4. How much is it after tax?
5. How much change does the customer get?
6. What is the return policy?

```
◆ MAYFIELD ◆
  DEPARTMENT STORE
        2/28/18

Women's Swimwear
1 swimsuit
Discount 30%          $59.99
Subtotal             -17.99
FL Sales Tax 6%       42.00
Total                  2.52
CASH                  44.52
Change
                      50.00
                       5.48
Returns must be made within
30 days of purchase.
```

B EXAMINE. Read the store ad. Then, look at the sales receipts. Identify the two mistakes.

```
◆ MAYFIELD ◆
  DEPARTMENT STORE
      7/25/2018

Men's swimwear     $25.00
1 swimsuit          -5.00
Discount 20%
                   $20.00
Subtotal             1.20
FL Sales Tax 6%
                    21.20
Total               21.20
CASH                 0.00
Change
```

```
◆ MAYFIELD ◆
  DEPARTMENT STORE
      7/26/2018

Children's swimwear
1 swimsuit         $32.00
Discount 50%       -16.00
Subtotal           $16.00
FL Sales Tax 6%       .96
Total              16.96
CASH               20.00
Change              3.04
```

C ▶ LISTEN. Then listen and repeat.

A: Excuse me. I think there's a mistake. The ad says all swimwear is 30 percent off.
B: Yes, that's right.
A: But my receipt says 20 percent off.
B: Oh, I'm sorry. I'll take care of that.

D ROLE-PLAY. Make a similar conversation about the incorrect sales receipt.

E GO ONLINE. Visit an online store. Find a sale ad.

What's on sale? How much can you save?

I can complete an online order and read a sales receipt. ■   I need more practice. ■

Lesson 5

Talk about plans

1 BEFORE YOU LISTEN

A **LABEL.** Look at the pictures. Where does the man go? Write the words under the pictures.

bank   hardware store   laundromat   supermarket

1. _____ 2. _____ 3. _____ 4. _____

B **BRAINSTORM.** What kinds of errands do people often run?

2 LISTEN

A ▶ **LISTEN FOR MAIN IDEA.** Complete the sentences.

1. They are talking about _____.
   a. plans   **b.** relaxing

2. _____ needs to go to the supermarket.
   a. Max   **b.** Deb

3. _____ is going to be busy.
   a. Max   **b.** Deb

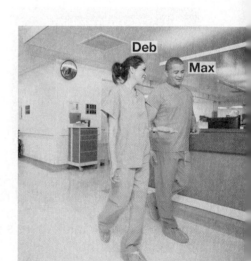

B ▶ **LISTEN FOR DETAILS.** Number Deb's errands in order.

_____ go to the supermarket

_____ go to the ATM

_____ go to the hardware store

C ▶ **EXPAND.** Listen to the whole conversation. Complete the sentence.

Max wants to _____.
a. take a nap   **b.** go to the ATM   **c.** stop at the supermarket

Listening and Speaking

3 PRONUNCIATION

A ▶ **PRACTICE. Listen. Then listen again and repeat.**

going to   I'm going to relax.
                    She's going to stop at the bank.

going to   I'm going to the post office.
                    You're going to the store with me.

> **Pronunciation of *going to***
>
> In informal conversation, *going to* often has the pronunciation "gonna" before another verb. It does not have this pronunciation before a noun.

B ▶ **APPLY. Listen to the sentences. Circle *going to* when it sounds like *gonna*.**

1. I'm going to stop at the deli.
2. I'm going to go to the bank.
3. We're going to the ATM.
4. She's going to run errands.

4 CONVERSATION

A ▶ **LISTEN AND READ. Then listen and repeat.**

A: So, what are your plans for tomorrow?
B: Nothing. I'm going to relax.
A: Well, I have a lot to do. First, I need to go to the ATM. Then I need to go to the hardware store. Then I'm going to stop at the deli at the supermarket.
B: Wow. You're going to be busy.

B **WORK TOGETHER. Practice the conversation.**

C **CREATE. Make new conversations. Use the words in the boxes.**

A: So, what are your plans for tomorrow?
B: Nothing. I'm going to ▮▮▮▮▮▮▮▮▮▮.
A: Well, I have a lot to do. First, I need to go to the ▮▮▮▮▮▮▮▮▮▮. Then I need to go to the ▮▮▮▮▮▮▮▮▮▮. Then I'm going to stop at the ▮▮▮▮▮▮▮▮▮▮.
B: Wow. You're going to be busy.

stay home
sleep late
watch TV

grocery store
deli
post office

bakery
gas station
laundromat

D **MAKE CONNECTIONS. Talk about errands.**

A: What are you going to do tomorrow?
B: First, I need to go to the gas station and then . . .

I can talk about plans. ▪	I need more practice. ▪

6

Grammar

Future with *be going to*

Future with *be going to*					
Affirmative			**Negative**		
I	**am**		I	**am**	
You We They	**are**	**going to** relax tomorrow.	You We They	**are**	**not going to** run errands.
He She	**is**		He She	**is**	

A COMPLETE. Write sentences with *be going to*. Use contractions.

1. She ＇s going to _____ take the package to the mail room.
2. I _____ cash my check after work.
3. They _____ return the files to their supervisor.
4. He _____ talk to his team leader.
5. We _____ prepare for the meeting.
6. You _____ check your schedule online.

Grammar Watch

I am = **I'm**
I am not = **I'm not**

he is = **he's**
he is not = **he isn't**

we are = **we're**
we are not = **we aren't**

For more contractions,
see page 258.

B APPLY. Complete the sentences with *be going to* and the words in parentheses.

1. Hector and Maria ___are going to get___ on-the-job training.

(get)

   They _____ it during the day at work.

(do)

2. My uniform is dirty. I'm _____ my clothes to the

(take)

   laundromat.

3. Tomorrow is a holiday, so a lot of people _____

(not come)

   to work. You're _____ almost alone in the office.

(be)

4. We need to run a lot of errands. We _____ time

(not have)

   to relax.

5. Sally _____ late. She _____ on time.

(work)   (not leave)

6. I _____ to work with a friend tomorrow.

(drive)

   I _____ the bus.

(not take)

Grammar

C **INTERPRET.** Look at the pictures. What are the people going to do? There is more than one correct answer.

In picture 1, the man is going to send a package.

D **WRITE.** Now write a sentence for each picture in Exercise C.

Show what you know!

1. **THINK ABOUT IT.** Make a list of errands you are going to run this week.

2. **TALK ABOUT IT.** Play charades. Take turns acting out an errand. Other students, guess the errand.

   A: What am I going to do?
   B: You're going to stop at the bank.
   A: No.
   C: You're going to . . .

3. **WRITE ABOUT IT.** Write sentences about what your classmates are going to do.

You're going to . . .

I can use future with *be going to.* ■ 　　　　　　　　I need more practice. ■

1 BEFORE YOU READ

A DECIDE. Complete the sentences with the words in the box.

cash	comparing	minimum	purchase

1. She's making a
   _____ .
   She's paying with
   _____ .

2. You don't have to pay
   the whole bill, but
   you have to pay the
   _____ .

3. He's _____
   TVs. Which one is best?

B MAKE CONNECTIONS. How do you pay when you go shopping? Do you use cash, a credit card, or another way to pay?

2 READ

▶ **LISTEN AND READ.**

Academic Skill: Identify Purpose

Authors write articles for different reasons. This is the author's purpose. Knowing the author's purpose helps you understand the main idea.

How Would You Like to Pay for That?

1 Are you thinking of making a big purchase soon, like a TV or a computer? What is the best way to pay for it? We interviewed three shoppers who just bought a new $475 Sonpanic TV. Read how each shopper 5 paid for the TV. Then compare how much it really cost them. You may be surprised!

Credit Card "I paid with my credit card. I use my credit card because it gives me time. I get a month to pay the bill. I always pay the total amount. That way I don't pay the credit card 10 company any interest. Credit card interest rates are too high. Like 20%!"

Brian

Sonpanic TV	$475.00
Sales tax	+ 23.75
Total cost	**$498.75**
(Sales tax = 5% in Brian's state)	

Credit Card "I paid with my credit card. I like to use my credit card because it gives me time to pay. I never have enough cash for big purchases. So I pay just the minimum every 15 month. The problem is, it can take years to pay off the whole bill! So I pay a lot of interest."

Cindy

Sonpanic TV	$475.00
Minimum monthly payment	$25.00
Number of months*	× 24
Cost of TV (including 20% interest)	$600.00
Sales tax	+ 30.40
Total cost	**$630.40**
(Sales tax = 6.4% in Cindy's state)	

Rent-to-Own "I bought my TV at the rent-to-own store because I don't have enough cash right now, and I don't have a credit card. At a rent-to-own store, I can get a new TV and bring it 20 home the same day. Every week, I pay $24 to the store for the TV. If I don't have the money, I return the TV to the store. But if I keep paying, at the end of the year, the TV will belong to me."

Craig

Sonpanic TV	$475.00
Weekly payment	$24.00
Number of weeks	× 52
Total cost of the TV	**$1,248.00**
(There's no sales tax in Craig's state.)	

*Source: http://www.bankrate.com

Reading

3 CLOSE READING

A IDENTIFY. What is the main idea?

When you make a big purchase, _____.

a. *how much* you pay depends on *how* you pay
b. it's best to pay for it in cash
c. you always have to pay sales tax

B CITE EVIDENCE. Complete the statements. Where is the information? Write the line numbers.

Lines

1. Brian doesn't like to _____.
   a. shop with a credit card
   b. pay the total amount of his credit card bill
   c. pay interest to his credit card company   _____

2. Cindy doesn't _____.
   a. have a credit card
   b. make big purchases with cash
   c. pay interest to her credit card company   _____

3. Cindy is unhappy because she _____.
   a. doesn't have a good TV
   b. pays a lot of interest on big purchases
   c. has only a little cash   _____

C INTERPRET. Complete the sentences about the chart.

1. The person who paid the most for the TV is _____.
   a. Brian
   b. Cindy
   c. Craig

2. The sales tax in Cindy's state is _____.
   a. 0%
   b. 6.4%
   c. 5%

4 SUMMARIZE

Complete the summary with the words in the box.

amount	interest	minimum	whole

Three shoppers all bought the same TV, but paid in different ways. Brian used a credit card and paid the (1) _____ bill at the end of the month: $475 plus sales tax. Cindy used a credit card, too. She made only the (2) _____ monthly payment, so she'll pay a lot of (3) _____. Her TV will cost $600 plus sales tax. Craig is renting a TV from a rent-to-own store. He'll pay the greatest (4) _____: $1,248.

Show what you know!

1. **THINK ABOUT IT.** Make a list of big purchases you want to make someday.
2. **TALK ABOUT IT.** Work with a partner. Compare your list of purchases. What is the best way to pay for them?
3. **WRITE ABOUT IT.** Write about a big purchase and the way to pay for it.

I can identify purpose. ■   I need more practice. ■

Lesson 8

Describe problems with purchases

1 BEFORE YOU LISTEN

MATCH. Look at the pictures. Match the pictures to the problems with the clothes.

| There's a hole in it. | It's too tight. | A button is missing. |
| They're too loose. | ~~The zipper is broken.~~ | A seam is ripped. |

The zipper is broken.

2 LISTEN

Anna   Bessy

A **PREDICT.** Look at the picture of two co-workers on a break. What are they talking about?

B ▶ **LISTEN FOR MAIN IDEA.** Listen to the conversation. Complete the sentence.

Anna and Bessy are going to _____.
a. buy clothes   **b.** return clothes

C ▶ **LISTEN FOR DETAILS.** Listen again. Read the sentences. Circle *True* or *False*.

1. Bessy needs to buy a jacket.   True   False
2. There is a problem with Bessy's jacket.   True   False
3. Anna wants to buy a dress.   True   False

D ▶ **EXPAND.** Listen to the whole conversation. Complete the sentence.

Anna's dress is really a _____.

Listening and Speaking

3 CONVERSATION

A ▶ **LISTEN AND READ.** Then listen and repeat.

A: Hi, Bessy. Are you going out at lunchtime?
B: Yeah, I need to run an errand. I'm going to Kohn's. I need to return this jacket.
A: How come?
B: The zipper is broken.
A: That's very annoying. . . . Actually, I need to go to Kohn's, too. I need to return a dress.
B: Really? What's wrong with it?
A: It's too short.

B **WORK TOGETHER.** Practice the conversation in Exercise A.

C **CREATE.** Make new conversations. Use the words in the boxes.

A: Hi, _____. Are you going out at lunchtime?
B: Yeah, I need to run an errand. I'm going to Kohn's to return
this _____.
A: What's the problem?
B: _____
A: That's very annoying. . . . Actually, I need to go to Kohn's,
too. I need to return a _____.
B: Really? What's wrong with it?
A: It's too _____.

cap
shirt
sweater

A button is missing.
A seam is ripped.
There's a hole in it.

sweatshirt
raincoat
jacket

tight
long
big

D **ROLE-PLAY.** Student A, talk about returning some clothes.
Student B, ask about the problem.

A: I need to return these pants.
B: What's the problem?

I can describe problems with purchases. ■   I need more practice. ☐

Adverbs of degree: *very* and *too*

Adverbs of degree: *very / too*		
That's	**very**	annoying.
It's	**too**	short.

Grammar Watch

- *very* = a lot
- *too* = more than you need or want

A **IDENTIFY.** Cross out the incorrect words.

1. This raincoat doesn't cost a lot. It's **very / ~~too~~** cheap.
2. She wears size 8. That dress is size 2. It's **very / too** small for her.
3. The prices at the clearance sale are **very / too** good. A lot of people are going to be there.
4. This sweater is **very / too** pretty. I want to buy it.
5. These shoes aren't good for walking to work. They're **very / too** tight.
6. This scarf is **very / too** colorful. It looks great with my coat.

B **COMPLETE.** Write *very* or *too*.

1. **A:** The coffee shop on Oak Street is ___very___ good. I get breakfast there a lot.

   B: That place is _____ slow. I'm always late for work when I stop there.

2. **A:** I like that blouse. It's _____ beautiful.

   B: Thanks. But it's _____ big. I need to exchange it for a smaller size.

3. **A:** I don't like to shop online. For me, it's _____ slow. When I want something, I don't want to wait.

   B: Really? I shop online all the time. It's _____ easy to order what you need, and a few days later it's at your door.

4. **A:** That coat is _____ warm. It's perfect for cold winter days.

   B: I know. I want it, but it's _____ expensive. It's $90, and I only have $60.

I can use adverbs of degree *very* and *too* in a sentence. ■   I need more practice. ■

Lesson 10 | Writing

Write about saving money

1 STUDY THE MODEL

READ. Answer the questions.

> Davit Babayan
>
> How I Save Money
>
> This is how I save money when I shop. I always buy things on sale. I pay with cash, not a credit card. I check the receipt to make sure the prices are correct.

1. What did Davit write about?
2. Why does Davit buy things on sale?
3. How does he pay?
4. Why does he check the receipt?

2 PLAN YOUR WRITING

WORK TOGETHER. Ask and answer the questions.

1. How do you save money when you shop?
2. Do you buy things on sale?
3. How do you pay for things?
4. Do you look at your receipts? Why or why not?

3 WRITE

Now write about how you save money. Use the model, the Writing Skill, and your ideas from Exercise 2 to help you.

Writing Skill: Use a topic sentence

Start your paragraph with a topic sentence. A topic sentence tells the main idea of the paragraph. For example:

This is how I save money when I shop.

4 CHECK YOUR WRITING

WORK TOGETHER. Read the checklist. Read your writing aloud. Revise your writing.

WRITING CHECKLIST

☐ The paragraph answers the questions in Exercise 2.

☐ The paragraph starts with a topic sentence.

I can use a topic sentence. ■   I need more practice. ■

Lesson 11

Listen Actively

1 MEET RITA

Read about one of her workplace skills.

I'm a good listener. I listen actively. For example, I ask questions to make sure I understand the customer's needs.

2 RITA'S PROBLEM

READ. Circle *True* or *False*.

Rita is a salesperson at an electronics store. A customer shows her a laptop and says, "I want to return this laptop. I bought it here two months ago." Rita knows that customers can return items up to two weeks after they buy them. But when something is wrong with an item, they can return it up to two months after they buy it.

1. Rita sells computers in an electronics store.	True	False
2. A customer bought his laptop two weeks ago in that store.	True	False
3. Customers can return all items two months after they buy them.	True	False

3 RITA'S SOLUTION

A **WORK TOGETHER.** Rita listens actively to understand her customers' needs. What does she say? Explain your answer.

1. Rita says, "Sorry. There are no returns after two weeks."
2. Rita says, "OK. Is there something wrong with the laptop?"
3. Rita says, "OK. Did you buy the laptop here?"
4. Rita _____.

B **ROLE-PLAY.** Look at your answer to 3A. Role-play Rita's conversation.

Show what you know!

1. **THINK ABOUT IT.** Do you listen actively? How do you listen actively in class? At work? At home?

2. **WRITE ABOUT IT.** Write an example in your Skills Log.

   I listen actively in class. I repeat and ask questions.

3. **PRESENT IT.** Tell the class how you listen actively.

I can give an example of how I listen actively. ◼

Unit Review: Go back to page 45. Which unit goals can you check off?

4 Small Talk

PREVIEW

Look at the picture. What do you see? Where are the people? What are they talking about?

UNIT GOALS

- [ ] Identify free-time activities
- [ ] Talk about free-time activities
- [ ] Read a community calendar
- [ ] Understand a schedule of events
- [ ] Communicate likes and dislikes

- [ ] Accept or decline an invitation
- [ ] **Academic skill:** Predict the topic
- [ ] **Writing skill:** Use details in your writing
- [ ] **Workplace soft skill:** Show how you are professional

Vocabulary

Free-time activities

A **PREDICT.** Look at the pictures. What are the people doing?

B ▶ **LISTEN AND POINT.** Then listen and repeat.

Vocabulary

Free-time activities

1. go swimming	**4.** go dancing	**7.** go to the gym	**10.** go to the park
2. go shopping	**5.** go running	**8.** go to the beach	**11.** go for a walk
3. go fishing	**6.** go out to eat	**9.** go to the zoo	**12.** go for a bike ride

C **ACT IT OUT.** Student A, act out a free-time activity. Other students, guess the activity.

Student A acts out "go dancing."
B: Go running?
A: No.
C: Go dancing?
A: Yes!

D **CATEGORIZE.** Look at the list of free-time activities. Which are outdoor activities? Which are indoor activities? Which can be both? Complete the chart.

Indoor
go to the gym

Both
go swimming

Outdoor
go to the park

> **Study Tip**
>
> **Write sentences**
> Look at the free-time activities. Which activities do you like to do? Write sentences.
> I like to go swimming.
> I don't like to go shopping.

Show what you know!

1. THINK ABOUT IT. Write three activities you do in your free time.

2. TALK ABOUT IT. Ask your classmates about their free-time activities.

A: What do you do in your free time?
B: I go to the beach.
A: Where do you go?
B: I go to Sunset Beach.
A: Really? How often do you go?

3. WRITE ABOUT IT. Now write about a classmate's free-time activities.

Wong goes to the beach in his free time. He likes Sunset Beach. He usually goes every weekend.

I can identify free-time activities. ■   I need more practice. ■

Listening and Speaking

Talk about free-time activities

1 BEFORE YOU LISTEN

LABEL. Look at the pictures. Write the names of the classes.

a business class   an auto mechanics class   a guitar class

1. _____ 2. _____ 3. _____

2 LISTEN

A ▶ **LISTEN FOR MAIN IDEA.** What are they talking about?

a. weekend plans
b. business
c. going hiking

B ▶ **LISTEN FOR DETAILS.** Listen again. Answer the questions.

1. Who does Bi-Yun usually see on Sunday?
   a. her family   b. her friends   c. her classmates

2. What does Mario usually do on Saturday mornings?
   a.   b.   c.

C ▶ **EXPAND.** Listen to the whole conversation. Answer the question.

Which level class do you think Mario is in?
a. beginning   b. intermediate   c. advanced

Listening and Speaking

3 PRONUNCIATION

A ▶ **PRACTICE. Listen. Then listen again and repeat.**

every	usually	interesting
(2 syllables)	(3 syllables)	(3 syllables)

> **Unpronounced syllables**
>
> Some words have a syllable that is not pronounced. For example, the word *family* looks like it has three syllables (fam·i·ly), but we pronounce it as two syllables (fam·i·ly).

B ▶ **APPLY. Listen. Write the number of syllables you hear.**

1. ____ evening   2. ____ favorite   3. ____ different

4 CONVERSATION

A ▶ **LISTEN AND READ. Then listen and repeat.**

A: What are you doing this weekend?
B: I'm going to go to the beach with my family.
A: Really? Sounds like fun.
B: Yeah. We usually go to the beach on Sunday in the summer. What about you?
A: Well, I have class on Saturday. I have a business class every Saturday morning.

B **WORK TOGETHER. Practice the conversation.**

C **CREATE. Make new conversations. Use the words in the boxes.**

A: What are you doing this weekend?
B: I'm going to _____ with my family.
A: Really? Sounds like fun.
B: Yeah. We usually _____ on Sunday.
   What about you?
A: Well, I have _____. I have
   _____ every _____.

> go out to eat
> go for a bike ride
> go hiking

> an auto mechanics class
> a cooking class
> a computer class

> Friday evening
> Saturday afternoon
> Sunday morning

D **MAKE CONNECTIONS. Think about three things you are going to do in your free time. Talk about your free-time activities.**

I can talk about free-time activities. ■   I need more practice. ■

Adverbs of frequency								
With action verbs				**With _be_**				
I We They	always usually often	go		I We They	am are	always usually often	at the beach.	
He She	sometimes hardly ever never	goes	to the beach.	He She	is	sometimes hardly ever never		

0%   100%

never   hardly ever   sometimes   often   usually   always

A **IDENTIFY. Cross out the incorrect words.**

1. She works on Saturday mornings. She **never / ~~often~~** sleeps late on Saturdays.

2. I can't go to the movies Thursday night. I **always / hardly ever** take a computer class after work on Thursdays.

3. There are very few good restaurants near my office. I **hardly ever / often** go out to eat for lunch.

4. Ty is an excellent worker. He **always / sometimes** finishes his projects on time.

5. My friend Tanya takes the bus to work. She **often / never** drives to her job.

6. He likes computer programming. He **sometimes / never** spends hours on the computer.

B **WRITE. Make sentences with the adverbs in parentheses.**

1. (always) The kids are busy. (usually) They get homework help after school.
   The kids are always busy. They usually get homework help after school.

2. (never) Marc is on time. (sometimes) He gets to work thirty minutes late.
   _____

3. (usually) They go dancing on weekends. (hardly ever) They stay home.
   _____

4. (never) They are home on Sundays. (always) They are at their cousin's house.
   _____

Grammar Watch

- Adverbs of frequency go _before_ action verbs.
- Adverbs of frequency go _after_ forms of _be_.

Grammar

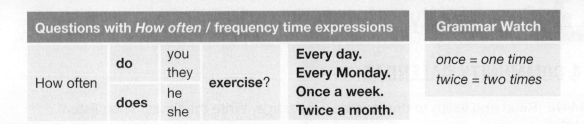

Questions with *How often* / frequency time expressions				Every day. Every Monday. Once a week. Twice a month.
How often	do	you they	exercise?	
	does	he she		

Grammar Watch

once = one time
twice = two times

C **INTERPRET.** Look at the calendar. Ask and answer five questions with *how often*.

A: How often does Felipe eat dinner with his cousins?
B: Once a week.

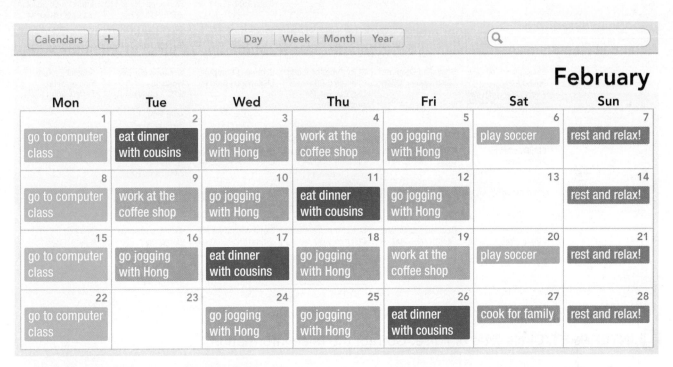

Calendars	+			Day	Week	Month	Year		🔍	

February

Mon	Tue	Wed	Thu	Fri	Sat	Sun
1 go to computer class	2 eat dinner with cousins	3 go jogging with Hong	4 work at the coffee shop	5 go jogging with Hong	6 play soccer	7 rest and relax!
8 go to computer class	9 work at the coffee shop	10 go jogging with Hong	11 eat dinner with cousins	12 go jogging with Hong	13	14 rest and relax!
15 go to computer class	16 go jogging with Hong	17 eat dinner with cousins	18 go jogging with Hong	19 work at the coffee shop	20 play soccer	21 rest and relax!
22 go to computer class	23	24 go jogging with Hong	25 go jogging with Hong	26 eat dinner with cousins	27 cook for family	28 rest and relax!

Show what you know!

1. **THINK ABOUT IT.** Write three questions about your classmates' free-time activities. Use *how often*.

   How often do you go to the movies?

2. **TALK ABOUT IT.** Ask your questions. Answer your classmates' questions.

3. **WRITE ABOUT IT.** Now write about your classmates' free-time activities.

   Safa rarely goes to the movies.

I can use adverbs of frequency in sentences and questions. ■   I need more practice. ■

Workplace, Life, and Community Skills

Community calendars and events

1 READ A COMMUNITY CALENDAR

A ▶ **EXAMINE.** Read and listen to the recorded message. Write the times. Then listen and repeat.

City Library Schedule of Events · March

Sun	Mon	Tue	Wed	Thu	Fri	Sat
				1 Beginning Computer Class 1:00–3:00 PM	**2** Writing a Resume Workshop 2:00–4:00 PM Teen Time 3–5:00 PM	**3** Citizenship Information Session 3:00 PM–5:00 PM
4	**5** ESL Classes for Adults from _6:00–8:00 PM_	**6** Beginning Computer Class 1:00–3:00 PM	**7** Story Time for Young Children 9:00 AM ESL Classes for Adults from _____	**8** Beginning Computer Class 1:00–3:00 PM	**9** Writing a Resume Workshop 2:00–4:00 PM Teen Time 3–5:00 PM	**10** Special Lecture: Finding Your Perfect Job
11	**12** ESL Classes for Adults from _____	**13** Beginning Computer Class 1:00–3:00 PM	**14** Story Time for Young Children 9:00 AM ESL Classes for Adults from _____	**15** Beginning Computer Class 1:00–3:00 PM	**16** Writing a Resume Workshop 2:00–4:00 PM Teen Time 3–5:00 PM	**17**
18	**19** ESL Classes for Adults from _____	**20** Beginning Computer Class 1:00–3:00 PM	**21** Story Time for Young Children 9:00 AM ESL Classes for Adults from _____	**22** Beginning Computer Class 1:00–3:00 PM	**23** Writing a Resume Workshop 2:00–4:00 PM Teen Time 3–5:00 PM	**24** Job Fair _____
25	**26**	**27**	**28**	**29**	**30**	**31**

B **INTERPRET.** Circle *True* or *False*. Correct the false information.

1. The Citizenship Information Session meets on the first Saturday of the month.   True   False
2. The Job Fair is twice a month.   True   False
3. The ESL Class for Adults meets every Monday and Wednesday.   True   False
4. The Beginning Computer Class meets twice a week.   True   False
5. The Beginning Computer Class meets from 9:00 to 1:00.   True   False
6. Story Time for Young Children meets every Wednesday afternoon.   True   False
7. There is a special lecture once a week.   True   False

C **WORK TOGETHER.** Ask and answer questions about the City Library Events Calendar.

A: When does the ESL Class for Adults meet?
B: It meets every Monday and Wednesday from 6 to 8 p.m.

I can read a community calendar. ■   I need more practice. ■

Workplace, Life, and Community Skills

2 UNDERSTAND A SCHEDULE OF EVENTS

A ▶ **LISTEN.** Check the events that will take place at Atlas Community College Library.

- ☐ ESL Conversation Classes
- ☐ Computer Classes
- ☐ Job Interview Workshop
- ☐ Story Time for Children

- ☐ Teen Time
- ☐ Job Application Workshop
- ☐ Job Interviews
- ☐ Résumé Writing Workshop

B ▶ **IDENTIFY.** Listen again and complete the table.

🌐 Atlas Community College Library: Upcoming Events   🔍 _____

Date	Event	Time	Location
Monday, May 14th	Open Computer Lab	1. _____	Computer Lab
	2. _____ _____	1:00 PM	Room 224
	ESL Conversation Class	3. _____	Classroom A
	ESL Conversation Class	6:30–8:30 PM	Classroom B
	Job Interview Workshop Series	4:00–6:00 PM	Computer Lab
Tuesday, May 15th	4. _____ _____	8:00 AM–1:00 PM	Computer Lab
	5. _____ _____	1:00–3:00 PM	Classroom A
	Completing a Job Application	6. _____	

C **WORK TOGETHER.** Invite a classmate to one of the college's library events.

D GO ONLINE. Find the website of your local library. Identify two events that interest you. Add those events to a digital calendar. Invite a friend to one of the events.

I can understand a schedule of events. ■   I need more practice. ■

Communicate likes and dislikes

1 BEFORE YOU LISTEN

MAKE CONNECTIONS. Look at the pictures. Which activities do you need to do at home or at work? What are some other activities that people need to do?

cook

vacuum

work outside

iron

2 LISTEN

A **PREDICT.** Look at the picture. What is the man's problem? What are some solutions?

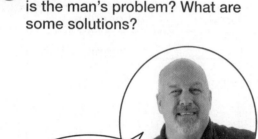

I need to drive a lot every day, but I really hate it.

B ▶ **LISTEN FOR MAIN IDEA.** What problem do the people discuss?

a. People often don't have a lot of free time.
b. People need to do things they don't enjoy.

C ▶ **LISTEN FOR DETAILS.** Listen to the whole podcast. Number the ideas in the order that you hear them.

a. _____ After you do something you hate, do something you like.

b. _____ Put a time limit on the activities you hate to do.

c. _____ When you need to do something you hate, do something you like at the same time.

D ▶ **EXPAND.** Listen to the whole podcast. Match the solutions and examples.

When you do something you hate:

1. _____ do something you like at the same time   **a.** work and then take a break

2. _____ put a time limit on it   **b.** work and talk to a friend

3. _____ do something you like after   **c.** work for two hours and then stop

Listening and Speaking

3 CONVERSATION

A ▶ **LISTEN AND READ. Then listen and repeat.**

A: You know, I really hate to do the laundry.
B: Me, too. And do you know what else I hate?
A: No. What?
B: I hate to iron.
A: Not me. I actually like it.
B: You're kidding.
A: No, really. I find it relaxing.

B **WORK TOGETHER. Practice the conversation in Exercise A.**

C **CREATE. Make new conversations. Use the words in the boxes.**

A: You know, I really hate to ▨▨▨▨▨▨▨.
B: Me, too. And do you know what else I hate?
A: No. What?
B: I hate to ▨▨▨▨▨▨.
A: Not me. I actually like it.
B: You're kidding.
A: No, really. I find it relaxing.

| clean the office |
| do the dishes |
| get up early |

| cook |
| vacuum |
| work outside |

D **PRESENT IT. Make a presentation about what you hate to do at work or at home. What are some solutions? Do the ideas in the podcast help? Which ideas are helpful? Explain you answer.**

I can communicate likes and dislikes. ■   I need more practice. ■

Lesson 6

Simple present: *love* / *like* / *hate* + infinitive

Simple present: *love* / *like* / *hate* + infinitive						
Affirmative			**Negative**			
I	**love**		I	**don't love**		
He	**likes**	to cook.	He	**doesn't like**	to vacuum.	
They	**hate**		They	**don't hate**		

Grammar Watch

love = 😊

like = ☺

not like = ☹

hate = 😠

A **COMPLETE.** Use the verbs to complete the sentences.

1. Zoya _____loves to go_____ to work every day.
   (love / go)

2. She _____ people.
   (like / help)

3. She _____ time with children.
   (love / spend)

4. She _____ them sick or hurt.
   (hate / see)

5. Her supervisor is supportive. She

   _____ unhappy employees.
   (not like / have)

6. But Zoya and her co-workers

   _____ long hours overnight.
   (not like / work)

7. The worst shift is midnight to noon.

   They all _____ that shift.
   (hate / work)

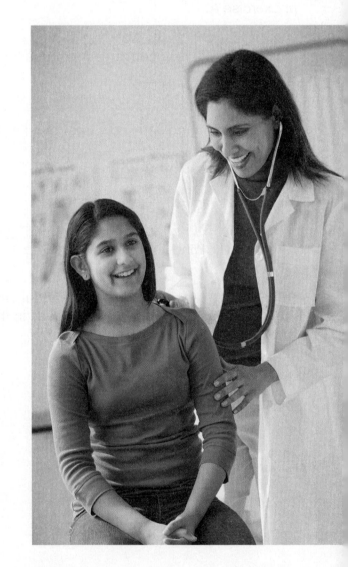

Grammar

B INTERPRET. Read the bar graph. Write three sentences about the information. Use *like to*, *love to*, and *hate to*.

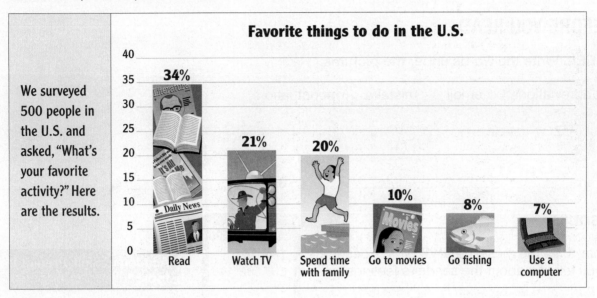

We surveyed 500 people in the U.S. and asked, "What's your favorite activity?" Here are the results.

Favorite things to do in the U.S.

- Read — 34%
- Watch TV — 21%
- Spend time with family — 20%
- Go to movies — 10%
- Go fishing — 8%
- Use a computer — 7%

Thirty-four percent of the people like to read.

Show what you know!

1. THINK ABOUT IT. Write four sentences about activities you like and dislike. Use *like, hate, love*.

2. TALK ABOUT IT. Talk about your likes and dislikes with your classmates.

A: I love to . . .
B: Not me. I love to . . .
A: Well, I don't like to . . .

3. WRITE ABOUT IT. Write four sentences about your partner's likes and dislikes.

Hu likes to go swimming. He doesn't like to go fishing.

I can use the simple present with *love* / *like* / *hate* + infinitive. ■   I need more practice. ■

1 BEFORE YOU READ

A LABEL. Write the words under the pictures.

> abbreviations   emoji   mistake   punctuation

· , ' ?

Great ~~Grate~~ job!

St. Ave. Rd.

1. an _____   **2.** _____   **3.** a _____   **4.** _____

B DISCUSS.

What does the message say? What does the emoji tell you about the sender's feelings?

THX 😎
C U L8R

Academic Skill: Predict the topic

You can often guess what an article is about by looking at the title and any pictures. This will get you ready to understand what you read.

2 READ

▶ **LISTEN AND READ.**

Different Writing Styles

1 Technology is changing the way people write in English. Some of the changes are happening because of text messages.

It isn't easy to write on a phone, so people keep messages
5 short. They do this in several ways:
- They make changes in spelling (like *cuz* for *because* or *prolly* for *probably*).
- They leave out words (like *Will call* for *I will call you.*).
- They leave out punctuation.
10 - They use abbreviations (like *am* for *morning* or *LMK* for *Let me know*).
- They use emojis to show feelings (for *That's funny!*).

People also leave out greetings, like "Dear Tom." They leave out closings, too, like "Best wishes." They usually don't sign
15 their name because the person getting the text knows them.

When you text a friend or family member, this style of writing is fine. Mistakes are usually okay, too. Text messages often have mistakes. That's because people write fast. They don't stop to check their message before they hit "Send."

20 But what about writing to other people? Do you ever write to a supervisor at work or a teacher at school? Some text messages or e-mails need a more formal writing style. It depends on your relationship with your reader. Sometimes you want to use a style that shows respect. Then you need
25 to take the time to write in a style that's clear and polite.

Dan Brown
RE: Meeting?

Hello Liz,

It was nice meeting you today and talking about the new project. I'd like to talk again soon. When are you free? Please text me at (202) 555-9876.

Best,

Dan

Hi Dan, Liz here. Happy to talk but this week not gd. Sorry. Mon @ 4 ok?

Clear and polite style	Friends and family style
Hello	Hey
Could you please	Cn u
I'm surprised!	WOW!!!
I'm sorry, but I'm afraid I'm going to be late.	Gonna be late. 😔

Reading

3 CLOSE READING

A **IDENTIFY. What is the main idea? Complete the sentence.**

There are different styles for writing messages in English.
The best style to use depends on _____.

a. who you are writing to   **b.** what you want to say   **c.** how you are feeling

B **CITE EVIDENCE. Complete the sentences. Where is the information? Write the line numbers.**

1. The way people write English is changing because of _____.   **Lines**
   a. new English words   **b.** writing on cell phones   **c.** changes in grammar   _____

2. When people write text messages, they often don't use _____.
   a. emojis   **b.** abbreviations   **c.** punctuation   _____

3. "Best wishes" is an example of _____.
   a. a mistake   **b.** a way to say hello   **c.** a way to end an e-mail   _____

4. "Cn u wait 4 me" is an example of _____ in a message to
   someone like a teacher or a supervisor.
   a. leaving out words   **b.** the wrong style   **c.** showing respect   _____

4 SUMMARIZE

Complete the summary with the words in the box.

leave out	mistakes	polite	style

Text messages are causing changes in the way people write English. When people

write texts to friends, they often (1) _____ letters, words, and punctuation.

They use "friends and family (2) _____." These messages are often full of

(3) _____. Sometimes writers need a more formal style that's more

(4) _____.

Show what you know!

1. **THINK ABOUT IT.** In the chart, write the names of people you e-mail or text. Which
   style is right for each person?

Friends and family style	
Clear and polite style	

2. **PRESENT IT.** Tell the class about the people in your chart. What is the right style
   for writing to each person? Why?

I can predict the topic. ■   I need more practice. ■

8 Accept or decline an invitation

1 BEFORE YOU LISTEN

A LABEL. Look at the pictures. Write the reasons that people say no to invitations.

> I have other plans.   I don't feel well.   I'm too busy.

1. _____ 2. _____ 3. _____

B MAKE CONNECTIONS. In the U.S., it is polite to give a reason when you decline an invitation. How about in your country?

2 LISTEN

A PREDICT. Look at the co-workers. Who looks like she is leaving? Who looks like she is staying?

B ▶ LISTEN FOR MAIN IDEA. Listen to the conversation. What does Meg ask?

a. "Do you want to get some lunch?"
b. "Do you have time to help me?"

C ▶ LISTEN FOR DETAILS. Listen again. Choose the correct answer.

1. _____ is very busy.
   a. Meg   **b.** Selda
2. Selda _____ go with Meg.
   a. can   **b.** can't

D ▶ EXPAND. Listen to the whole conversation. Answer the questions.

1. Who called Selda?
   a. her husband   **b.** her friend   **c.** her co-worker
2. What is Selda going to do?
   a. finish her work   **b.** go to lunch with Meg   **c.** go to lunch with Bob

Listening and Speaking

3 PRONUNCIATION

A ▶ **PRACTICE. Listen. Then listen again and repeat.**

have to   I have to finish some work.
has to   She has to make some calls.

B ▶ **CHOOSE. Listen to the sentences. Circle the words you hear.**

1. **a.** have to
   b. have a

2. **a.** have to
   b. have a

3. **a.** has to
   b. has a

4. **a.** has to
   b. has a

4 CONVERSATION

A ▶ **LISTEN AND READ. Then listen and repeat.**

A: Do you want to get some lunch?
B: Sorry, I can't. I have to finish some work.
A: Oh. Are you sure?
B: Yes, I'm sorry. I'm really too busy.
A: Well, how about a little later?
B: Thanks, but I don't think so. Not today.

B **WORK TOGETHER. Practice the conversation in Exercise A.**

C **CREATE. Make new conversations. Use the words in the boxes.**

A: Do you want to _____?
B: Sorry, I can't. I have to _____.
A: Oh. Are you sure?
B: Yes, I'm sorry. I really can't.
A: Well, how about a little later?
B: Thanks, but I don't think so. Not today.

> walk over to the deli
> take a walk
> get some coffee

> go to a meeting
> run some errands
> make some calls

D **ROLE-PLAY. Make your own conversations. Student A, invite your partner to do something. Student B, accept or decline the invitation.**

> To accept an invitation, you can say:
> • Sure. I'd love to.
> • That sounds like fun.
> • Sounds great.

I can accept or decline an invitation. ■   I need more practice. ■

Grammar

Modal: *Have to*

Modal: *have to*						
Affirmative			**Negative**			
I			I			
You	**have to**		You	**don't have to**		
We		**finish** some work.	We			**go** to a meeting.
They			They			
He	**has to**		He	**doesn't have to**		
She			She			

A **DECIDE.** Complete the sentences. Use the verbs in the box.

drive	get up	~~go~~	study	stay	visit

1. We don't have _____*to go*_____ to the grocery store. We have a lot of food.

2. He has _____ tonight. There's a big test tomorrow.

3. Kara doesn't have _____ to work. She takes the bus every day.

4. They start work at 6:00 in the morning. They have _____ _____ early.

5. Jon has _____ home from work today. He's sick.

6. I have _____ my co-worker. She's in the hospital.

B **APPLY.** Complete the sentences. Use *have to* and the words in parentheses.

1. I'm coming home on time tonight. I ___*don't have to work late*___.
   (not work late)

2. Bik _____ _____ home with her son. He's sick.
   (stay)

3. I can help you finish. You _____ all the work.
   (not do)

4. Monica __ _____ this weekend. She can go to the zoo with us.
   (not work)

5. Omar ___ _____ the bus to work. He doesn't have a car.
   (take)

6. The movie theater is always crowded. We _____ tickets early.
   (buy)

C **SELF-ASSESS.** Compare your answers.

Grammar Watch

- Use *have to* / *has to* + the base form of the verb.
- Use *have to* / *has to* when something is necessary.
- Use *don't* / *doesn't have to* when something is not necessary.

I can make sentences with the modal *have to.* ■   I need more practice. ■

Write about a free-time activity

1 STUDY THE MODEL

READ. Answer the questions.

> Nestor Cruz
>
> My Free Time
>
> In my free time, I like to go fishing. I usually go on Sunday mornings. I go fishing with my brother and my son. We go to different places, like Spring River and Silver Lake. I like to fish because it is relaxing.

1. What does Nestor like to do in his free time?
2. How often does he do this activity?
3. Who does he go with?
4. Where does he go?

2 PLAN YOUR WRITING

WORK TOGETHER. Ask and answer the questions.

1. What do you like to do in your free time?
2. How often do you do this activity?
3. Who do you go with?
4. Where do you go?

3 WRITE

Now write about your free time. Use the model, the Writing Skill, and your ideas from Exercise 2 to help you.

4 CHECK YOUR WRITING

WORK TOGETHER. Read the checklist. Read your writing aloud. Revise your writing.

Writing Skill: Use details in your writing

Put details in your writing. Write details about time, people, and places. For example:

No details: I go fishing.
With details: I go fishing with my brother and my son.

WRITING CHECKLIST

☐ The paragraph answers the questions in Exercise 2.

☐ The paragraph starts with a topic sentence.

☐ There are details about time, people, and places in the writing.

I can use details in my writing. ■   I need more practice. ■

Be professional

1 MEET ASAD

Read about one of his workplace skills.

I am professional. For example, when I'm at work, I always take care of the customer. The customer's needs come first.

2 ASAD'S PROBLEM

READ. Circle *True* or *False*.

Asad works in a supermarket. There is a big sale today. Asad's supervisor told him to prepare items for the sale, and there isn't much time. Then a customer comes to Asad and says, "Excuse me. I can't find the coffee. Can you show me where it is?" But Asad still has a lot of work to do.

1. Asad has a very busy day today.	True	False
2. Asad's supervisor is helping him with the display.	True	False
3. The customer needs Asad's help.	True	False

3 ASAD'S SOLUTION

A **WORK TOGETHER.** Asad is professional. What does he say to the customer? Explain your answer.

1. Asad says, "Sure. Come with me."
2. Asad says, "I'm sorry, I'm busy. Can you ask someone else?"
3. Asad says, "I need to finish this. Then I can help you."
4. Asad _____.

B **ROLE-PLAY.** Look at your answer to 3A. Role-play Asad's conversation.

Show what you know!

1. **THINK ABOUT IT.** Are you professional? How are you professional at work? Give examples.

2. **WRITE ABOUT IT.** Write an example in your Skills Log.

I am professional at work. For example, I stop talking to my co-workers when a customer needs help.

I can give an example of how I am professional. ☐

Unit Review: Go back to page 65. Which unit goals can you check off?

5 At Home

PREVIEW

Look at the picture. What do you see? What is the woman doing? What is the problem?

UNIT GOALS

- [ ] Identify household problems
- [ ] Describe household problems
- [ ] Read apartment ads
- [ ] Read a utility bill
- [ ] Ask about an apartment
- [ ] Get directions
- [ ] **Academic skill:** Skimming
- [ ] **Writing skill:** Structure paragraphs and use indents
- [ ] **Workplace soft skill:** Show how you take initiative

Vocabulary

Household problems

A **PREDICT.** Look at the pictures. What do you see? What are the household problems?

B ▶ **LISTEN AND POINT.** Then listen and repeat.

Vocabulary

Household Problems

1. The ceiling is leaking.
2. The faucet is leaking.
3. The toilet is clogged.
4. The sink is clogged.
5. The lock is broken.
6. The mailbox is broken.
7. The window is stuck.
8. The door is stuck.
9. The washing machine isn't working.
10. The stove isn't working.
11. There's no heat.
12. There's no hot water.

C **WORK TOGETHER.** Look at the pictures. Student A, point to a picture and ask, "What's the problem?" Student B, say the problem.

Student A points to Picture 2.
A: What's the problem?
B: The ceiling is leaking.
A: No, it isn't.
B: The faucet is leaking.
A: Right!

D **CATEGORIZE.** Complete the chart. Use the words in the box. Some words can be in more than one column.

ceiling	~~faucet~~	sink	washing machine
door	lock	toilet	window

Things that leak	Things that get stuck	Things that get clogged
faucet		

Study Tip

Use the flashcards on MyEnglishLab

Click on each flashcard. Say the household problem. Play the audio to check your answer. To practice pronunciation, play the audio and repeat.

Show what you know!

1. **THINK ABOUT IT.** Read the list of household problems again. Put a star (★) next to two small household problems.

2. **TALK ABOUT IT.** Talk about small household problems.

   A: The toilet is clogged. That's a small problem.
   B: I agree. The window is stuck. That's a small problem, too.
   C: I don't think so. It is dangerous.

3. **WRITE ABOUT IT.** Write a list of small household problems.

   Small Household Problems

   _____

   _____

I can identify household problems. ■　　　　　I need more practice. ■

Lesson 2 — Listening and Speaking

Describe problems in your home

1 BEFORE YOU LISTEN

A **LABEL.** Write the words under the pictures.

| a locksmith | an electrician | a building manager | a plumber |

1. _____ 2. _____ 3. _____ 4. _____

B **MAKE CONNECTIONS.** When there is a problem in your home, who fixes it?

2 LISTEN

Harry

A **PREDICT.** Look at the picture. What is the man doing?

B ▶ **LISTEN FOR MAIN IDEA.** Complete the sentence.

Harry is talking to _____.
a. a plumber
b. the building manager
c. his friend

C ▶ **LISTEN FOR DETAILS.** Listen again. What does Joe say?

a. Call the building manager.
b. Buy a new radiator.
c. Fix the radiator.

D ▶ **EXPAND.** Listen to the whole conversation. Why can't Harry follow Joe's advice?

a. His phone doesn't work.
b. He doesn't have the manager's number.
c. He is the building manager.

3 CONVERSATION

A ▶ **LISTEN AND READ. Then listen and repeat.**

A: Hello?
B: Hi, Harry. It's Joe.
A: Oh, hi, Joe. Can I call you back?
B: Sure. No problem.
A: Thanks. My radiator is broken and I'm trying to fix it.
B: You should call the building manager for your apartment.

B **WORK TOGETHER. Practice the conversation in Exercise A.**

C **CREATE. Make new conversations. Use the words in the boxes.**

A: Hello?
B: Hi, _____. It's
_____.
A: Oh, hi, _____. Can I
call you back?
B: Sure. No problem.
A: Thanks. ▇▇▇▇▇▇
and I'm trying to fix it.
B: You should call
▇▇▇▇▇▇▇.

My lock is broken	a locksmith
My bathroom light isn't working	an electrician
My faucet is leaking	a plumber

D **MAKE CONNECTIONS. Make your own conversations about a problem in your home.**

I can describe problems in my home. ▇   I need more practice. ▇

Grammar

Present continuous

Present continuous						
Affirmative				**Negative**		
I	**am**			I	**am**	
You				You		
We	**are**	**fixing** the radiator now.		We	**are**	**not calling** the building manager.
They				They		
He	**is**			He	**is**	
She				She		

A COMPLETE. Use the present continuous and the verbs in parentheses to complete the sentences.

1. The oven is broken. The electrician (look for) ___*is looking for*___ the problem.

2. The plumber (fix) _____ the sink.
   It (not leak) _____ now.

3. The dishwasher (not work) _____.
   It (make) _____ a loud noise.

4. That lock is broken. The locksmith (try) _____ to fix it.

5. Be careful! The paint is still wet, and you (sit) _____ on it.

6. We (not wait for) _____ the building manager to fix the broken light. My husband and I (fix) _____ it right now.

7. You (do) _____ all the work yourself. Do you want some help?

8. The painters (work) _____, but they (not paint) _____ very quickly.

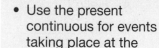

Grammar Watch

- Use the present continuous for events taking place at the present time.
- See page 258 for spelling rules with *-ing* verbs.
- See page 258 for contractions with forms of *be*.

B EVALUATE. Correct the mistake in each sentence.

1. The sink is ~~leak~~. *leaking*

2. We're are looking for a good plumber.

3. I not calling the building manager.

4. The stove in my apartment not working.

5. The building manager are fixing the problem.

6. They're not use the broken sink.

Grammar

C **APPLY.** Complete the text messages. Use the present continuous and the words in the box.

come	not stop
leak	~~not work~~
make	try
not call	watch

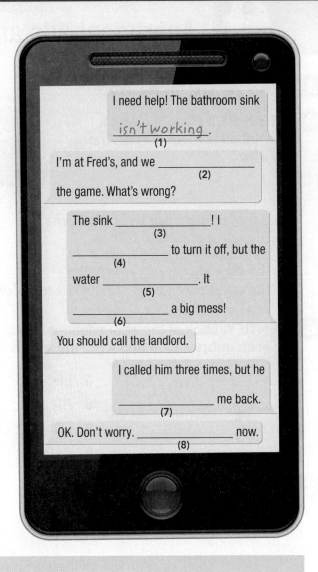

I need help! The bathroom sink _isn't working_ .
(1)

I'm at Fred's, and we _____ (2) the game. What's wrong?

The sink _____ ! I
(3)
_____ to turn it off, but the
(4)
water _____ . It
(5)
_____ a big mess!
(6)

You should call the landlord.

I called him three times, but he
_____ me back.
(7)

OK. Don't worry. _____ now.
(8)

Show what you know!

1. **THINK ABOUT IT.** Look at the picture. List three problems.

2. **TALK ABOUT IT.** Talk about the picture. Share your list of problems. What are the people doing?

   A: The window is stuck.
   B: A man is trying to close it.

3. **WRITE ABOUT IT.** Now write three sentences about what is happening in the picture.

I can use the present continuous in affirmative and negative sentences. ■

I need more practice. □

1 READ APARTMENT ADS

A **INTERPRET.** Read the ad for a rental apartment. Circle *True* or *False*.

2 bedroom/2 bathroom apartment, living room, dining room, eat-in kitchen. 1200 square feet. Air-conditioning. Washer and dryer. Utilities included. Near transportation. Pets allowed. No fee. $1200 per month. One month's rent security deposit. CONTACT: Kim at kchan@yehee.com

1. The apartment has two bathrooms.	True	False
2. The rent includes all utilities.	True	False
3. It's not okay to have a pet.	True	False
4. The security deposit is $1200.00.	True	False
5. The apartment does not have a washer or dryer.	True	False

B **IDENTIFY.** Look at the abbreviations. Then look at the ad above. Circle the words for each abbreviation and write the words on the line.

1. A/C _____
2. apt. _____
3. DR _____
4. BA _____

5. EIK _____
6. BR _____
7. LR _____
8. W/D _____

9. util. incl. _____
10. trans. _____
11. sec.dep. _____
12. sq. ft. _____

C **COMPARE.** Read about the family. Read the ads. Which apartment is better for the family? Why?

> ### The Chens
> The Chens are a family of three with a small dog (a mother and two children). Mrs. Chen works in the South End. She can spend $1450 a month on rent and utilities. She can pay $2000 for a security deposit. She doesn't have a car.

A.

South End. Large 2 BR, LR, EIK, 2 BA. 1200 square feet. W/D. Ht. + hw. not incl. Pets allowed. No fee. $1,200/mo. 1 mo. sec. dep. Near transportation. Available immediately. Call Rick 207-555-1212.

B.

North Square. Nice 2 BR, LR, DR. No pets. $1,200/mo. Util. incl. Near schools. Fee + 2 mo. sec. dep. Maven Realty Sam@mavenrealty.com

D GO ONLINE. Search for an apartment in your town or city.

Find an apartment that you like. How much is it? What is included? How much is the security deposit?

I can read apartment ads. ■   I need more practice. ■

Workplace, Life, and Community Skills

2 READ A UTILITY BILL

A DISCUSS. What is a utility bill? What utility bills do most people need to pay?

B MATCH. Read the descriptions. Then read the utility bill. Match the descriptions with the words.

1. __c__ getting something brought to your house or apartment
2. ____ a period of time
3. ____ the number that identifies your service
4. ____ the amount of money you need to pay
5. ____ the amount of money you already paid
6. ____ how much of something you get

a. credits
b. account number
c. ~~delivery~~
d. dates of service
e. supply
f. total charges

Georgia Electric

Dates of service:
June 2, 2019–July 1, 2019

Name: Lin Guo   **Account number:** 12 3456 7890

Charges:

Delivery:	$26.72
Supply:	$36.43
Previous balance:	$74.22
Subtotal:	**$137.37**
Credits:	$74.22
Total charges:	**$63.15**

Due by July 22, 2019

C INTERPRET. Review the utility bill. Answer the questions.

1. What is the bill for? _____
2. Who is the bill for? _____
3. What time period does the bill cover? _____
4. What is the account number? _____
5. How much money was paid? _____
6. When should the bill be paid? _____
7. How much money needs to be paid? _____

I can read a utility bill. ■   I need more practice. ■

Lesson 5 Ask about an apartment

1 BEFORE YOU LISTEN

MAKE CONNECTIONS. Read the questions. What other questions can you ask a rental agent about an apartment for rent?

10:15

How much is the rent?

How many bedrooms are there?

Is there a laundry room?

Are there two bathrooms?

2 LISTEN

Maria

Rental agent

A **PREDICT.** Look at the picture. Who do you think is making the phone call?

B ▶ **LISTEN FOR MAIN IDEA.** Why is the woman calling?

a. She wants information about an apartment.
b. She has a question about her rent.
c. She has a problem with her apartment.

C ▶ **LISTEN FOR DETAILS.** Circle *True* or *False*.

1. There are two bedrooms.	True	False
2. There's a large living room.	True	False
3. There's a laundry room in the building.	True	False
4. There's a bus stop around the corner.	True	False

D ▶ **EXPAND.** Listen to the whole conversation. How much is the rent?

a. $2,000 a month   b. $200 a month   c. $500 a month

3 PRONUNCIATION

A ▶ PRACTICE. Listen. Then listen and repeat.

• **bus** stop   • **laundry** room   • **dish**washer   • **living** room

> **Stress in two-word nouns**
>
> Sometimes we put two words together to make a noun. The first word is usually stressed.

B ▶ APPLY. Listen. Put a dot (•) above the stressed syllable.

1. washing machine   2. mailbox   3. locksmith   4. rental agent   5. microwave

4 CONVERSATION

A ▶ LISTEN AND READ. Then listen and repeat.

A: Hello?
B: Hi, I'm calling about the apartment for rent. Can you tell me about it?
A: Sure. There are two bedrooms and a large living room.
B: Is there a laundry room?
A: No, there isn't. But there's a laundromat down the street.
B: I see. Is there a bus stop nearby?
A: Yes, there is—just around the corner.

B WORK TOGETHER. Practice the conversation.

C CREATE. Make new conversations. Use the words in the boxes.

A: Hello?
B: Hi, I'm calling about the apartment for rent. Can you tell me about it?
A: Sure. There are two bedrooms and a ▓▓▓▓▓▓▓▓▓▓.
B: Is there a ▓▓▓▓▓▓▓▓▓▓?
A: No, there isn't. But there's ▓▓▓▓▓▓▓▓▓▓.
B: I see. Is there a ▓▓▓▓▓▓▓▓▓▓ nearby?
A: Yes, there is—just around the corner.

sunny kitchen	dishwasher	a microwave	subway stop
new bathroom	parking lot	free parking on the street	shopping center
big closet	balcony	a big window in the living room	supermarket

D ROLE-PLAY. Make your own conversations. Student A, you are going to rent your house or apartment. Student B, you want to rent a house or apartment. Ask and answer questions.

I can ask about an apartment. ☐   I need more practice. ☐

There is / There are

Affirmative		Negative	
There is a	bus stop nearby.	**There isn't a** **There's no**	park near here.
There are	two bedrooms.	**There aren't any** **There are no**	restaurants in the neighborhood.

Questions			Short answers			
	Is there **Are there**	a laundry room? a lot of windows?	Yes,	**there is.** **there are.**	No,	**there isn't.** **there aren't.**
How many bedrooms	**are there?**		Two. (**There are** two.) One. (**There's** one.)			

A **IDENTIFY.** Cross out the incorrect words.

1. **There is / ~~There are~~** a bus stop near the apartment.
2. **Are there / Is there** a lot of children in the neighborhood?
3. **Is there / Are there** a bathtub?
4. **There is / There are** two windows in the kitchen.
5. **There's / There isn't** no elevator in the building.
6. **There aren't / There isn't** a lot of traffic on this street.

B **COMPLETE.** Use *there is / there are* to complete the conversation.

A: So, tell me about your new apartment. How many bedrooms ___*are there*___?

B: _____ two. And they're nice and big.

A: That's good. How are the neighbors?

B: Well, _____ an older woman next door. She seems very friendly.

A: And how's the neighborhood?

B: I like it a lot. _____ a lot of stores around the corner.

A: That's convenient. _____ any supermarkets?

B: No, _____, but _____ a convenience store down the street.

> ### Grammar Watch
>
> We use *there is* and *there are* to say that something is in a place or to talk about how many things are in a place.

Grammar

C **WRITE.** Read the answers. Write questions with *Is there*, *Are there*, or *How many*.

1. **A:** *Is there a bus stop near the apartment?* _____
   B: Yes, there is. The #2 bus stop is across the street.

2. **A:** _____
   B: No. There are no families with children in the building.

3. **A:** _____
   B: Yes, there is. There's a supermarket 10 minutes from here.

4. **A:** _____
   B: Sorry. There aren't any furnished apartments available.

5. **A:** _____
   B: Yes, there is. There's a laundry room in the basement.

6. **A:** _____
   B: Four. There are four big closets in the apartment.

Show what you know!

1. **THINK ABOUT IT.** Imagine that you have an apartment for rent. Look at the chart. Complete the column under *My Apartment*.

	My Apartment	My Partner's Apartment
Number of bedrooms?		
Number of bathrooms?		
Laundry room? (yes or no)		
Parking? (street or lot)		

2. **TALK ABOUT IT.** Student A, ask questions about your partner's apartment. Write the answers in the last column. Student B, use your chart and answer the questions. Take turns.

3. **WRITE ABOUT IT.** Write four sentences about your partner's apartment.

   There is one bathroom in Nico's apartment.

I can make sentences and ask and answer questions with *there is / there are*. ■   I need more practice. ■

1 BEFORE YOU READ

A DECIDE. Complete the sentences with the words in the box.

> homeowners   investments   renter   value

1. The _____ of a house is how much it sells for.

2. They are new _____.

3. A _____ pays rent to live in a house or apartment.

4. People make _____ so that their money will grow over time.

B MAKE CONNECTIONS.

In your native country, do most people live in houses? Are most adults homeowners or renters?

2 READ

▶ Listen and read.

Academic Skill: Skimming

Skimming means you do not read every word. Instead, you read quickly to get the general idea of the article.

Rent or Own?

1 In many countries, most people live in homes that they own. In China, for example, 90% of homes are owner-occupied. They belong to the people who live in them. In the United States, only about 63% of homes are owner-occupied. Renters
5 live in the other 37%.

Young adults often rent. Most American adults under age 35 are renters. After age 35, that changes. In the 35 to 44 age group, there are more homeowners than renters. People over 65 are the group most likely to own their homes.

10 Many renters don't like renting. Only 32% of renters say they rent because they want to. Most renters say they want to buy a home in the future (72%).

Who Rents in the U.S.?

Source: Pew Research Center

65%	41%	28%	21%
Younger than 35	Age 35-44	Age 45-64	Age 65+

Which is better, renting a home or owning one? It depends. There are good reasons to buy a home, but there are good
15 reasons to rent, too.

Reasons to Buy a House

• A house can be a good investment. The value of a house usually goes up over time.

• If you stay in the house for three or more years, you'll
20 probably save money.

• You can make any changes you want to your home when you own it.

• Homeowners can save money on their taxes.

Reasons to Rent

25 • A house can be a bad investment. Sometimes the value of a house drops.

• It is easier to move (for another job or to a better home, for example).

• You don't have to spend time or money on home repairs.

30 • You don't have to pay property tax.

Reading

3 CLOSE READING

A **IDENTIFY. What is the main idea?**

About 63% of U.S. homes are owner-occupied, _____.
a. so most Americans are renters
b. but it's usually better to rent
c. and most renters want to be homeowners

B **CITE EVIDENCE. Complete the statements. Where is the information? Write the line numbers.**

1. About _____ of homes in the United States are owner-occupied.	**Lines**
a. 10% **b.** 63% **c.** 90%	_____
2. About _____ of U.S. renters are happy to be renters.	
a. 32% **b.** 37% **c.** 72%	_____
3. Buying a house is a good investment when the value of the house _____.	
a. goes up **b.** goes down **c.** stays the same	_____

C **INTERPRET. Complete the sentences about the bar graph.**

1. In the U.S., about _____ of people in the 35 to 44 age group are renters.
   a. 60%   **b.** 40%   **c.** 20%

2. Less than 30% of people aged _____ living in the U.S. rent houses.
   a. 45 to 64   **b.** 35 to 44   **c.** 35 and younger

4 SUMMARIZE

Complete the summary with the words in the box.

investment	likely	owner-occupied	rented

About 63% of the homes in the United States are (1) _____. The rest (37%) are (2) _____. Most adults under age 35 are renters. Older people are more (3) _____ to own their homes. It can be a good (4) _____ to own your home, but sometimes it's better to rent.

Show what you know!

1. **THINK ABOUT IT.** What are some good reasons to buy a house? What are some good reasons to rent?

2. **WRITE ABOUT IT.** Is it better to rent or own a home? Explain your reasons.

   I think it's better to _____ because _____.

3. **PRESENT IT.** Give a short presentation on reasons to buy a home. Present reasons to rent. What is good and bad about each one?

I can skim an article. ■   I need more practice. ■

1 BEFORE YOU LISTEN

A **LABEL.** Look at the pictures. Write the words under the pictures.

Turn right.   Turn left.   ~~Go straight.~~   Go through one traffic light.

 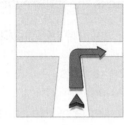  

1. _Go straight._   2. _____   3. _____   4. _____

B **MAKE CONNECTIONS.** How do you usually get directions? Do you use a map? Your phone? Other?

2 LISTEN

A **PREDICT.** Look at the map. What information do you see?

B ▶ **LISTEN FOR MAIN IDEA.** Listen to the directions. Number the directions in the order you hear them.

__1__ go straight

____ turn right

____ turn left

____ go straight

____ go through one traffic light

C ▶ **LISTEN FOR DETAILS.** Start at the red dot [•] on the map. Follow the directions. Draw the route on the map.

D ▶ **EXPAND.** Listen to the complete directions. Where are you going? Circle the building.

Listening and Speaking

3 PRONUNCIATION

A ▶ **PRACTICE.** Listen. Then listen and repeat.

Then turn right.   It's on the left.
It's on Third Street.   Thanks.

B ▶ **CHOOSE.** Listen. How does the *th* in these words sound? Check (✓) the column.

> **Voiced and voiceless *th***
>
> There are two *th* sounds in English. To feel the difference, put your hand on your throat. When you say the *th* sound in *thanks,* you don't feel anything. (This is called a voiceless sound.) When you say the *th* sound in *then,* you feel a vibration in your throat. (This is a voiced sound.)

	voiced *th* (like *then*)	voiceless *th* (like *thanks*)		voiced *th* (like *then*)	voiceless *th* (like *thanks*)
1. there	✓		**4.** theater		
2. this			**5.** the		
3. things			**6.** third		

4 CONVERSATION

A ▶ **LISTEN AND READ.** Then listen and repeat.

A: Can you give me directions to Save-Rite Pharmacy?
B: Sure. Go straight on Third Street.
A: OK. Go straight on Third Street.
B: Yep. At the stop sign, turn right onto Davis Road.
A: Turn right onto Davis Road.
B: Exactly. Save-Rite Pharmacy is on the left.

B **WORK TOGETHER.** Practice the conversation.

C **CREATE.** Make new conversations. Use the directions on the maps.

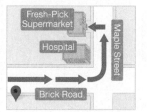

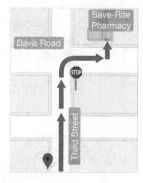

A: Can you give me directions to _____?

B: Sure. Go straight on _____.

A: OK. Go straight on _____.

B: Yep. At the _____, turn _____ onto _____.

A: At the _____, turn _____ onto _____.

B: Exactly. _____ is on the left.

D **MAKE CONNECTIONS.** Make your own conversations. Ask for and give directions from school to places in your community.

| I can get directions. ■ | I need more practice. ■ |

Lesson 9 Grammar

Imperatives

Imperatives	
Affirmative	**Negative**
Turn left at the stop sign.	**Don't turn** right.

Grammar Watch

- Use the imperative for instructions and directions.
- The imperative is the base form of the verb.
- Use *don't* + the base verb for the negative.

A LABEL. Write the words under the pictures.

| Don't park. | Don't text. | Don't walk. | Go straight. | Stop. |

1. _Don't park._ 2. _____ 3. _____ 4. _____ 5. _____

B INTERPRET. Look at the pictures. Complete the instructions. Use the words in the box.

| be | not go | not smoke | not use | turn | watch for |

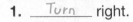  

1. _Turn_ right. 2. _____ straight. 3. _____ people walking.

4. _____. 5. _____ your phone. 6. _____ quiet.

I can use affirmative and negative imperatives. ■   I need more practice. ■

Writing

Write about your home

1 STUDY THE MODEL

READ. Answer the questions.

Anissa Bel

My Home

I like my home. I live in an apartment. It has a large kitchen and many windows. There is a laundry room in the building. There is a bus stop nearby.

There are also some problems with my apartment. Sometimes the elevators don't work. The neighbors are noisy. The school is far away.

1. What did Anissa write about?
2. Where does Anissa live?
3. What does she like about her home?
4. What are some problems with her home?

2 PLAN YOUR WRITING

WORK TOGETHER. Ask and answer the questions.

1. What will you write about?
2. Where do you live?
3. What do you like about your home?
4. What are some problems with your home?

Writing Skill: Structure paragraphs and use indents

The first line of a paragraph is indented. It begins a little bit in from the left. For example:

I like my home.

There are also some problems with my apartment.

3 WRITE

Now write about your home. Use the model, the Writing Skill, and your ideas from Exercise 2 to help you.

WRITING CHECKLIST

☐ The paragraphs answer the questions in Exercise 2.

☐ Each paragraph starts with a topic sentence.

☐ The first line of each paragraph is indented.

4 CHECK YOUR WRITING

WORK TOGETHER. Read the checklist. Read your writing aloud. Revise your writing.

I can use the correct structure and indents in my writing. ■   I need more practice. ■

Take initiative

1 MEET YUSEF

Read about one of his workplace skills.

> I take initiative. For example, I try to fix problems at work. When I can't fix the problem myself, I find someone to help me fix it.

2 YUSEF'S PROBLEM

READ. Circle *True* or *False*.

Yusef has a new job. He is a cleaner in a grocery store. He works alone at night. Last night, his supervisor showed him all the cleaning equipment. Then the supervisor went home. Yusef vacuumed some of the floors in the building, but in the middle of the night the vacuum cleaner stopped working.

1. Yusef is a new employee in the building.	True	False
2. Yusef has many co-workers.	True	False
3. Yusef finished vacuuming all the floors.	True	False

3 YUSEF'S SOLUTION

WORK TOGETHER. Yusef takes initiative. What does he do? Explain your answer.

1. Yusef tries to fix the vacuum cleaner so he can finish cleaning the floors.
2. Yusuf calls his supervisor and leaves a voice message about the broken cleaner.
3. Yusef doesn't do anything about the vacuum cleaner.
4. Yusef _____.

Show what you know!

1. **THINK ABOUT IT.** Do you take initiative? How do you take initiative in class? At work? At home? Give examples.

2. **WRITE ABOUT IT.** Write an example in your Skills Log.

   I take initiative in class. For example, when there aren't enough chairs in the classroom, I get some chairs from another classroom.

I can give an example of how I take initiative. ■

Unit Review: Go back to page 85. Which unit goals can you check off?

6 In the Past

PREVIEW

Look at the picture. What do you see? What are the people looking at? What are they talking about?

UNIT GOALS

- ☐ Identify events
- ☐ Talk about past activities
- ☐ Recognize U.S. holidays
- ☐ Talk about milestones
- ☐ Talk about something that happened

- ☐ **Academic skill:** Scan for information
- ☐ **Writing skill:** Use commas with dates
- ☐ **Workplace soft skill:** Show how you are dependable

Vocabulary

Events

A PREDICT. Look at the pictures. What do you see? What events are these?

B ► LISTEN AND POINT. Then listen and repeat.

Vocabulary

Events

1. a birthday party	**4.** a funeral	**7.** a barbecue
2. a wedding	**5.** a family reunion	**8.** a holiday party
3. an anniversary party	**6.** a graduation	**9.** a retirement party
		10. a surprise party

C **WORK TOGETHER.** Look at the pictures. Student A, point to a picture. Student B, name the event.

Student A points to Picture 3.
A: What event is this?
B: It's an anniversary party.
A: Right!

D **MAKE CONNECTIONS.** Do you usually bring gifts to these events? Check (✓) your response. Talk about it with your classmates.

Event	Gifts	No Gifts
1. a birthday party		
2. a wedding		
3. an anniversary party		
4. a funeral		
5. a family reunion		
6. a graduation		
7. a holiday party		
8. a barbecue		
9. a retirement party		
10. a surprise party		

> **Study Tip**
>
> **Self-test**
>
> Close your book. Write the name of events from the list. Open your book. Check your spelling.

Show what you know!

1. THINK ABOUT IT. List two of your favorite events.

2. TALK ABOUT IT. Talk about your favorite events. Why do you like them?

I like weddings. I love dancing, and people are happy.

3. WRITE ABOUT IT. Write about your favorite kind of event. Explain why it is your favorite event.

I can identify events. ■   I need more practice. ■

Lesson 2 | Listening and Speaking

Talk about past activities

1 BEFORE YOU LISTEN

MAKE CONNECTIONS. Look at the pictures. Which of these activities do you do with your family or friends?

listen to family stories

look at old photos

stay up late

dance all night

2 LISTEN

A **PREDICT.** Look at the picture. The people are probably _____.

a. married   **b.** family   **c.** co-workers

B ▶ **LISTEN FOR MAIN IDEA.** What are the people talking about?

a. the weekend   **b.** a meeting   **c.** a problem

Rose   Sam

C ▶ **LISTEN FOR DETAILS.** Listen again. Circle *True* or *False*.

1. Rose asks Sam about his weekend.	True	False
2. Sam was at a wedding last weekend.	True	False
3. Sam watched old movies last weekend.	True	False
4. Sam listened to family stories.	True	False

D ▶ **EXPAND.** Listen to the whole conversation. What did Rose do last weekend?

a.

b.

Listening and Speaking

3 PRONUNCIATION

A ▶ **PRACTICE. Listen. Then listen and repeat.**

Extra syllable	No extra syllable	
in·vit·ed	looked	danced
need·ed	dropped	showed

> **Extra syllable for -ed endings**
>
> The past tense -ed ending adds an extra syllable after the sound /t/ or /d/. It does not add an extra syllable after other sounds.

B ▶ **IDENTIFY. Listen. Circle the words with an extra -ed syllable.**

1. called   **2.** visited   **3.** watched   **4.** wanted   **5.** talked   **6.** stayed

4 CONVERSATION

A ▶ **LISTEN AND READ. Then listen and repeat.**

A: How was your weekend? How was the family reunion?
B: It was really nice, thanks. My whole family showed up.
A: Sounds great.
B: Yeah, it was fun. We looked at old pictures and listened to family stories.

B **WORK TOGETHER. Practice the conversation in Exercise A.**

C **CREATE. Make new conversations. Use the information in the boxes.**

A: How was your weekend? How was the   ?
B: It was really nice, thanks. My whole family showed up.
A: Sounds great.
B: Yeah, it was fun. We   and   .

anniversary party	watched family movies	talked about old times
barbecue	cooked a lot of food	played games
wedding	stayed up late	danced all night

D **MAKE CONNECTIONS. Talk about a special event. What did you do?**

I can talk about past activities. ■   I need more practice. ■

Simple past: Regular verbs

Simple past: Regular verbs	
Affirmative	**Negative**
I You He She **invited** some co-workers over. We They	I You He She **didn't plan** a party. We They

Grammar Watch

- For the simple past, regular verbs, add *-ed*.
- For example:
  want → want**ed**
- For verbs that end in *-e*, add *-d*.
- For example:
  invite → invite**d**

A COMPLETE. Use the simple past of the words in parentheses.

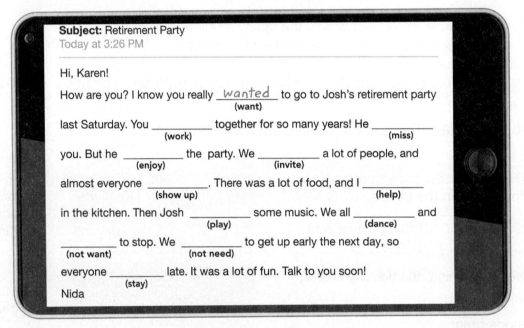

Subject: Retirement Party
Today at 3:26 PM

Hi, Karen!

How are you? I know you really __wanted__ to go to Josh's retirement party
                                                         (want)

last Saturday. You _____ together for so many years! He _____
                                (work)   (miss)

you. But he _____ the party. We _____ a lot of people, and
                        (enjoy)   (invite)

almost everyone _____. There was a lot of food, and I _____
                                (show up)   (help)

in the kitchen. Then Josh _____ some music. We all _____ and
                                            (play)   (dance)

_____ to stop. We _____ to get up early the next day, so
    (not want)   (not need)

everyone _____ late. It was a lot of fun. Talk to you soon!
                        (stay)
Nida

B APPLY. Complete the conversation with the past tense form of the words in the box.

clean up	finish	not leave	visit	watch
decide	need	stay up	want	~~work~~

A: You look a little tired this morning.

B: Yeah, I _____worked_____ late last night. My supervisor _____ some help, so

I _____ to stay. We _____ the work, but the place was a mess!

So then we _____. We _____ until really late. You look a little

tired, too.

A: I am. I _____ my cousin last night. We _____ a soccer game on

TV. I _____ to see the end so I _____ late.

Grammar

C **INTERPRET.** Look at the pictures. Then read Sofia's to-do list and check the things she did.

To Do +

- ☐ visit Mrs. Parker
- ☐ call supervisor
- ☐ watch a movie
- ☐ respond to work e-mails
- ☐ look at work schedule online
- ☐ walk the dog
- ☐ go to the supermarket
- ☐ bake cookies

D **DISCUSS.** Talk about what Sofia did and did not do after work.

A: Sofia visited Mrs. Parker.
B: She didn't call her supervisor.

E **WRITE.** Now write four sentences about what Sofia did and did not do after work.

Show what you know!

1. **THINK ABOUT IT.** Complete the sentence about a past activity. Use the simple past.

   I _____ last week.

2. **TALK ABOUT IT.** Play the Memory Game. What did you do last weekend?

   Talib: I visited my sister.
   Alex: Talib visited his sister. I cooked dinner for my wife.
   Ying: Talib visited his sister. Alex cooked dinner for his wife. I worked Saturday and Sunday.

3. **WRITE ABOUT IT.** Now write one sentence about each person's weekend. Use the simple past.

   Talib visited his sister. Alex cooked dinner for his wife.

I can use the simple past with regular verbs. ■   I need more practice. ■

4

Workplace, Life, and Community Skills

U.S. holidays

1 RECOGNIZE U.S. HOLIDAYS

A **MATCH.** Look at the calendars. Write the name of each holiday on the correct line.

Christmas Day	Columbus Day	Independence Day	Labor Day
Martin Luther King, Jr. Day	Memorial Day	~~New Year's Day~~	Presidents' Day
Thanksgiving Day	Veterans Day		

1. _____ New Year's Day _____

2. _____

3. _____

4. _____

5. _____

6. _____

7. _____

8. _____

9. _____

10. _____

B ▶ **SELF-ASSESS.** Listen and check your answers. Then listen and repeat.

C ▶ **IDENTIFY.** Look at the calendars. Listen. Which U.S. holidays is she talking about? Write the name of each holiday.

1. _____

2. _____

3. _____

4. _____

5. _____

Workplace, Life, and Community Skills

2 READ ABOUT HOLIDAYS

A **INTERPRET.** Read the article. Then read the sentences. Circle *True* or *False*. Correct the false information.

○○○

Q&A   HOME | TOPICS | FEEDS | BOOKMARKS   (🔍 Holidays in the U.S.)   **Add Question**

Q. How many national holidays are there in the United States?

A. There are ten national holidays, but most people don't know that because many businesses stay open on national holidays. Schools, banks, and government offices such as the post office are closed on all ten days. Many U.S. businesses observe only the "Big Six:" New Year's Day, Memorial Day, Independence Day, Labor Day, Thanksgiving Day, and Christmas Day.   More

Q. Which holidays celebrate specific people?

A. Presidents' Day, Martin Luther King, Jr. Day, and Columbus Day celebrate specific people. Presidents' Day celebrates George Washington, the first president of the United States, and Abraham Lincoln, the sixteenth president. Martin Luther King, Jr. Day celebrates Dr. King's work for the equality of all people. Columbus Day celebrates the day Columbus arrived in the Americas in 1492.   More

Q. What's the difference between Veterans' Day and Memorial Day?

A. Both holidays celebrate the U.S. military. On Veterans' Day, we celebrate all people in the U.S. military. On Memorial Day, we remember U.S. military personnel who died in wars.   More

---

1. There are ten national holidays.	True	False
2. All businesses in the U.S. are closed on national holidays.	True	False
3. Government offices are closed on national holidays.	True	False
4. Presidents' Day celebrates the life of Martin Luther King, Jr.	True	False
5. Columbus Day celebrates the day Columbus arrived in 1942.	True	False
6. Veterans' Day celebrates all people in the U.S. military.	True	False

B GO ONLINE. Search for other U.S. holidays. Select a holiday you are not familiar with. What is the holiday? When is it celebrated? What does it celebrate?

I can recognize U.S. holidays. ■   I need more practice. ■

Lesson 5

Talk about milestones

1 BEFORE YOU LISTEN

LABEL. Write the words under the pictures.

getting a job	growing up
getting married	being born
having children	graduating from school

1. _____being born_____

2. _____

3. _____

4. _____

5. _____

6. _____

2 LISTEN

Daniel
Amber

A **PREDICT.** Look at the picture. Where are the people? What are they doing?

B ▶ **LISTEN FOR MAIN IDEA.** Look at the milestones in Exercise 1. Which milestones do the people talk about?

C ▶ **LISTEN FOR DETAILS.** Listen to the podcast again. Complete the sentences.

1. Daniel says his _____ isn't interesting.
   a. job   **b.** life

2. Daniel was born in _____.
   a. California   **b.** Colorado

3. Daniel went to _____.
   a. college   **b.** acting classes

4. He wanted to be _____ when he was a child.
   a. an actor   **b.** a plumber

D ▶ **EXPAND.** Listen to the whole podcast. Complete the sentences.

1. Daniel _____ last night.
   a. went to a party   **b.** stayed home

2. Daniel says he is _____.
   a. a glamorous person   **b.** a regular guy

Listening and Speaking

3 PRONUNCIATION

A ▶ **PRACTICE. Listen. Then listen and repeat.**

You were born in California?

Sarah came to the U.S. last year?

Daniel always wanted to be an actor?

You got a job in a supermarket?

Statements as questions

Sometimes we say a statement as a question. The voice goes up at the end.

B ▶ **APPLY. Listen to the sentences. Add a period (.) to statements. Add a question mark (?) to questions.**

1. Maria grew up in Houston
2. You came to the U.S. in 2015
3. Ali graduated from college two years ago
4. She got married last year
5. Rob became a home caregiver in 2017
6. You got your first job last month

4 CONVERSATION

A ▶ **LISTEN AND READ. Then listen and repeat.**

A: So, tell me . . . Where are you from?
B: China. I was born in a small village, but I grew up in Beijing.
A: And you came to the U.S. five years ago?
B: Right. First, my wife and I got an apartment in Long Beach. Then we moved to San Francisco.
A: Your English is very good. Did you study English in China?
B: Yes, I did, but I didn't practice speaking a lot.

B **WORK TOGETHER. Practice the conversation in Exercise A.**

C **MAKE CONNECTIONS. Make new conversations. Ask a classmate about milestones in his or her life. Take turns.**

Angela: Where are you from?
Yu: China . . .

D **PRESENT. Tell the class about your partner.**

Yu is from China. He studied English in China.

I can talk about milestones. ■	I need more practice. ■

Simple past: Irregular verbs

Simple past: Irregular verbs			
Affirmative		**Negative**	
I		I	
You		You	
He		He	
She	**went to bed early.**	She	**didn't go to a party.**
We		We	
They		They	

Grammar Watch

Here are some examples of irregular past-tense forms. See page 259 for more past tense forms.

Base form	Past-tense form
begin	**began**
come	**came**
do	**did**
go	**went**
get	**got**
grow	**grew**
have	**had**
leave	**left**
make	**made**
take	**took**

A **IDENTIFY. Cross out the incorrect words.**

1. I ~~don't grow~~ / **didn't grow** up in the U.S. I ~~grow~~ / **grew** up in India.

2. Rosa **meets / met** Carlos in 2016, and they **get / got** married in 2018.

3. My co-worker **took / takes** some college classes last year, but he didn't **graduated / graduate**.

4. Last year, they **leave / left** Colombia, and they **came / come** to the U.S.

5. Mike **goes / went** to Los Angeles, and he **finds / found** a good job there.

6. She **have / had** a good job, but she didn't **have / had** a nice supervisor.

B **COMPLETE. Write the simple past of the words in parentheses.**

I _____was born_____ in Venezuela in 1997. I _____ up
    1. (be born)   **2. (grow)**

in Caracas. My family _____ a small store there. In
                     3. (have)

2015, my family left Venezuela, and we _____ to the
                                    4. (come)

U.S. I _____ find a job, but I _____ English
      5. (have to)   **6. (not speak)**

very well. So I _____ classes. A supermarket near my
             7. (take)

house needed cashiers. I _____ to the store, and I
                8. (go)

_____ an interview that day. I _____ the job.
  9. (have)   **10. (get)**

Today, I still work at the supermarket, but now I'm a manager.

Grammar

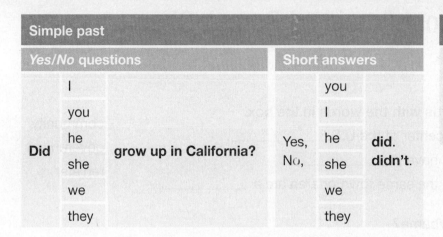

Simple past						
Yes/No questions			**Short answers**			
	I				you	
	you				I	
Did	he	grow up in California?	Yes,	No,	he	**did.**
	she				she	**didn't.**
	we				we	
	they				they	

Grammar Watch

Remember how to form past tense questions with *be*.

A: Were you born in Myanmar?

B: Yes, I **was.**

C **WRITE.** Make questions and answers. Use the simple past of the verbs.

1. **A:** _Did you grow up in a big city?_
   (you / grow up / in a big city)
   B: No, _I didn't_ .

2. **A:** _____
   (Ana / take / English classes)
   B: Yes, _____.

3. **A:** _____
   (they / move / to San Diego)
   B: No, _____.

4. **A:** _____
   (Mr. Jung / get / a new job)
   B: Yes, _____.

Show what you know!

1. THINK ABOUT IT. Write four questions about milestones in your partner's life.

Did you grow up in Angola?

2. TALK ABOUT IT. Ask and answer the questions. Take turns.

A: *Did you grow up in Angola?*
B: *No, I didn't. I grew up in the Democratic Republic of the Congo.*

3. WRITE ABOUT IT. Write four sentences about your partner's life.

David grew up in the Democratic Republic of the Congo.

I can use the simple past with irregular verbs. ■   I need more practice. ■

1 BEFORE YOU READ

A **DECIDE.** Complete the words with the words in the box.

1. Washington, D.C., is the center of the U.S. _____.
2. Before you can vote, you have to _____.
3. All the people who live in the same town or area are a _____.

community
government
register

B **DISCUSS.** Who is Barack Obama?

2 READ

▶ Listen and read.

Academic Skill: Scan for Information

Scanning an article means reading it quickly to find specific information, such as names and dates.

PRESIDENT BARACK OBAMA

1 "It doesn't matter who you are or where you come from or what you look like. . . . You can make it here in America if you're willing to try." *President Barack Obama*

"America is a place where all things are possible!"
5 said Barack Obama. And he knows. Barack Obama was the first African-American president of the United States!

His Unusual Early Life
As a child, Obama learned about different races,
10 languages, and countries. He was born in Hawaii in 1961. His mother was a white woman from Kansas. His father was a black man from Kenya. They divorced, and his mother married a man from Indonesia. The family lived in Indonesia for four
15 years. At age 10, Obama returned to Hawaii and lived with his grandparents.

Helping People Build Better Lives
Obama went to college in New York. After he graduated in 1983, he became a community organizer
20 in Chicago. He helped poor people register to vote, get job training, and get into college.

In 1988, Obama went to law school. He became a lawyer and taught law in Chicago, Illinois. Finally, he decided to go into politics. Working in government,
25 he could help more people. First, he worked for the people of Illinois. In 2009, he became president of the United States.

His Years in the White House
During his time in office, many changes happened.
30 Obama is famous for the Affordable Care Act. It's often called "Obamacare." This law helped millions of Americans get health insurance. The economy got better, too. Obama worked hard to improve U.S. relationships with other countries. He won the 2009
35 Nobel Peace Prize.

President Obama left the White House in 2017. He worked very hard while he was president.

Reading

3 CLOSE READING

A **IDENTIFY. What is the main idea?**

Barack Obama, the first African-American president of the United States, _____.
a. came to the United States from Africa
b. cared about helping people have better lives
c. was a poor boy who became a rich man

B **CITE EVIDENCE. Complete the statements. Where is the information? Write the line numbers.**

Lines

1. President Obama's father was from ____.
   a. Hawaii   b. Kansas   c. Kenya   _____

2. As a boy, Obama lived for four years in ____ with his mother and stepfather.
   a. Kenya   b. Indonesia   c. Illinois   _____

3. From age 10 until college, Obama lived in Hawaii with his ____.
   a. mother   b. father   c. grandparents   _____

4. Obama worked first as a community organizer and then as a lawyer in ____.
   a. Hawaii   b. Chicago   c. the White House   _____

5. Obama decided to go into politics because it's a way to ____.
   a. help people   b. make money   c. become famous   _____

4 SUMMARIZE

Complete the summary with the words in the box.

early	famous	health insurance	politics	president

Barack Obama was the first African-American (1) _____ of the United States.
He learned a lot from his (2) _____ life in Hawaii and Indonesia. After college, he
became a lawyer. He decided to work in (3) _____ to help people. As president,
he was (4) _____ for helping millions of Americans get (5) _____ with
the Affordable Care Act.

Show what you know!

1. **TALK ABOUT IT.** Scan the article for important dates in President Obama's life.
   Mark five or more important events in his life on the timeline.

Born in Hawaii
•————————————————————————————————————
1961

2. **WRITE ABOUT IT.** Use your timeline to write about events in President Obama's life.

1983 was an important year in President Obama's life because _____.

I can scan for information. ■   I need more practice. ■

1 BEFORE YOU LISTEN

A **LABEL.** Write the words under the pictures.

I got stuck in traffic.   I forgot my lunch.   I lost my keys.
I took the wrong train.   I overslept.   ~~I had car trouble.~~

1. _I had car trouble._

2. _____

3. _____

4. _____

5. _____

6. _____

B **MAKE CONNECTIONS.** What are some other things that can happen before work?

2 LISTEN

A **PREDICT.** Look at the picture. How does Adam feel?

  a. sick   **b.** stressed out   **c.** nervous

B ▶ **LISTEN FOR MAIN IDEA.** What happened to Adam before work?

  a. He had some free time.
  b. He had a lot of problems.
  c. He had a big breakfast.

C ▶ **LISTEN FOR DETAILS.** Listen again. Put the events in the correct order.

____ Adam got stuck in traffic.

____ Adam got to work late.

____ Adam lost his car keys.

D ▶ **EXPAND.** Listen to the whole conversation. Circle the answers.

1. What day is it?
   a. Tuesday.　　　　　　　　　　**b.** Thursday.

2. What mistake did Adam make?
   a. He went to work on his day off.　　**b.** He didn't go to work.

3 CONVERSATION

A ▶ **LISTEN AND READ.** Then listen and repeat.

A: Is everything OK? You look stressed out.
B: Well, I had a rough morning.
A: Why? What happened?
B: First, I lost my car keys.
A: Oh, no!
B: Then I got stuck in traffic.
A: When did you get to work?
B: At 10:00. I was really late.

B **WORK TOGETHER.** Practice the conversation in Exercise A.

C **CREATE.** Make new conversations. Use the words in the boxes.

A: Is everything OK? You look _____.
B: Well, I had a rough morning.
A: Why? What happened?
B: First, I _____.
A: Oh, no!
B: Then I _____.
A: When did you get to work?
B: At 10:00. I was really late.

upset
unhappy
exhausted

lost my wallet
overslept
forgot my lunch

had car trouble
missed the bus
took the wrong train

D **ROLE-PLAY.** Make your own conversations.

I can talk about something that happened. ■	I need more practice. ■

Grammar

Simple past: Information questions

Simple past: Information questions		
When **did**	I / you / he / she / we / they	**get** to work?

Grammar Watch

Question words
What
What time
Why
When
Where

- Use a question word + *did* and the base form of the verb.
- Answer with a short answer (At 10:00.) or a full sentence (I got to work at 10:00.).

A WRITE. Make questions about the past. Use the words in parentheses.

1. (What time / you / get up yesterday) _What time did you get up yesterday?_
2. (Where / you / go this morning) _____
3. (What / you / have for lunch yesterday) _____
4. (What time / you / get to work this morning) _____
5. (What / you / do last night) _____

B WORK TOGETHER. Ask and answer the questions in Exercise A.

A: *What time did you get up yesterday?*
B: *I got up at 7:00.*

C WRITE. Read the answers. Then write questions about the underlined words.

1. A: _What did Saul forget?_
   B: Saul forgot his wallet.
2. A: _____
   B: Jane finished work at 10:45.
3. A: _____
   B: Brad missed the bus because he overslept.
4. A: _____
   B: Lan found her keys in the kitchen.

I can ask information questions with the simple past. ■   I need more practice. ■

Write a biography

1 STUDY THE MODEL

READ. Answer the questions.

Pablo Rivera

My Mother

My mother's name is Frida. She was born in 1955, in a small town in Mexico. In 1975, she moved to Mexico City and met my father. They got married in 1978. Then I was born in 1979. In 1985, my parents opened a store. They worked in the store for 30 years. In 2015, my father died, and my mother moved back to her small town in Mexico.

1. Who did Pablo write about?
2. Where was she born? In what year?
3. Where did she move? In what year?
4. When did she get married?
5. When did she have children?
6. Where did she work?

2 PLAN YOUR WRITING

WORK TOGETHER. Ask and answer the questions.

1. Who will you write about?
2. Where was the person born? In what year?
3. Did the person move? When and where?
4. Did the person get married? When?
5. Did the person have children? When?
6. Does the person work? Where?

Add more details about the person.

> **Writing Skill: Use commas with dates**
>
> When you begin a sentence with a date, add a comma. For example:
> In 1985, my parents opened a store.
> When you end a sentence with a date, do not add a comma. For example:
> I was born in 1979.

3 WRITE

Now write about a person you know well. Use the model, the Writing Skill, and your ideas from Exercise 2 to help you.

4 CHECK YOUR WRITING

WORK TOGETHER. Read the checklist. Read your writing aloud. Revise your writing.

> **WRITING CHECKLIST**
>
> ☐ The paragraph answers the questions in Exercise 2.
>
> ☐ There is a comma after a date at the beginning of a sentence.
>
> ☐ There is no comma next to a date at the end of a sentence.

I can use commas with dates. ■   I need more practice. ■

Be dependable

1 MEET CHUNHUA

Read about one of her workplace skills.

I am dependable. People can count on me. For example, when I am going to be late, I always let people know.

2 CHUNHUA'S PROBLEM

READ. Circle *True* or *False*.

Chunhua takes the bus to work every morning. This morning, her alarm did not go off, and she overslept. She hurried, but she couldn't get to the bus stop in time. She missed the bus, and she is going to be late for work.

1. Chunhua always takes the bus to work.   True   False
2. Chunhua didn't set her alarm.   True   False
3. Chunhua can get to work on time today.   True   False

3 CHUNHUA'S SOLUTION

WORK TOGETHER. Chunhua is dependable. What does she do? Explain your answer.

1. Chunhua takes the next bus. She hopes no one will see that she is late.
2. Chunhua calls her supervisor and says she is going to be late for work.
3. Chunhua calls her supervisor and says she can't come to work today.
4. Chunhua _____.

Show what you know!

1. **THINK ABOUT IT.** Are you dependable? How are you dependable in class? At work? At home? Give examples.

2. **WRITE ABOUT IT.** Write an example in your Skills Log.

I am dependable. When I am going to meet a friend and I'm running late, I always call to let my friend know.

I can give an example of how I am dependable. ■

Unit Review: Go back to page 105. Which unit goals can you check off?

7 Health Watch

PREVIEW

Look at the picture. What do you see?
What is the problem?

UNIT GOALS

- ☐ Describe health problems
- ☐ Identify health problems
- ☐ Make a doctor's appointment
- ☐ Read medicine labels
- ☐ Talk about an injury

- ☐ Call about missing work
- ☐ **Academic skill:** Use formatting cues
- ☐ **Writing skill:** Give a reason
- ☐ **Workplace soft skill:** Show how you respect others

Vocabulary

Health Problems

A **PREDICT.** Look at the pictures. What do you see? What are the health problems?

B ▶ **LISTEN AND POINT.** Then listen and repeat.

Health problems

1. a headache
2. a sore throat
3. a cough
4. a cold
5. a fever
6. a rash
7. an earache
8. an upset stomach
9. the flu
10. high blood pressure
11. heartburn
12. chest pains

Vocabulary

C ▶ **ANALYZE. Listen to the sentences. Write the words you hear. Circle the words** *a, an, the*. **Find and circle those words in the "Health Problems" list.**

1. I have _____.
2. I have _____.
3. I have _____.
4. I have _____.

D **WORK TOGETHER. Look at the pictures. Student A, point to a picture and ask, "What's the matter?" Student B, say the problem. Take turns.**

Student A points to Picture 1.
A: What's the matter?
B: She has a headache.
Student B points to Picture 12.
B: What's the matter?
A: He has chest pains.

> **Study Tip**
>
> **Translate**
>
> Look at the list of health problems. Make cards for five new words. Write the word in English on one side of the card. Write the word in your native language on the other side.

Show what you know!

1. **THINK ABOUT IT. For some health problems you need to go to an emergency room immediately. For some health problems you can wait to see a doctor. Other health problems get better with rest. Look at the health problems again. Complete the chart.**

Go to the Emergency Room	Call for an appointment	Wait a couple of days
		headache

2. **TALK ABOUT IT. Use your chart. Talk about health problems.**

   A: Wait a couple of days when you have a headache.
   B: I don't agree. A headache can be very serious. Some people have to go to the emergency room.

3. **WRITE ABOUT IT. Now write three sentences about health problems.**

   Wait a couple of days when you have _____.
   Call your doctor for an appointment when you have _____.
   Go to the emergency room when you have _____.

| I can describe health problems. ■ | I need more practice. ■ |

Lesson 2

Make a doctor's appointment

1 BEFORE YOU LISTEN

LABEL. Write the words under the pictures.

| It's itchy. | It's swollen. | He's nauseous. | She's dizzy. |

1. _____ 2. _____ 3. _____ 4. _____

2 LISTEN

Receptionist   Roberto

A PREDICT. Look at the pictures. Where is the woman? Where is the man?

B ▶ LISTEN FOR MAIN IDEA. What does the woman say?

a. What are your symptoms?
b. What's the matter?

C ▶ LISTEN FOR DETAILS. Check (✓) the man's symptoms.

☐ He has a fever.   ☐ He's nauseous.
☐ He has heartburn. ☐ He's dizzy.

D ▶ EXPAND. Listen to the whole conversation. Write the day and time of the appointment.

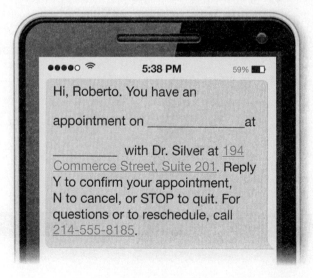

●●●●○ 🛜   5:38 PM   59% 🔋

Hi, Roberto. You have an

appointment on _____ at

_____ with Dr. Silver at 194
Commerce Street, Suite 201. Reply
Y to confirm your appointment,
N to cancel, or STOP to quit. For
questions or to reschedule, call
214-555-8185.

Listening and Speaking

3 PRONUNCIATION

A ▶ **PRACTICE.** Listen. Then listen and repeat.

I have a fever.

I need to make an appointment.

Please come at eight.

We close at noon on Friday.

B ▶ **APPLY.** Listen. Draw lines to connect sounds that are linked in speech.

1. He has a fever.

2. I have an upset stomach.

3. My hand is itchy.

4. She's a medical assistant.

4 CONVERSATION

A ▶ **LISTEN AND READ.** Then listen and repeat.

A: Hello. Westview Clinic.
B: Hi. This is Roberto Cruz. I'm sick, and I need to make an appointment, please.
A: All right. What's the matter?
B: I have a fever and I'm nauseous.
A: OK. How about Tuesday morning? At 9:00?
B: Yes, that's fine.

B **WORK TOGETHER.** Practice the conversation.

C **CREATE.** Make new conversations. Use the words in the boxes.

A: Hello. Westview Clinic.
B: Hi. This is _____. I'm sick, and I need to make an appointment, please.
A: All right. What's the matter?
B: I have a _____ and _____.
A: OK. How about _____? At _____?
B: Yes, that's fine.

cough	my throat is swollen	on Thursday	noon
headache	I'm dizzy	this afternoon	3:00
rash	my leg is itchy	first thing tomorrow	8:30

D **ROLE-PLAY.** Make your own conversations.

| I can make a doctor's appointment. ☐ | I need more practice. ☐ |

Prepositions of time: *on / at / by / in / from . . . to*		
Are you available	**on**	Tuesday morning?
The appointment is	**at**	9:00 A.M.
Please get here	**by**	5:00 today.
I'm going to see the doctor	**in**	an hour.
The pharmacy is open	**from**	8:00 A.M. **to** 9:00 P.M.

Grammar Watch

- Use *on* with a day or date.
- Use *at* with a specific time on the clock.
- Use *by* with a specific time in the future. It means *at that time or earlier*.
- Use *in* with an amount of time in the future.
- Use *from . . . to* with a starting time and an ending time.

A **IDENTIFY. Cross out the incorrect words.**

1. The appointment is ~~on~~ / at 9:15 A.M. on April 1.
2. You need to get here by / in 5:00.
3. The clinic is open from 8:00 A.M. at / to 5:00 P.M.
4. The office is closed on / in Saturday and Sunday.
5. The doctor can see you from / in an hour.
6. Dr. Evans has openings at / from 3:40 P.M. to 5:00 P.M.
7. My appointment is at / in 2:30 this afternoon.

B **DECIDE. Complete the sentences with *on, at, by, in,* or *from . . . to*.**

1. The dentist has appointments available __on__ June 6 and 7.
2. The doctor can call you back _____ a few minutes.
3. The appointment is _____ 4:30 today.
4. The clinic has openings _____ 3:30 _____ 5:00 tomorrow afternoon.
5. The doctor's office closes _____ noon for lunch.
6. Please come _____ Monday.
7. The doctor wants to see you again _____ a week.
8. The drugstore is open _____ 9:00 A.M. _____ 7:00 P.M.
9. You need to call _____ 5:00 P.M. because the office closes then.
10. Is the office open _____ Saturdays?

C **INTERPRET.** Look at the text message. Answer the questions. Use *on*, *at*, *by*, *in*, or *from . . . to*.

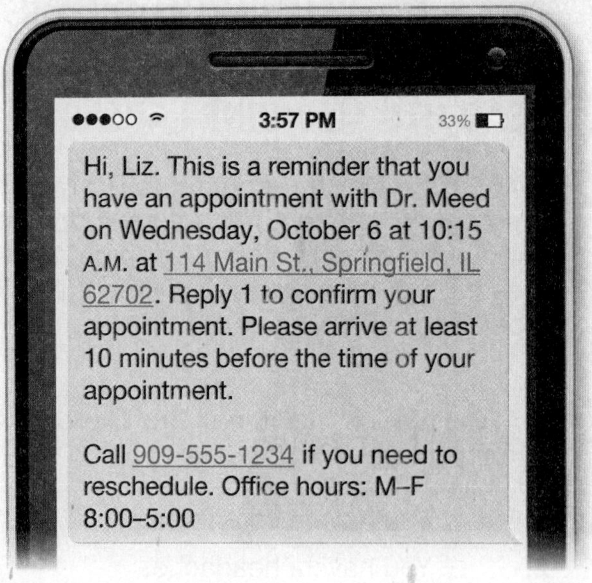
3:57 PM
33%
Hi, Liz. This is a reminder that you have an appointment with Dr. Meed on Wednesday, October 6 at 10:15 A.M. at 114 Main St., Springfield, IL 62702. Reply 1 to confirm your appointment. Please arrive at least 10 minutes before the time of your appointment.
Call 909-555-1234 if you need to reschedule. Office hours: M–F 8:00–5:00

1. What day is Liz's appointment?
   It is *on Wednesday*.
2. What time is her appointment?
   It is ________________.
3. When is the doctor's office open?
   It is open ________________.
4. It is now 8:15 A.M. on October 6. How soon is Liz going to see the doctor?
   She is going to see him ________________.
5. What time does Liz need to arrive at the doctor's office?
   She should be there ________________.

Show what you know!

1. **THINK ABOUT IT.** On the first appointment card, write your partner's name. Choose a time and date for your partner's appointment. Write them on the card. Write your name on the second card.
2. **TALK ABOUT IT.** Ask questions with *When* and *What time*. Write the information on the second card. Take turns.
   A: When is the appointment?
   B: It's on Friday, January 15.
3. **WRITE ABOUT IT.** Write two sentences about the day and time of your appointment.
   My appointment is on Friday, January 15. It's at 3:30 P.M.

1
Appointment for ____________
Date: ____________
Time: ____________

2
Appointment for ____________
Date: ____________
Time: ____________

I can use prepositions of time. ☐ I need more practice. ☐

Lesson 4 — Medicine labels

1 READ OTC MEDICINE LABELS

A IDENTIFY. Over-the-counter (OTC) medicine is medicine you can buy from any drugstore. For other medicine, you need to get a prescription from a doctor. Circle the OTC medicine you buy or have at home.

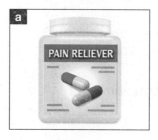
a. PAIN RELIEVER

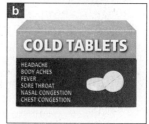
b. COLD TABLETS
HEADACHE
BODY ACHES
FEVER
SORE THROAT
NASAL CONGESTION
CHEST CONGESTION

c. COUGH SYRUP

d. Throat Lozenges
16 Lozenges

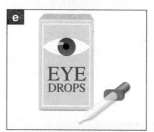
e. EYE DROPS

f. OINTMENT

B MATCH. Which medicine from Exercise A should you take?

1. __d__ You have a sore throat.
2. ____ You have a headache.
3. ____ Your skin itches.
4. ____ You have a cold.
5. ____ You have a cough.
6. ____ You have red eyes.

C MATCH. Read the medicine label. Match the questions and answers.

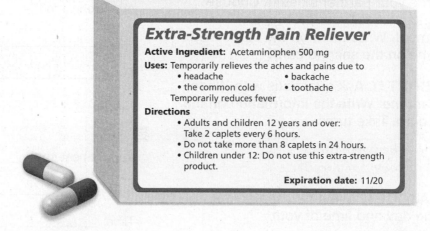

Extra-Strength Pain Reliever

Active Ingredient: Acetaminophen 500 mg

Uses: Temporarily relieves the aches and pains due to
- headache
- backache
- the common cold
- toothache
Temporarily reduces fever

Directions
- Adults and children 12 years and over: Take 2 caplets every 6 hours.
- Do not take more than 8 caplets in 24 hours.
- Children under 12: Do not use this extra-strength product.

Expiration date: 11/20

1. ____ What is this medicine for?
2. ____ Who can take this medicine?
3. ____ What is the dosage?
4. ____ Who cannot use this product?
5. ____ What is the expiration date?

a. November, 2020
b. Aches and pains, and fever
c. Two caplets every six hours
d. Adults and children over 12
e. Children under 12

Workplace, Life, and Community Skills

2 READ PRESCRIPTION MEDICINE LABELS

A **INTERPRET.** Look at the prescription and the medicine label. Answer the questions.

1. Who wrote the prescription?
2. Who is it for?
3. What is the dosage?
4. Where can you get this medicine?
5. What information is on the label?

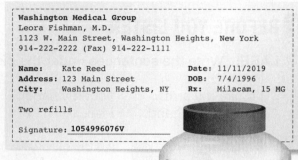

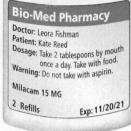

B **MATCH.** Read the medicine label in Exercise A again. Match the questions and answers.

1. ____ What is the name of the medicine?
2. ____ How often do I take it?
3. ____ What is the dosage?
4. ____ What is the expiration date?
5. ____ How many refills can I get?

a. Two
b. Two tablespoons
c. November 20, 2021
d. Once a day
e. Milacam

C ▶ **SELF-ASSESS.** Listen and check your answers. Then listen and repeat.

D **ACT IT OUT.** With a partner, take turns being the customer and the pharmacist. Ask and answer the questions in Exercise B about these prescriptions.

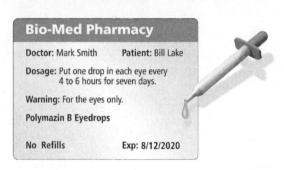

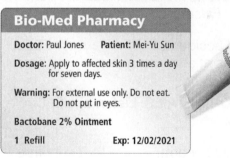

E GO ONLINE. Search for an online pharmacy. On the website, find information on a medicine you saw in an advertisement. Check the instructions on how to take the medicine.

I can read medicine labels. ■   I need more practice. ■

1 BEFORE YOU LISTEN

LABEL. Write the sentences under the pictures.

I broke my arm.	I cut my finger.	I hurt my head.
I burned my hand.	~~I fell.~~	I sprained my ankle.

1. _I fell._

2. _____

3. _____

4. _____

5. _____

6. _____

2 LISTEN

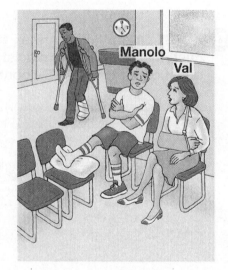

A **PREDICT.** Look at the picture. Where are the people?

B ▶ **LISTEN FOR MAIN IDEA.** Read the sentences. Circle *True* or *False*.

1. Val had an accident.	True False
2. Manolo was at a soccer game.	True False

C ▶ **LISTEN FOR DETAILS.** Listen again. Circle *True* or *False*.

1. Val sprained her arm.	True False
2. Manolo thinks he broke his ankle.	True False

D ▶ **EXPAND.** Listen to the whole conversation. What happened to Manolo? Circle the letter.

a.

b.

Listening and Speaking

3 PRONUNCIATION

A ▶ **PRACTICE. Listen. Then listen and repeat.**

What are you doing here?

I was at a soccer game.

What's the matter?

> **_t_ between two vowel sounds**
>
> When the letter _t_ is between two vowel sounds, it often sounds like a quick /d/.

B ▶ **CHOOSE. Listen. Which _t_'s have the sound /d/? Circle the words.**

1. What about you?
2. I hurt my ankle.
3. That's too bad.
4. See you later.

4 CONVERSATION

A ▶ **LISTEN AND READ. Then listen and repeat.**

A: Hi, Val. What are you doing here?
B: Oh, hi, Manolo. I had an accident. I broke my arm.
A: Oh, no! I'm sorry to hear that.
B: Thanks. What about you?
A: I hurt my ankle at a soccer game. I think I sprained it.

B **WORK TOGETHER. Practice the conversation.**

C **CREATE. Make new conversations. Use the words in the boxes.**

A: Hi, _____. What are you doing here?
B: Oh, hi, _____. I had an accident.
�_____

A: Oh, no! I'm sorry to hear that.
B: Thanks. What about you?
A: I hurt my _____ at a soccer game.
I think I sprained it.
B: That's too bad.

I cut my hand	foot
I burned my finger.	wrist
I fell.	back

D **ROLE-PLAY. Make your own conversations.**

I can talk about an injury. ■	I need more practice. ■

Grammar

Simple past: More irregular verbs

Simple past: More irregular verbs		
She	**had**	an accident.
	broke	her arm.
	got	hurt.
	hurt	her ankle.

Grammar Watch

Common irregular verbs

Base form	Past-tense form
break	**broke**
cut	**cut**
fall	**fell**
get	**got**
have	**had**
hurt	**hurt**

- See page 259 for more past-tense forms.

A COMPLETE. Write the past-tense forms of the words in parentheses.

1. I (get) _____got_____ hurt on my way to work last week. I was in a hurry, and I (fall) _____ down the stairs. My foot (hurt) _____ for a few days after that, but I (not go) _____ to the doctor.

2. The floor in the bathroom at work was wet. Nishi slipped, and she (fall) _____. She (hurt) _____ her hand pretty bad, but she (not break) _____ it.

3. Luis (have) _____ an accident at his job in the restaurant. He (cut) _____ his finger. It was serious, and he (go) _____ to the hospital.

4. Ling was out of the office yesterday. She (have) _____ a sore throat, and her head (hurt) _____. She (not have) _____ any medicine at home, so I (get) _____ some for her at the pharmacy.

B APPLY. Make sentences about the past. Use the words in the box.

~~break~~	cut	fall	get	have	hurt

1. Oscar / his ankle _Oscar broke his ankle._____
2. The kitchen manager / her finger with a knife _____
3. You / a fever last night _____
4. My co-worker and I / sick on the same day _____
5. The patient / in the bathroom _____
6. Lan / her arm _____

Grammar

C **DESCRIBE.** Look at the pictures. What happened last weekend?

Jessica had an accident in the kitchen. She . . .

1. _____

2. _____

3. _____

4. _____

D **WRITE.** Make two sentences about what happened in each picture in Exercise C.

Show what you know!

1. THINK ABOUT IT. Complete the questions.

Did you ever hurt _____?

Did you ever break _____?

Did you ever have _____?

2. TALK ABOUT IT. Ask your questions. Take notes.

A: Did you ever break your toe?
B: No, but I broke my finger at work last year.

3. WRITE ABOUT IT. Write two sentences about your classmates' injuries.

_____

_____

I can talk about an injury. ■   I need more practice. ■

1 BEFORE YOU READ

A **DECIDE. Complete the sentences with the words in the box.**

attitude	avoid	situation	sources	stress

1. When you feel _____, you worry and you can't relax.
2. Things that cause stress are called _____ of stress.
3. Anna's co-workers always try to do their best work. They have a good _____.
4. Tom's car won't start and he's late for an important meeting. He's in a bad _____.
5. Doctors say to _____ eating junk food.

B **MAKE CONNECTIONS.**

What's happening in the photo? Are you ever in the same situation? When do you feel stressed?

2 READ

► Listen and read.

> **Academic Skill: Use formatting cues**
>
> Authors sometimes use formatting such as **boldface** type, bullets (•), and color to help readers find the main point.

STRESS

1 Everyone feels stress sometimes. That *can* be a good thing. For example, stress about important things, like a job interview or a test, can make you work hard
5 to prepare for it. But some people feel so much stress that they become sick.

What causes stress?

Change The biggest source of
10 stress is change. It may be a bad change, like losing a job or getting divorced. But even a good change, like going on vacation, causes stress.

15 **Loss of Control** You also feel stress in situations that you can't control. Maybe you are stuck in traffic or your kids are sick. When you can't change bad things in your life, then you feel stress.

Negative Attitudes The way you think can cause stress.
20 For example, you worry a lot or you think about only the bad things in your life. These kinds of negative attitudes cause stress.

Unhealthy Habits The way you live can cause stress. Do you eat too
25 much junk food? Do you work too many hours? Unhealthy habits like these add stress to your life.

How can you manage stress?

Pay attention to the times you feel
30 stressed. Look for what causes stress in your life.

Think about ways to change the things that cause you stress.

Accept the things you can't change. Some-
35 times you can't avoid a stressful situation.

Get regular exercise. It will help you relax. You'll also sleep better.

Talk about your stress with a family member, friend, counselor, or doctor.

Reading

3 CLOSE READING

A **IDENTIFY.** What is the main idea?

Everybody feels stress but _____.
a. not all stress is bad
b. you can learn to manage it
c. you just have to accept it

B **CITE EVIDENCE.** Complete the sentences. Where is the information? Write the line numbers.

Lines

1. The thing that causes the most stress is _____.
   a. a person's job   b. change   c. a negative attitude   _____

2. Being in a car stuck in traffic is an example of _____.
   a. something you   b. avoiding a   c. a situation that
      can change   stressful situation   you cannot control   _____

3. Eating junk food is an example of _____.
   a. an unhealthy habit   b. a good way to relax   c. a thing you have
                                                              to accept   _____

4. Start managing the stress in your life by _____.
   a. understanding the   b. avoiding all   c. thinking about
      sources of your stress   changes   happy things only   _____

5. Try talking about your stress with a friend, family member, doctor,
   or _____.
   a. employer   b. pharmacist   c. counselor   _____

4 SUMMARIZE

Complete the summary with the words in the box.

accept   attitudes   control   manage   sources

Too much stress is bad for you. Big (1) _____ of stress are change, loss of
(2) _____, negative (3) _____, and unhealthy habits. There are things
you can do to (4) _____ the stress in your life, but sometimes you have to
(5) _____ things you can't change.

Show what you know!

1. **THINK ABOUT IT.** What causes you stress? How do you manage stress?

2. **WRITE ABOUT IT.** Write about your sources of stress and how you can
   manage stress.

   I feel stress when _____. To manage my stress, I _____.
   I can also _____.

3. **PRESENT IT.** Make a presentation about the five ways to manage stress in the
   article. Which ones are the most helpful? What are other ways to manage stress?

I can use formatting cues. ■   I need more practice. ■

Lesson 8

Call in when you have to miss work

1 BEFORE YOU LISTEN

A **LABEL.** Write the sentences under the pictures.

> I have a checkup.
> I have to go to the dentist.
>
> I'm getting my flu shot.
> My child is sick.

1. _____   2. _____   3. _____   4. _____

B **MAKE CONNECTIONS.** What are some other reasons that people miss work? Did you ever have to miss work or school?

2 LISTEN

Sung   Eva

A **PREDICT.** Look at the picture. Who is Sung calling?

B ▶ **LISTEN FOR MAIN IDEA.** Why is Sung calling?

   a. She's going to be late.
   b. She's not going to work today.
   c. She has an emergency.

C ▶ **LISTEN FOR DETAILS.** Answer the questions.

  1. Where is Sung going?
    a. to the hospital   **b.** to the doctor's   **c.** to the dentist's
                          office   office

  2. What is the problem?
    a. Sung doesn't   **b.** Sung's son   **c.** Sung forgot
        feel well.   is sick.   her appointment.

  3. What does the supervisor say?
    a. Take your   **b.** See you   **c.** Take care
        medicine.   tomorrow.   of yourself.

D ▶ **EXPAND.** Listen to the whole conversation. Answer the questions.

  1. What does the supervisor ask?
    a. When is your appointment?   **b.** Do you feel better?   **c.** Do you think you'll be
                                                                      in tomorrow?

  2. What will Sung do later?
    a. call her supervisor again   **b.** go to work   **c.** call the doctor

Listening and Speaking

3 PRONUNCIATION

A ▶ **PRACTICE. Listen to the sentences. Then listen and repeat.**

I'm sorry / to hear that.
Do you think / you'll be in / tomorrow?
I have to / take my son / to the clinic.

B ▶ **APPLY. Listen. Draw lines to separate the thought groups.**

1. I can't come in today.
2. She has an appointment.
3. Thanks for calling.
4. Take care of yourself.

> **Using pauses**
>
> We use pauses to break sentences into smaller thought groups. These pauses make sentences easier to say and understand.

4 CONVERSATION

A ▶ **LISTEN AND READ. Then listen and repeat.**

A: Hello. Eva Pérez speaking.
B: Hi, Eva. This is Sung. I can't come in today because I have to go to the doctor. I don't feel well.
A: Sorry to hear that. Thanks for calling, and take care of yourself.
B: Thanks.

B **WORK TOGETHER. Practice the conversation in Exercise A.**

C **CREATE. Make new conversations. Use the words in the boxes.**

A: Hello. _____ speaking.
B: Hi, _____. This is _____. I can't come in today because I have to _____. _____.
A: Sorry to hear that. Thanks for calling, and _____.
B: Thanks.

go to the dentist
take my son to the clinic
take care of my mother

I broke my tooth
He has a fever
She's sick

good luck
I hope he feels better
I hope she gets well soon

D **ROLE-PLAY. Make your own conversations.**

I can call in when I have to miss work. ■   I need more practice. ■

Ways to express reasons

Ways to express reasons		
Sung missed work yesterday	**because**	she didn't feel well.
She went to the doctor	**for**	a prescription.

Grammar Watch
• Use *because* + a subject and a verb. • Use *for* + a noun.

A COMPLETE. Write *because* or *for*.

1. I can't go to work ___because___ I have a cold.
2. We have to go to the pharmacy _____ some medicine.
3. My co-worker is going to the doctor _____ a blood test.
4. Carlo went to the clinic _____ he hurt his back.
5. You went to the store _____ cold medicine.
6. Our supervisor wasn't at work yesterday _____ she had a fever.

B WRITE. Where do they have to go? Write one sentence with *because* and one with *for*. Use the words in parentheses.

1. (Jack / the pharmacy / some medicine)

   Jack has to go to the pharmacy because he needs some medicine.
   _____

2. (Ping / the doctor / a flu shot)

   _____
   _____

3. (Grace / the dentist / a checkup)

   _____
   _____

I can express reasons with *because* and *for*. ■	I need more practice. ■

1 STUDY THE MODEL

READ. Answer the questions.

> Hasti Kumar
>
> Treating a Cough
>
> There are three things I do when I have a cough. I drink a lot of hot tea. The tea relaxes my chest. Also, I wear a scarf because it keeps my chest warm. I take cough medicine at night. It helps me sleep. I usually feel better in a couple of days.

1. What is Hasti's health problem?
2. What does Hasti drink? Why?
3. What does Hasti wear? Why?
4. What medicine does Hasti take? Why?

2 PLAN YOUR WRITING

WORK TOGETHER. Ask and answer the questions.

1. Think of a health problem. What is it?
2. What's one thing you do to get better? Why?
3. What's another thing you do to get better? Why?
4. What's one more thing you do to get better? Why?

Writing Skill: Give a reason

Give a reason why you do something. For example:
I drink a lot of hot tea. The tea relaxes my chest.

3 WRITE

Write about how you treat a health problem. Use the model, the Writing Skill, and your ideas from Exercise 2 to help you.

WRITING CHECKLIST

☐ The paragraph answers the questions in Exercise 2.

☐ There is a topic sentence.

☐ There is a reason for each thing the writer does.

4 CHECK YOUR WRITING

WORK TOGETHER. Read the checklist. Read your writing aloud. Revise your writing.

I can give reasons in my writing. ■   I need more practice. ■

Lesson 11 Respect others

1 MEET BELVIE

Read about one of her workplace skills.

> I show respect for others. For example, I respect my co-workers' needs, and I try not to cause problems for them.

2 BELVIE'S PROBLEM

READ. Circle *True* or *False*.

Belvie works at a factory. She is ready to start work, but she suddenly feels very sick. Belvie thinks she has the flu. She can work today, but then she will probably give the flu to her co-workers. She can go home, but then she will lose a day's pay.

1. Belvie is late for work.	True	False
2. Belvie probably has the flu.	True	False
3. Belvie might make her co-workers sick.	True	False

3 BELVIE'S SOLUTION

WORK TOGETHER. Belvie shows respect for others. What does she do? Explain your answers.

1. Belvie starts to work. She doesn't say that she is sick.
2. Belvie tells her supervisor that she's sick. Then she goes home.
3. Belvie starts to work. She tells everyone she's sick.
4. Belvie _____.

Show what you know!

1. **THINK ABOUT IT.** Do you respect others? How do you show respect for others in class? At work? At home? Give examples.

2. **WRITE ABOUT IT.** Write an example in your Skills Log.

   I show respect for others in class. For example, I turn off my phone during class. I don't want someone to call me and interrupt the class.

I can give an example of how I show respect for others. ■

Unit Review: Go back to page 125. Which unit goals can you check off?

8 Job Hunting

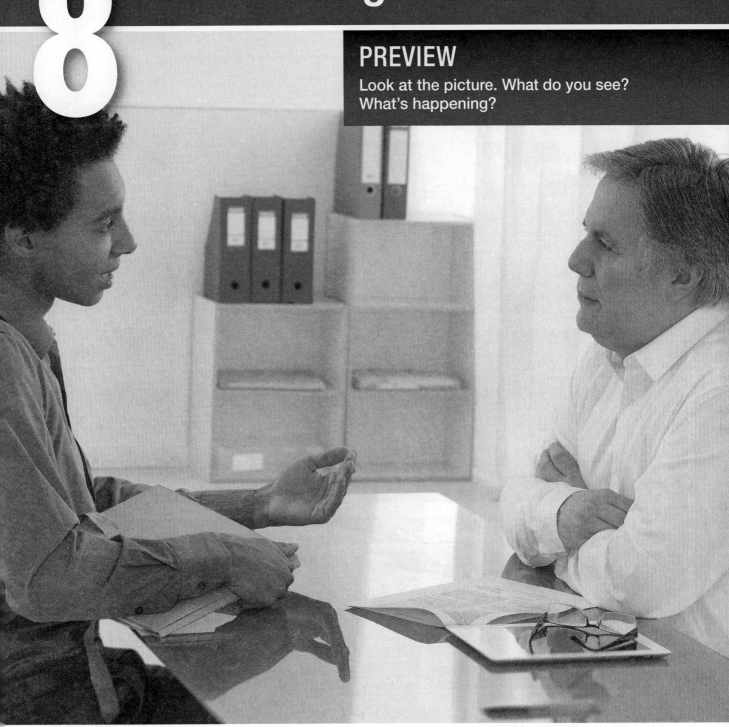

PREVIEW
Look at the picture. What do you see?
What's happening?

UNIT GOALS

- [ ] Identify job titles and duties
- [ ] Talk about your job skills
- [ ] Read help-wanted ads
- [ ] Identify job requirements
- [ ] Answer questions about work history

- [ ] Answer questions about availability
- [ ] **Academic skill:** Predict the topic
- [ ] **Writing skill:** Use the correct tense
- [ ] **Workplace soft skill:** Show how you are honest

Job titles and duties

A **PREDICT.** Look at the pictures. What do you see? What are the jobs? What do the people do in each job?

B ▶ **LISTEN AND POINT.** Then listen and repeat.

Vocabulary

Job titles and duties

1. computer system administrator
   A install computer systems
   B problem solve

2. nursing assistant
   A take care of patients
   B record patient information

3. warehouse worker
   A receive shipments
   B unload materials

4. stock clerk
   A assist customers
   B stock shelves

5. receptionist
   A greet visitors
   B handle phone calls

6. food service worker
   A prepare food
   B clean kitchen equipment

7. manager
   A supervise employees
   B plan work schedules

C **IDENTIFY.** Student A, say a job title. Student B, say the job duties for that job.

A: Manager.
B: Plan work schedules. Supervise employees.

D **EXTEND.** Think of jobs. Write the job duties.

assist: _visitors, patients_   prepare: _____

clean: _the dishes, the floor_   record: _____

greet: _____   stock: _____

handle: _____   supervise: _____

install: _____   unload: _____

> ### Study Tip
>
> **Make connections**
> Make cards for job duties. Write a job title on the front of the card. Write two job duties of that job on the back.

Show what you know!

1. **THINK ABOUT IT.** What job do you want in five years? What are the job duties?

   Job title: _____

   Job duties: _____   _____   _____

2. **WRITE ABOUT IT.** Now write about the job you want.

   A medical assistant takes care of patients.

3. **PRESENT IT.** Tell your classmates about the job you want.

   I want to be a medical assistant. A medical assistant takes care of patients.

I can identify job titles and duties. ■   I need more practice. ■

1 BEFORE YOU LISTEN

A **LABEL.** Write the words under the pictures.

operate a forklift	speak Spanish	use a computer
order supplies	use a cash register	work as a team

1. _____

2. _____

3. _____

4. _____

5. _____

Hablo español.

6. _____

2 LISTEN

A **PREDICT.** Look at the picture. Who is the supervisor?
a. Albert
b. Manny

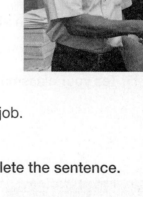

Albert   Manny

B ▶ **LISTEN FOR MAIN IDEA.** Complete the sentence.

Manny is at the store _____.
a. to buy something
b. for a job interview

C ▶ **LISTEN FOR DETAILS.** Complete the sentences.

1. Albert is a _____.
   a. salesperson
   b. store manager

2. Albert asks about Manny's _____.
   a. job duties
   b. customer experience

3. Manny assists customers and _____ at his job.
   a. stocks shelves
   b. orders supplies

D ▶ **EXPAND.** Listen to the whole conversation. Complete the sentence.

Manny _____ _____ use a cash register.
a. can
b. can't

Listening and Speaking

3 PRONUNCIATION

A ▶ **PRACTICE. Listen. Then listen and repeat.**

I can't use a cash register.   I can learn.
Can you speak Chinese?   Yes, I can.

B ▶ **CHOOSE. Listen. Circle** *can* **when it has a strong pronunciation.**

1. I can't plan work schedules.
2. Can you handle phone calls?
3. Yes, I can.
4. My manager can supervise employees.

Pronunciation of *can* **and** *can't*

- *Can* often has a weak pronunciation when another word comes after it. It sounds like "c'n" because "a" becomes short and quiet.
- *Can* has a strong pronunciation at the end of a sentence.
- *Can't* always has a strong pronunciation.

4 CONVERSATION

A ▶ **LISTEN AND READ. Then listen and repeat.**

A: Manny? Hi, I'm Albert Taylor, the store manager. Please have a seat.
B: Thank you. It's nice to meet you.
A: I have your application here. I see that you're working now. What are your job duties?
B: Well, I assist customers and stock shelves.
A: OK. Tell me about your skills. Can you use a cash register?
B: No, I can't, but I can learn.

B **WORK TOGETHER. Practice the conversation in Exercise A.**

C **CREATE. Make new conversations. Use the words in the boxes.**

A: _____? Hi, I'm _____, the
store manager. Please have a seat.
B: Thank you. It's nice to meet you.
A: I have your application here. I see that
you're working now. What are your job
duties?
B: Well, I _____ and _____.
A: OK. Tell me more about your skills. Can
you _____?
B: No, I can't, but I can learn.

receive shipments	unload materials	operate a forklift
greet visitors	handle phone calls	use a computer
prepare food	clean equipment	order supplies

D **ROLE-PLAY. Make your own conversations.**

I can talk about my skills at a job interview. ☐   I need more practice. ☐

Grammar

Can to express ability

Can to express ability		
Affirmative		
I / She / They	**can**	stock shelves.
Negative		
I / She / They	**cannot** **can't**	speak Chinese.

Yes/No questions				**Short answers**
Can	you	**use**	a cash register?	**Yes**, I **can**. **No**, I **can't**.

Grammar Watch

- Use *can* + the base form of the verb.
- *Can't* = *cannot*. We use *can't* more often.

A **WRITE.** Look at the pictures. Write one question for each picture. Use *can*.

1. Can Pat lift heavy boxes?
2. _____
3. _____
4. _____
5. _____
6. _____

B **WORK TOGETHER.** Ask and answer the questions in Exercise A.

A: Can Pat lift heavy boxes?
B: No, she can't.

Grammar

C **INTERPRET.** Look at Amy's job application. Ask and answer questions about her skills. Use *can*.

A: *Can Amy help with computer problems?*
B: *No, she can't.*

○○○

Amy Ruiz
Please check the skills you have.

Office skills
○ help with computer problems
● use a computer
● record information

Warehouse skills
○ operate a forklift
● sort materials
○ lift up to 50 lbs.

D **WRITE.** Make sentences about Amy's skills. Use *can* and *can't*.

1. *Amy can't help with computer problems.*
2. _____
3. _____
4. _____
5. _____
6. _____

E **MAKE CONNECTIONS.** Describe your skills. Use *can* and *can't*.

1. _____
2. _____
3. _____
4. _____

Show what you know!

1. THINK ABOUT IT. Complete the questions.

Question	Name	Answer
Can you use a computer?	Paola	Yes
1. Can you _____?		
2. Can you _____?		
3. Can you _____?		

2. TALK ABOUT IT. Interview each member of your group. Ask questions and complete the chart.

3. WRITE ABOUT IT. Now write one sentence about each person's skills.

Paola can use a computer.

I can use *can* to express ability. ■   I need more practice. ■

Lesson 4

Help wanted ads and job requirements

1 READ HELP WANTED ADS

A **IDENTIFY.** Read the help wanted ads. Where can you find these ads? Where else can people find out about jobs?

CAR SERVICE DRIVERS NEEDED

Job description: Drivers for evening and weekend airport car service. Experience: 1 year of driving service. Part-time. Pay: $12/hr. For more information, and to apply, please send a letter of interest to Jonna Kern at jkern@carservice.org

Office Assistant

Responsibilities: handle phone calls, greet visitors, and organize customer files. Preferred experience: 1 year of working in a busy office environment and formal training in computer application software. Class and hours: Full-time, M-F, 8 am-5 pm. Health benefits. Required materials: Cover letter, résumé, and list of references. Send to: erinhubs@hroffice.com. For full consideration, apply by 1/31.

B **MATCH.** Connect the sentence parts.

1. _____ A full-time employee works
2. _____ Responsibilities are
3. _____ A résumé includes
4. _____ A cover letter is
5. _____ Experience is
6. _____ References are
7. _____ Health benefits are

a. people who can describe you and your work.
b. a list of your job experiences and skills.
c. when your company pays some of your health insurance.
d. the activities and things you will do at a job.
e. a way to introduce yourself to your future employer.
f. your past work activities.
g. 40 hours a week.

C **INTERPRET.** Read the ads again. Answer the questions.

1. Which job is full-time? _____
2. What should someone do to apply for the car service driver position? _____
3. Which job requires evening and weekend work? _____
4. What is the pay for Car Service Drivers? _____
5. What are the responsibilities of an office assistant? _____
6. What kind of experience is preferred for the Office Assistant position? _____
7. When does the Office Assistant need to be able to work? _____

I can read help wanted ads. ■   I need more practice. ■

2 IDENTIFY JOB REQUIREMENTS

A **WORK TOGETHER.** Look at the résumés. Which job from 1A is each candidate applying for? Write your answers on the lines. How do you know?

B **COMPARE.** Look at the résumés. Answer the questions.

Which candidate is best qualified for the Car Service Driver job? Why?

Which candidate is best qualified for the Office Assistant job? Why?

C **ROLE-PLAY.** Act out a job interview. Choose a job from 1A. Student A, you are the interviewer. Student B, you are the applicant. Take turns.

D GO ONLINE. Search for a job posting website. Find a job you are interested in.

What are the job responsibilities? What experience do you need? How can you apply for the job?

Jin Mong
1234 New Moon Road, New Jersey 11112

Education: Jones Community College
Major: Hospitality
Work experience: OMBER Driver, June 2018-present, Moon Gas, gas station attendant, June 2017-June 2018
Languages: English and Chinese
Skills: can operate a cash register

Ann Lopez
42 North Shore Road, Boynton Beach, FL
alopez@qmail.com

Education: Palm Beach High School, currently enrolled in Palm Beach State College, Office Technology
Work Experience: Starland Coffee Shop, server January 2018-present.
Relevant Experience: Work with customers, handle customer problems, train new staff
Languages: Spanish and English
Skills: Can type, order supplies, use a cash register

Kim Kiska
22 West Lane Street, #3A
Stockton, CA
kimkas@yippe.com

Education: Stockton High School, A.A in Office Systems and Technology.
Work Experience: Office Assistant, Gem Restaurant Supply, March 2017-present
Responsibilities: Handle phone calls, organize file room, work with customers; Office Clerk, Bel Blue Office Systems, October 2015-March 2017.
Responsibilities: Greet customers, enter new data in database
Languages: Polish, Russian, and English
Skills: Fluent in all Office Software Systems

Bin Fang
807 Kates Place, #21. Chicago, IL binfang@macro.com

Education: Jones Driving School, C-License
Work Experience: John's Taxi Service, September 2018-present; Roberto's Car Service, December 2015-present
Skills: Can type, use a computer, operate a commercial vehicle

---

I can identify job requirements. ■   I need more practice. ■

Lesson 5

Answer questions about work history

1 BEFORE YOU LISTEN

A **READ.** What are the reasons people change jobs?

B **MAKE CONNECTIONS.** Have you ever changed jobs? What was the reason?

1. I'd like to make more money.

2. I'd like a different schedule.

3. I'd like a job closer to home.

4. I'd like to do something different.

2 LISTEN

A **PREDICT.** Look at the picture. What are they talking about?

a. things Manny wants to buy
b. Manny's work experience

B ▶ **LISTEN FOR MAIN IDEA.** Put Manny's experiences in the correct order. Write numbers on the lines.

1. _____ got a job as a stock clerk

2. _____ came to the U.S.

3. _____ got a job as a gardener

C ▶ **LISTEN FOR DETAILS.** Why does Manny want to change jobs?

a. He wants to be a stock clerk.
b. He wants to do something different.

Manny

Albert

D ▶ **EXPAND.** Listen to the whole conversation. Answer the questions.

1. When was Manny unemployed?
   a. two months ago   **b.** two years ago

2. Why was Manny unemployed?
   a. His mother was sick. **b.** He was sick.

3. How long was Manny unemployed?
   a. for two years   **b.** for two months

3 CONSONANT

A ▶ LISTEN AND READ. Then listen and repeat.

A: So, tell me more about your work experience.
B: Well, I came to the U.S. three years ago. First, I got a job as a gardener. Then last year I got a job as a stock clerk.
A: OK. So now you're a stock clerk. Why are you looking for another job?
B: Things in my life have changed, and now I'd like to do something different.

B WORK TOGETHER. Practice the conversation in Exercise A.

C CREATE. Make new conversations. Use the words in the boxes.

A: So, tell me more about your work experience.
B: Well, I came to the U.S. _____ ago. First, I got a job as a _____. Then last year I got a job as a _____.
A: OK. So now you're a _____. Why are you looking for another job?
B: Things in my life have changed, and now I'd like _____.

a year	warehouse worker	truck driver	to make more money
a few years	nurse assistant	receptionist	a different schedule
ten months	food service worker	cook	a job closer to home

D ROLE-PLAY. Make your own conversations.

I can answer questions about my work history. ■   I need more practice. ■

Time expressions with *ago*, *last*, *in*, and *later*

Time expressions with *ago*, *last*, *in*, and *later*				
I got a job	three years 10 months	ago.	One month	later, I got a better job.
	last	year. week.	Two days	
	in	July. the fall.	A week	

A **DECIDE.** Use the words in the boxes to complete the sentences.

1.
| ago |
| in |
| last |

Luz came to the U.S. two years ___ago___ She studied English _____ year. She got a job _____ December.

2.
| ago |
| last |
| later |

Six months _____, Meng came to the U.S. She started working in a factory one month _____. She left that job _____ week because she got a better job.

3.
| in |
| last |
| later |

_____ 2004, Omar came to the U.S. One year _____, he got a job in a supermarket. He got a new job in a warehouse _____ month.

B **APPLY.** Write each sentence a different way. Use *ago* or *in*.

1. Tina got a new job last month. *Tina got a new job a month ago.* _____
2. She learned to take care of patients in 2015. _____
3. Frank got his job a year ago. _____
4. He left his job in January. _____
5. They started school six months ago. _____
6. Yan changed jobs last week. _____

Grammar

C **WRITE.** Look at Aram's timeline. Write sentences. Use *in*, *ago*, and *later*.

| May 2015 came to the U.S. | June 2015 started English classes | January 2016 got his first job | July 2017 got a better job | December 2018 became a supervisor |

1. _Aram came to the U.S. in May 2015._
2. _Later he_
3. _____
4. _____
5. _____

Show what you know!

1. **THINK ABOUT IT.** Answer the question about yourself. When did you start learning English? Use *in* or *ago*.

2. **TALK ABOUT IT.** Take turns asking *When did you start learning English?* Draw a time line to show each person's answer.

Victor   Dani
July 2017   September   today

Victor: I started learning English in July, 2017.
Dani: I started learning English four months ago.

3. **WRITE ABOUT IT.** Now write a sentence about when each person started learning English.

_____
_____
_____

I can use time expressions with *ago*, *last*, *in*, and *later*. ▪   I need more practice. ▪

Read about jobs in the U.S.

1 BEFORE YOU READ

A LABEL. Label the pictures with the words in the box.

| agriculture | health care | manufacturing | technology |

1. _____   2. _____   3. _____   4. _____

B MAKE CONNECTIONS. Think about the fields of employment in A. Which fields have the most jobs these days? What kinds of jobs are they?

2 READ

▶ **LISTEN AND READ.**

> **Academic Skill: Predict the topic**
>
> You can often guess what an article is about by looking at the title and pictures. This will prepare you to understand what you read.

Today's Hot Jobs

1 The U.S. job market is changing fast. At one time, most workers in the U.S. had jobs on farms. Now, less than 2 percent of workers have agricultural jobs. In 1960, 25 percent of workers had jobs in manufacturing. 5 Now, only 10 percent of workers are making things in factories. So where are the jobs today?

Health Care
Many of the fastest-growing jobs 10 are in health care. The U.S. population is getting older. These older Americans need 15 medical care and help with daily living. The greatest need is for personal care aides. There may be more than 750 thousand new jobs of this kind by 2026. Personal care aides take care of people in their homes or in 20 day programs. They sometimes work with people with disabilities or long-term illnesses. On average, they make about $22,000 a year. There are other fast-growing jobs in health care, too. For example, by 2026, there may be a need for 437 thousand 25 more registered nurses. On average, they make about $69,000 a year.

Computer and Information Technology
There are also many fast-growing jobs in computer and information technology. By 2026, there may be 30 more than 546 thousand new jobs in this field. Almost 300 thousand of those jobs will be for software developers. Some software developers create programs for computers and cell phones. Others design computer networks (where many 35 computers work together). On average, they make more than $100,000 a year.

Many of today's fastest-growing jobs are in these two fields. Where will tomorrow's jobs be?

Source: U.S. Department of Labor

Percentage of Growth in Jobs

Home health aides	47%
Physical therapist assistants	31%
Application software developers	31%
Occupational therapy assistants	29%

Reading

3 CLOSE READING

A IDENTIFY. What is the main idea?

The fastest-growing jobs in the United States _____.
a. are in health care and in computer and information technology
b. are some of the highest-paid jobs in the United States
c. are jobs creating programs for computers and cell phones

B CITE EVIDENCE. Answer the questions. Where is the information? Write the line numbers.

			Lines
1. The number of jobs in manufacturing today is _____ it was in the past.			_____
a. higher than	b. lower than	c. the same as	
2. Personal care aides make about _____ on average.			_____
a. $2026 a month	b. $22,000 a year	c. $69,000 a year	
3. By 2026, there will probably be _____ new jobs for software developers.			_____
a. about 100,000	b. more than 546,000	c. almost 300,000	

C INTERPRET. Complete the sentences about the bar graph.

1. The bar graph shows _____.
   a. growing jobs in numbers
   b. growing jobs in percentage
   c. dying jobs in percentage   _____

2. The growth in jobs for application software developers _____.
   a. is higher than for home health aides
   b. is lower than for occupational therapy assistants
   c. is the same as for physical therapist assistants   _____

4 SUMMARIZE

Complete the summary with the words in the box.

| employment | health care | job market | software | technology |

The (1) _____ in the U.S. is changing. Two fields of (2) _____ are
growing fast. There will be many new jobs in (3) _____, especially jobs for
personal care aides. There will also be many new jobs in computer and information
(4) _____, especially for (5) _____ developers.

Show what you know!

1. **THINK ABOUT IT.** What job do you want to have in five years? Why? What do you need to do to get that job?

2. **TALK ABOUT IT.** Talk about the jobs you want. Talk about how to get those jobs.

   In five years, I want to be a software developer. I need to learn about technology.

3. **WRITE ABOUT IT.** Now write about the job you want in five years.

I can predict the topic. ■   I need more practice. ■

Lesson 8

Answer questions about availability

1 BEFORE YOU LISTEN

MATCH. Read the information about job interviews. Then match the words with the definitions.

> At a job interview, the interviewer asks you about your **availability**. For example, "Which shift can you work, day or night? and "Can you work on weekends?" The interviewer may ask if your hours are **flexible**. For example, "Can you work different hours if the schedule changes?" The interviewer also asks when you can start. If you are working, you should give your boss one or two weeks' **notice** that you are leaving your job. This will help your boss find a new employee to fill your position when you leave.

1. _____ easy to change
2. _____ when you can work
3. _____ information or warning that something will happen
4. _____ a scheduled period of work time

a. availability
b. shift
c. flexible
d. notice

2 LISTEN

A **PREDICT.** Look at the picture. What do you think is happening?

B ▶ **LISTEN FOR MAIN IDEA.** What does Albert ask? Check the questions.

☐ Do you prefer mornings or afternoons?
☐ Are you flexible?
☐ Can you work on weekends?
☐ When could you start?

Albert   Manny

C ▶ **LISTEN FOR DETAILS.** Circle *True* or *False*.

1. Manny prefers to work in the morning. True False
2. Manny can work on weekends. True False
3. Manny can start working today. True False

D ▶ **EXPAND.** Listen to the whole conversation. Does Manny know if he got the job?

3 PRONUNCIATION

A ▶ **PRACTICE.** Listen. Then listen and repeat.

Do you prefer mornings or afternoons?

Can you work first shift or second shift?

Do you work days or nights?

> **Intonation of questions with *or***
>
> Some questions with *or* ask the listener to make a choice. In these questions, the voice goes up on the first choice and down on the last choice.

B ▶ **APPLY.** Listen and draw arrows where the voice goes up and down.

1. Do you work the morning shift or the night shift?

2. Are you a sales associate or a stock clerk?

3. Do you prefer to work Saturday or Sunday?

4 CONVERSATION

A ▶ **LISTEN AND READ.** Then listen and repeat.

A: Let me ask you a few questions about your availability.
    Do you prefer mornings or afternoons?
B: Well, I prefer mornings, but I'm flexible.
A: All right. Can you work on weekends?
B: Yes, I can.
A: Great. And when could you start?
B: In two weeks. I need to give two weeks' notice at my job.

B **WORK TOGETHER.** Practice the conversation in Exercise A.

C **CREATE.** Make new conversations. Use the words in the boxes.

A: Let me ask you a few questions about your availability.
    Do you prefer ⬛⬛⬛⬛⬛?
B: Well, I prefer ⬛⬛⬛⬛⬛, but I'm flexible.
A: All right. Can you work on ⬛⬛⬛⬛⬛?
B: Yes, I can.
A: Great. And when could you start?
B: In two weeks. I need to give two weeks' notice at my job.

| first or second shift |
| days or nights |

| first shift |
| days |

| Saturdays |
| Sundays |

D **ROLE-PLAY.** Make your own conversations.

> I can answer questions about availability. ⬛   I need more practice. ⬛

Ways to express alternatives: *or, and*			
He can They can	work Saturdays	**or** **and**	Sundays.
I can't		**or**	

Grammar Watch

Use *or* (not *and*) in negative statements.

A COMPLETE. Write *and* or *or*.

1. **A:** Which shift do you prefer?

   B: I'm flexible. I can work first shift ____*or*____ second shift.

2. **A:** Can you work weekends?

   B: Sure! I can work both Saturday _____ Sunday. I want a lot of hours.

3. **A:** Can you work both Saturday and Sunday?

   B: I'll be happy to work Saturday _____ Sunday, but I can't work both days.

4. **A:** Can you take classes in the morning _____ in the evening?

   B: In the morning. I can't take classes in the evening because I work second shift.

B INTERPRET. Look at the job applications. Write two sentences about each person's availability. Use *or* with *can* and *can't*.

1. Carlos can work second shift or third shift.
2. _____

   ○○○

   Carlos Hernández

   When can you work? Check the boxes.

   ○ first shift ● second shift ● third shift ○ weekends

3. _____
4. _____

   ○○○

   Mila Pérez

   When can you work? Check the boxes.

   ● first shift ● second shift ○ third shift ○ weekends

C WRITE. Now write two sentences about your work availability. Use *or* with *can* and *can't*.

I can express alternatives with *or* and *and.* ☐   I need more practice. ☐

1 STUDY THE MODEL

READ. Answer the questions.

Ana Pino

My Job History

I have a long job history. From 2012 to 2014, I was a stock clerk at Nexo in Mexico City. I stocked the shelves in the store. Three years later, I became a sales associate there. I helped customers and used the cash register. Now, I live in Houston, Texas. I am a store manager at World Mart. I supervise employees and plan work schedules.

1. Where did Ana work?
2. What did she do?
3. Where does Ana work now?
4. What does she do?

2 PLAN YOUR WRITING

WORK TOGETHER. Ask and answer the questions.

1. Where did you work in the past?
2. What did you do?
3. Where do you work now?
4. What do you do?

3 WRITE

Now write about your job history. Use the model, the Writing Skill, and your ideas from Exercise 2 to help you.

Writing Skill: Use the correct tense

Use the simple past to explain your previous jobs. Use the present tense to explain your current job. For example:

Past: I was a stock clerk at Nexo in Mexico City.

Present: Now, I am a store manager at World Mart.

4 CHECK YOUR WRITING

WORK TOGETHER. Read the checklist. Read your writing aloud. Revise your writing.

WRITING CHECKLIST

☐ The paragraph answers all the questions in Exercise 2.

☐ The paragraph is indented.

☐ The verbs tenses are correct.

I can use the correct tense to describe my job history. ■   I need more practice. ■

11 Soft Skills at Work

Lesson **11**

Be honest

1 MEET RODRIGO

Read about one of his workplace skills.

> I am honest. I always tell the truth. I admit when I am wrong, and I try to learn from my mistakes.

2 RODRIGO'S PROBLEM

READ. Circle *True* or *False*.

Rodrigo wants to work at a company. He is in a job interview at the company. At his last job, he had a problem. He made a mistake, and his boss fired him. Rodrigo was upset, but he knows he made the mistake.

The interviewer asks, "Why did you leave your last job?" Rodrigo is not sure what to say.

1. Rodrigo is working at a company now.	True	False
2. Rodrigo's boss told him to leave his last job.	True	False
3. Rodrigo did something wrong at his last job.	True	False

3 RODRIGO'S SOLUTION

A **WORK TOGETHER.** Rodrigo is honest. He knows it is important to tell the truth. What does he say?

1. Rodrigo says, "My last job was awful, so I decided to leave."
2. Rodrigo says, "I was fired," and then he explains why his boss made a mistake.
3. Rodrigo says, "I was fired," and then he explains what he learned from the experience.
4. Rodrigo says, _____.

B **ROLE-PLAY.** Look at your answer to 3A. Role-play Rodrigo's conversation.

Show what you know!

1. THINK ABOUT IT. How are you honest in class? At work? At home? Give examples.

2. WRITE ABOUT IT. Write an example in your Skills Log.

I am honest in class. When I don't know the answers in a test, I don't copy the answers from a classmate. I get the answers wrong and then learn from my mistakes.

I can give an example of how I am honest. ■

Unit Review: Go back to page 145. Which unit goals can you check off?

9 Parents and Children

PREVIEW

Look at the picture. What do you see?
Who are the people? What are they doing?

UNIT GOALS

- Identify school subjects
- Make plans for school events
- Leave a phone message
- Talk about school progress
- Discuss your child's behavior in school

- **Academic skill:** Use information in graphs and tables
- **Writing skill:** Use commas between words in a list
- **Workplace soft skill:** Show how you plan well

Vocabulary

School subjects

A **PREDICT.** Look at the pictures. What school subjects are the students learning in each picture?

B ▶ **LISTEN AND POINT.** Then listen and repeat.

Vocabulary

School subjects

1. math
2. English language arts
3. P.E. (physical education)
4. social studies/history
5. art
6. music
7. technology
8. community service
9. world languages
10. science

C **WORK TOGETHER.** Choose a school subject. What do students learn in that subject? Make a list. Talk about your list with the class.

science
the earth
the sun
health
electricity

Show what you know!

1. **THINK ABOUT IT.** What are three very important subjects for all students to learn? Why?

_____   _____   _____

2. **WRITE ABOUT IT.** Write two sentences about an important subject.

I think _____ is an important school subject.

3. **PRESENT IT.** Make a presentation to your classmates about three important subjects to learn and why they are important.

I think science is important. There are a lot of jobs in science. You can work with computers. You can be a nursing assistant.

I can identify school subjects. ■   I need more practice. ■

Lesson 2

Listening and Speaking

Make plans for school events

1 BEFORE YOU LISTEN

MATCH. Write the words next to the definitions.

| notice | parent-teacher conference | PTO |

1. _____ meeting with a student's teacher and his or her parents
2. _____ Parent-Teacher Organization; group of teachers and parents of students in a school
3. _____ information that something will happen

2 LISTEN

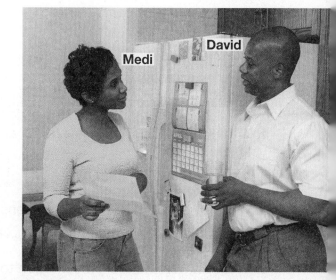

A **PREDICT.** Look at the picture. What are they talking about?

a. dinner plans
b. a problem with the refrigerator
c. a notice from school

B ▶ **LISTEN FOR MAIN IDEA.** What happens in two weeks?

a. There is a PTO meeting.
b. There is a parent-teacher conference.
c. They will get a notice.

C ▶ **LISTEN FOR DETAILS.** Listen again. Answer the questions.

1. When is the parent-teacher conference?
   a. Tuesday the 19th at 6:00
   b. Thursday the 19th at 6:00
   c. Thursday the 19th at 9:00

2. What does David have to do on the day of the conference?
   a. go to work
   b. go to class
   c. watch the kids

D ▶ **EXPAND.** Listen to the whole conversation. What is David going to do on Monday the 23rd?

a. go to work   b. go to a parent-teacher conference   c. go to a band concert

3 PRONUNCIATION

A ▶ **PRACTICE. Listen. Then listen and repeat.**

I'll try. She'll meet him there.
We'll both go. My mother will watch the kids.
He'll be at work.

Pronunciation of *will*

The word *will* usually has a short, weak pronunciation. After a pronoun (such as *I* or *we*), we usually use the contraction *'ll*.

B ▶ **CHOOSE. Listen and circle the words you hear.**

1. **She will / She'll** send a notice.
2. **I'll / I will** be there after work.
3. **We'll / We will** go to the meeting.
4. **They will / They'll** meet next Tuesday.

4 CONVERSATION

A ▶ **LISTEN AND READ. Then listen and repeat.**

A: Carlo brought a notice home from school today. There's a parent-teacher conference in two weeks.
B: Oh yeah? What day?
A: Thursday the 19th at 6:00. My mother will watch the kids. That way we can both go.
B: Oh, I have to work that day until 9:00, but I'll try to change my shift.

B **WORK TOGETHER. Practice the conversation in Exercise A.**

C **CREATE. Make new conversations. Use the words in the boxes.**

A: Carlo brought a notice home from school today. There's a _____ in two weeks.
B: Oh, yeah? What day?
A: Thursday the 19th at 6:00. My mother will watch the kids. That way we can both go.
B: Oh, I have to be at work that day until 9:00, but I'll _____.

school play
PTO meeting
science fair

switch hours with someone
ask if I can leave early
change my schedule

D **ROLE-PLAY. Make your own conversations.**

I can make plans for school events. ■	I need more practice. ■

Grammar

Future with *will*

Future with *will*				
Affirmative			**Negative**	
I	**will** / **'ll**	**try** to change my shift.	I	**will not** / **won't** **be** late.

Grammar Watch

- Use *will* + the base form of a verb.
- *won't* = *will not*.
- Use contractions *'ll* and *won't* for speaking and informal writing.

A COMPLETE. Use *will* and the words in parentheses to talk about the future.

1. Abe _____will work_____ the evening shift this week.
   (work)

2. Her manager _____ the supplier about the problem.
   (call)

3. They _____ a meeting tomorrow.
   (have)

4. Rico _____ at work this morning. He has an appointment.
   (not / be)

5. The office _____ on Monday because it is a holiday.
   (not / open)

6. Drew _____ late for dinner.
   (be)

7. Kids _____ school on Friday, so a lot of people _____
   (not / have)   (take)
   that day off work.

B APPLY. Complete the sentences with the words in the box and *will* to talk about the future.

meet	go	send	not be	~~see~~	check	talk about

A: I _____'ll see_____ you at the PTO meeting on
Thursday night, right?

B: I'm sorry, I _____ there. I have to
work.

A: That's too bad. We _____ some
important things.

B: Well, you _____ again next month,
right?

A: I think so. I _____ the date of the
next meeting, and I _____ you a text.

B: Yes, please. I _____ to the next
meeting. I promise.

Grammar

C **COMPLETE. Use *will* and the words in parentheses.**

To: jane@abc.com
Subject: Invitation

Hi Jane,

Thank you for inviting us to Sue's school play next Friday night. Unfortunately, Jack has a class, so he __won't be__
                                                                                                                    1. (not / be)

there. But the kids and I _____. I usually get out of work at around 6:30, but I _____ early if I can. The
                            2. (come)   **3. (leave)**

kids and I_____ a quick dinner, and we _____ to the school around 8:00. Don't worry—we
            4. (eat)   **5. (get)**

_____ late! I'm going out now, so I _____ you tonight. I _____ you on Sunday, and we
6. (not / be)   **7. (not / call)**   **8. (call)**

_____ some more then.
  9. (talk)
Anita

Show what you know!

1. **THINK ABOUT IT. Look at the chart. Choose two tasks
   that you can do for a bake sale at school.**

Event: School Bake Sale	
Event task	**Group member**
get permission from the school	
design a flyer	
decide who will bring what	
set up before the event	
clean up after the event	

a school bake sale

2. **TALK ABOUT IT. Work in a group. Decide who will do
   each task in the chart. Complete the chart.**

   A: Who wants to get permission from the school?
   B: I'll call the principal tomorrow.

3. **WRITE ABOUT IT. Now write a sentence about what each person will do.**

   Marta will call the principal tomorrow.

I can use the future with *will*. ■   I need more practice. ■

4

Workplace, Life, and Community Skills

Lesson | **Voicemail messages**

1 LEAVE A PHONE MESSAGE

A **PREDICT.** Look at the picture. Why is the woman calling the school?

B ▶ **LISTEN.** Was your guess in Exercise A correct?

C ▶ **IDENTIFY.** Read the phone messages. Listen to the conversation again. Circle the number of the correct message.

Winter Hill Elementary School.

OFFICE

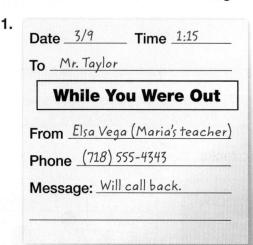

1.

Date __3/9__   Time __1:15__

To __Mr. Taylor__

While You Were Out

From __Elsa Vega (Maria's teacher)__

Phone __(718) 555-4343__

Message: __Will call back.__

2.

Date __3/9__   Time __1:15__

To __Mr. Taylor__

While You Were Out

From __Elsa Vega (Maria's mom)__

Phone __(718) 555-4343__

Message: __Please call back.__

2 LEAVE A VOICEMAIL MESSAGE

A ▶ **LISTEN.** The teacher leaves Ms. Vega a message on her mobile phone. Complete the missing information.

●●●○○ 🔋   3:57 PM   33% 🔋

‹   **Voicemail**   +

John Taylor
May 23 at 2:15 PM

▶ ●———————————

Transcript
"Ms. Vega, this is Mr. Taylor. I'm returning your call. Since Maria was home sick today, she _____ need to complete next week's unit, but she _____ need to complete this week's unit. _____ take the quiz on Tuesday. Please _____ me or _____ me at jtaylor@winterhill.edu. if you have questions."

I can leave a phone message. ■   I need more practice. ■

172 Unit 9, Lesson 4

B INTERPRET. Read the voicemail messages below. Circle *True* or *False*.

1.

●●●●○ 🗢 1:25 PM 92% 🔋

< **Voicemail** +

Laura Jeffrey
May 27 at 3:46 PM

▶━●━━━━━━━━

Transcript
Hello, Ms. Vega. This is Laura Jeffrey. I am a PTO officer, and I wanted to make sure you knew about our meeting this coming Friday. We will meet in the conference room at 4:00. We'll discuss the upcoming special events. The meeting won't be long. If you have any questions, please feel free to call me at 777-0099.

2.

●●○○○ 🗢 3:18 PM 52% 🔋

< **Voicemail** +

Sasha Burton
June 16 at 9:15 PM

▶━●━━━━━━━━

Transcript
Hi, Elsa. It's Sasha. Will you be at the meeting on Friday? I won't be there. I have to work. Can you get an extra copy of the special events calendar for me? I'll get it from you when I see you on Sunday. Thanks!

1. The first message is for Ms. Vega. True False
2. The PTO officer invites Elsa to a meeting. True False
3. The meeting will be long. True False
4. Sasha will be at the meeting on Friday. True False
5. Sasha asks her friend for help. True False
6. The friends will see each other on Sunday. True False

C APPLY. Take turns leaving messages or voicemails. Use the information in the chart below.

What you need	You need a ride home from work	The homework assignment for tomorrow
Who you need to call	Mario	Lin
The reason you need something	Your car is broken	You missed class
How to contact you	Call back at 555-1122	E-mail happyday@gletter.com

D GO ONLINE. Search how to set up a personal voicemail greeting message on your mobile phone. If you don't have a greeting message, set one up.

I can leave a voicemail message. ■ I need more practice. ■

Lesson **5**

Talk about progress in school

1 BEFORE YOU LISTEN

A **READ.** How can students get extra help in school?

> Sometimes students have trouble in their classes. Students can get help from their parents and older brothers and sisters. Sometimes they can get extra help from teachers or older students before or after school. Most local libraries also have programs to help students with their schoolwork.

2 LISTEN

A **PREDICT.** Look at the picture. Where are they? Who is Mr. Thompson?

Mr. Thompson

Medi

B ▶ **LISTEN FOR MAIN IDEA.** Answer the questions.

1. What does Medi say?
   a. How are you doing? **b.** How's Carlo doing?

2. What are they talking about?
   a. Carlo's progress **b.** the parent-teacher conference

C ▶ **LISTEN FOR DETAILS.** Listen again. Answer the questions.

1. What subject is Carlo doing well in?

   _____

2. What subject *isn't* Carlo doing well in?

   _____

D ▶ **EXPAND.** Listen to the whole conversation. What does Carlo's teacher suggest?

a. help from older students
b. extra homework
c. help from his parents

3 CONVERSATION

A ▶ **LISTEN AND READ. Then listen and repeat.**

A: Hi, I'm Harold Thompson, Carlo's teacher. Nice to meet you.
B: I'm Carlo's mother. Nice to meet you, too. So, how's Carlo doing?
A: Carlo's a good student. I enjoy having him in class.
B: That's good to hear.
A: He does very well in math. He works carefully.
B: He likes math a lot. What about social studies?
A: Well, he's having a little trouble in that class. He needs to do his homework.
B: OK. I'll talk to him.

B **WORK TOGETHER. Practice the conversation in Exercise A.**

C **CREATE. Make new conversations. Use the words in the boxes.**

A: Hi, I'm _____, Carlo's teacher. Nice to meet you.
B: I'm Carlo's _____. Nice to meet you, too.
   So, how's Carlo doing?
A: Carlo's a good student. I enjoy having him in class.
B: That's good to hear.
A: He does very well in _____. He _____.
B: He likes _____ a lot. What about _____?
A: Well, he's having a little trouble in that class.
   He needs to _____.
B: OK. I'll talk to him.

science	learns quickly	language arts	ask more questions
social studies	studies hard	science	spend extra time on it
language arts	writes well	math	study a little more

D **ROLE-PLAY. Make your own conversations.**

I can talk about progress in school. ■	I need more practice. ■

Adverbs of manner

Adverbs of manner					
Adjective			**Adverb**		
Carlo is a	**careful**	worker.	Carlo works	**carefully**.	
	quick			**quickly**.	
	good			**well**.	

Grammar Watch

- To create most adverbs of manner, add *-ly* to the adjective. See page 259 for more spelling rules.
- A few adverbs of manner are irregular:

  good → **well**
  hard → **hard**
  fast → **fast**

A **COMPLETE. Change the underlined adjectives to adverbs of manner. Then complete the sentences.**

1. Sonia is a <u>careless</u> worker. She works _____carelessly_____.
2. Kevin's pronunciation is <u>clear</u>. He speaks _____.
3. Amad is a <u>fast</u> learner. He learns _____.
4. Your children are <u>good</u> students. They do _____ in school.
5. My team leader is a <u>hard</u> worker. He works _____.
6. Chi is very <u>quiet</u>. She does her work _____.
7. Luke's handwriting is <u>neat</u>. He writes _____.

B **APPLY. Change the adjectives to adverbs of manner. Then complete the sentences.**

careful	creative	good	hard	quick	~~slow~~

1. Chen isn't fast. He works _____slowly_____.
2. Mona gets good grades. She does _____ in school.
3. We don't have much time. Please work _____.
4. Nan is very careful with her schoolwork. She does her work _____.
5. Nelson has great ideas to solve problems at work. He always thinks _____.
6. John has a test tomorrow. He needs to study _____.

I can use adverbs of manner. ■　　　　　　　　　　I need more practice. ■

Grammar

Object pronouns

Object pronouns			
Singular		**Plural**	
Can you help	**me**?	Come with	**us**.
I need to see	**you.** **him.** **her.**	I am proud of all of	**you.** **them.**
You can do	**it.**		

Grammar Watch

- An object pronoun takes the place of a noun.
- Use an object pronoun after a verb or a preposition.

C **DECIDE. Look at the underlined noun. Write the correct object pronoun.**

1. Ms. Carson was at the parent-teacher conference. I met _____ *her* _____.
2. There is a PTO meeting on Friday. We can't attend _____.
3. Emily and Mary are doing very well in school. We're proud of _____.
4. My daughter is not doing well in science. I am worried about _____.
5. My son needs help in math class. Can you help _____?
6. Are you busy? I need to talk to _____.
7. When we don't understand something, our teacher helps _____.
8. Art class is hard for me. I don't like _____.
9. My son does his homework every day. I never have to remind _____.

Show what you know!

1. **THINK ABOUT IT.** Look at the skills in the first column of the chart. Look at the adjectives in the second column. Write adverbs of manner.

2. **TALK ABOUT IT.** Which classmates or co-workers have these skills? Write their names in the third column.

3. **WRITE ABOUT IT.** Now write one sentence about a person with each skill.

   Mimi speaks English well.

Skill	Adjective / Adverb	Name
speaks English	good / ___ *well* ___	
studies	hard / _____	
learns	quick / _____	
writes	neat / _____	
listens	careful / _____	

I can use adverbs of manner and object pronouns. ■   I need more practice. ■

Read about going to college

1 BEFORE YOU READ

A **MATCH. Write the words in the box next to the correct definitions.**

college degree	non-profit	private	profit

1. _____ = owned by a person or group (not by the government, not public)

2. _____ = the money you get by doing business (after your costs have been paid)

3. _____ = making money to help people (instead of making money to keep)

4. _____ = what a student gets after completing a course of study at a university, college, or community college

	Community College	College	University
Degrees offered	Certificate (Up to 1 year)		Bachelor's Degree (4 years)
		Bachelor's Degree (4 years)	Master's Degree (1-2 more years)
	Associate's Degree (2 years)		Ph.D.* (3-8 more years)

*Doctor of Philosophy

B **MAKE CONNECTIONS. What kinds of colleges are there in your community?**

2 READ

▶ Listen and read.

GOING TO COLLEGE

1 Are you thinking of going to college*? Here are some things you should know.

Rising Numbers of Students Going to College
In 1990, 59 percent of U.S. high school graduates
5 went to college. In 2007, over 66 percent went to college. In 2016, almost 70 percent went to college. Every year, more and more Americans decide that going to college is their way to a better future.

The Cost of College
10 But going to college costs a lot. Today, the average cost of tuition is between $4,800 and $34,000 a year. This does not include the cost of books, housing, food, or transportation. These can cost $12,000 to $20,000 more a year.

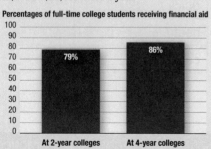

Percentages of full-time college students receiving financial aid

At 2-year colleges: 79%
At 4-year colleges: 86%

Source: National Center for Education Statistics

Type of school	Average cost of tuition (1 year)
Public community college	About $3,520
Public college or university	About $10,000
Private non-profit college or university	About $33,000
For-profit college or university	About $16,000

15 **Paying for College**
How do people pay for college? Most students get financial aid—scholarships, grants, and loans.

Scholarships and grants are the best kind of financial aid. You don't have to pay them back.
20 Some students get scholarships because their grades are good. Some students get grants because their income is low. About half of all college students receive some form of scholarship or grant. Students usually get them from their college, a state
25 program, or a community group.

Most students get loans. You have to pay back loans after you graduate.

Most students use a combination of scholarships, grants, and government loans to pay the high cost
30 of college.

College is a general word for community colleges, colleges, and universities.
Sources: The College Board, the U.S. Census Bureau

Academic Skill: Use Information in Graphs and Tables

Authors sometimes use graphs and tables to present information. This information supports the author's main ideas.

Reading

3 CLOSE READING

A **IDENTIFY. What is the main idea?**

More and more Americans are going to college, and most of them _____.
a. say college is their way to a better future
b. probably think the cost of college is too high
c. get some form of financial aid to help pay for it

B **CITE EVIDENCE. Complete the statements. Where is the information? Write the line numbers.**

1. The average _____ is between $4,800 and $34,000.   **Lines**
   a. cost of a college   b. college tuition for   c. amount of   _____
      education   one year   financial aid
2. _____ can get scholarships.
   a. Some students   b. Students who   c. About half of   _____
      with good grades   work part-time   all students
3. Some students can get grants because they're _____.
   a. lucky   b. full-time   c. low-income   _____
4. Community groups sometimes give college students _____.
   a. good advice   b. scholarships or   c. low-cost loans   _____
                                   grants
5. Students who get _____ have to pay it back.
   a. any financial aid   b. a scholarship   c. a loan   _____
                                   or grant

4 SUMMARIZE

Complete the summary with the words in the box.

costs	degree	loans	scholarship	tuition

Many Americans believe a college (1) _____ is the way to a better future.
But college is expensive. College (2) _____ is thousands of dollars a year,
and there are other (3) _____, too, like books and transportation. About half
of all college students get some form of (4) _____ or grant. Most students
get (5) _____.

Show what you know!

1. **THINK ABOUT IT.** Is going to college one of your goals? Why or why not? If yes,
   what type of college would be best for you to reach your goals?
2. **TALK ABOUT IT.** Explain your educational goals. Tell how you plan to reach your goals.
3. **WRITE ABOUT IT.** Write about your educational goals.
   _I want to _____ because _____. I plan to _____._

I can use information in graphs and tables. ■   I need more practice. ■

1 BEFORE YOU LISTEN

LABEL. Write the words under the pictures.

be disrespectful	fool around in class	bully other kids
skip class	not pay attention	not get along with others

☐ _____

☐ _____

☐ _____

☐ _____

☐ _____

☐ _____

2 LISTEN

A **PREDICT.** Look at the picture. What do you think happened? Complete the sentence.

Ana and Tito's son Luis _____.
a. got a good report card
b. is in trouble at school
c. finished his homework early

B ▶ **LISTEN FOR MAIN IDEA.** What trouble is Luis having? Check the boxes in Before You Listen.

C ▶ **LISTEN FOR DETAILS.** Listen again. Complete the sentence.

Luis's parents are going to _____.
a. talk to him
b. call the principal
c. go to a parent-teacher conference

D ▶ **EXPAND.** Listen to the whole conversation. Complete the sentence.

Luis usually _____ at school.
a. does well
b. has problems
c. talks a lot

Listening and Speaking

3 PRONUNCIATION

A ▶ **PRACTICE. Listen. Then listen and repeat.**

my boss**'s** name	his friend**'s** house
Alex**'s** friend	Sue**'s** homework
George**'s** class	her aunt**'s** car

> **Extra syllables with 's**
>
> The **'s** possessive ending adds an extra syllable after the sounds at the end of *Luis*, *Liz*, *Josh*, *Mitch*, *George*, and *Felix*. It does not add an extra syllable after other sounds.

B ▶ **CHOOSE. Listen. Circle the possessive nouns that add a syllable.**

1. Lucas's computer
2. the department's meetings
3. the class's assignment
4. our supervisor's office
5. the employee's tasks
6. Aziz's schedule
7. the language's sounds

4 CONVERSATION

A ▶ **LISTEN AND READ. Then listen and repeat.**

A: Where's Luis?
B: He's at a friend's house. Why? What's up?
A: Well, his teacher called. He's having some trouble at school.
B: Uh-oh. What kind of trouble?
A: She said he's not paying attention and skipping class.
B: What? Well, we need to talk to him right away.
A: Definitely. Let's all talk tonight after dinner.

B **WORK TOGETHER. Practice the conversation in Exercise A.**

C **CREATE. Make new conversations. Use the words in the boxes.**

A: Where's Luis?

B: He's at a friend's house. Why? What's up?

A: Well, his teacher called. He's having some trouble at school.

B: Uh-oh. What kind of trouble?

A: She said he's _____ and _____ .

B: What? Well, we _____ right away.

A: Definitely. Let's all talk tonight after dinner.

> not getting along with others
> getting to school late
> being disrespectful to his teachers

> bullying some other kids
> not doing his homework
> fooling around in class

> have to find out what's going on
> need to have a talk with him
> need to have a family meeting

D **DISCUSS. What should Luis's parents do? What would you do in their situation?**

I can discuss a child's behavior in school. ■   I need more practice. ■

Possessive nouns			
Singular		**Plural**	
Their son**'s**	name is Luis.	Their sons**'**	names are Luis and Lucas.
The child**'s**		The children**'s**	

Grammar Watch

To form a possessive noun:
• Add 's to most singular nouns.
• Add only an apostrophe to plural nouns that end in -s.
• Add 's to plural nouns that do not end in -s.
• See page 260 for more spelling rules.

A IDENTIFY. Cross out the incorrect words.

1. Who is your ~~daughters~~ / **daughter's** teacher?
2. My **sons** / **son's** are in the first and second grades.
3. The **teachers** / **teacher's** first name is Alex.
4. Sometimes a teacher calls a **students** / **student's** parents.
5. I know the names of all my **classmates** / **classmates'**.
6. My **daughter's** / **daughters'** names are Alicia and Rita.
7. The guidance **counselor's** / **counselors'** name is Ms. White.

B EVALUATE. Find and correct the error in each sentence.

1. My ~~sons~~ son's grades are poor, so I need to talk to his teacher.
2. The new teacher's names are Ms. Gómez and Ms. Bates.
3. Where is the school nurse' office?
4. My daughters report card was good, but my son is having a hard time.
5. The principal will try to answer all the parents's questions.
6. Teachers like to meet their students parents.

I can use possessive nouns. ■   I need more practice. ■

Lesson 10 | Writing
Write about school

1 STUDY THE MODEL

READ. Answer the questions.

Tam Dang

My School

New Neighbors is a school for adult students in Boston, Massachusetts. It has classes in English, citizenship, and computer skills. Classes are in the mornings, in the evenings, and on Saturdays. The classes are free. I am taking English and computer skills classes there so I can get a job as a software developer.

1. What's the name of Tam's school?
2. What classes does it have?
3. When are the classes?
4. How much does it cost?
5. What is Tam's goal?

2 PLAN YOUR WRITING

WORK TOGETHER. Ask and answer the questions.

1. What's the name of the school?
2. What classes does it have?
3. When are the classes?
4. How much do they cost?
5. Are you taking classes there?
6. What is your goal?

3 WRITE

Now write about a school. Use the model, the Writing Skill, and your ideas from Exercise 2 to help you.

4 CHECK YOUR WRITING

WORK TOGETHER. Read the checklist. Read your writing aloud. Revise your writing.

Writing Skill: Use commas between words in a list

Put commas between words in a list. For example:

It has classes in English, citizenship, and computer skills.

WRITING CHECKLIST

☐ The paragraph answers the questions in Exercise 2.

☐ There is a topic sentence.

☐ There are commas between words in lists.

I can use commas between words in a list. ■   I need more practice. ■

1 MEET RASHA

Read about one of her workplace skills.

> I plan well. For example, I plan my schedule so that I can both complete all my work and also be available for important family events.

2 RASHA'S PROBLEM

READ. Circle *True* or *False*.

Rasha is at work. Her son Omar plays soccer on his school team. He calls her and says, "Mom, we won the game! Our team is going to be in the final!" Rasha says, "That's great! When's the final?" Omar says, "It's on Friday afternoon at 4 p.m." Rasha wants to go to the final game because she knows it is important to Omar, but she always works on Friday at 4 p.m.

1. Rasha and Omar are at work.	True	False
2. Omar will play soccer on Friday.	True	False
3. Rasha has to work on Friday.	True	False

3 RASHA'S SOLUTION

Ⓐ **WORK TOGETHER.** Rasha plans well. What does she say to her son? Explain your answer.

1. Rasha says, "OK. I'll ask a co-worker to change shifts with me on Friday."
2. Rasha says, "I can't come to the game. I have to work on Friday."
3. Rasha says, "OK. I'll plan to tell my supervisor I'm sick on Friday."
4. Rasha should _____.

Ⓑ **ROLE-PLAY.** Look at your answer to 3A. Role-play Rasha's conversation.

Show what you know!

1. **THINK ABOUT IT.** Do you plan well? How do you plan well in class? At work? At home? Give examples.

2. **WRITE ABOUT IT.** Write an example in your Skills Log.

   I plan well in class. When I have class and my son is home, I ask my neighbor to watch him. Then I can go to class.

I can give an example of how I plan well. ☐

Unit Review: Go back to page 165. Which unit goals can you check off?

10 Let's Eat!

PREVIEW

Look at the picture. What do you see?
Where is this person? What is he doing?

UNIT GOALS

☐ Identify food containers and quantities
☐ Ask for quantities of food
☐ Read food labels
☐ Compare information in food ads
☐ Order food in a restaurant

☐ **Academic skill:** Get meaning from context
☐ **Writing skill:** Use *like* and *such as* to introduce examples
☐ **Workplace soft skill:** Show how you ask for help

A **PREDICT.** Look at the pictures. What do you see?

There's a bag of potato chips.
There's a box of cereal.

B ▶ **LISTEN AND POINT.** Then listen and repeat.

C ▶ **IDENTIFY.** Listen. Check (✓) the foods you hear.

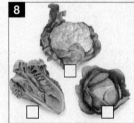

Vocabulary

Food containers and quantities

1. bag	**3.** can	**5.** jar	**7.** bunch	**9.** pound	**11.** quart	**13.** gallon
2. box	**4.** bottle	**6.** container	**8.** head	**10.** pint	**12.** half-gallon	**14.** dozen

D **CATEGORIZE.** Which foods come in these containers?

a bag of	a box of	a can of	a jar of
oranges			

Show what you know!

1. **THINK ABOUT IT.** What foods do you have at home now? Make a list.

2. **TALK ABOUT IT.** Work with a partner. Talk about the food you have at home. Take notes. Circle the foods you both have at home.

   A: I have a gallon of milk and boxes of cereal.
   B: Me too! I have cans of tomatoes and tuna.
   A: I don't. What else do you have?

3. **WRITE ABOUT IT.** Now write about the food both you and your partner have at home.

   We both have _____.

I can identify food containers and quantities. ■   I need more practice. ■

1 BEFORE YOU LISTEN

A **LABEL.** Write the words under the pictures.

> a convenience store   an outdoor market   a supermarket

1. _____   2. _____   3. _____

B **MAKE CONNECTIONS.** Where do you go food shopping? Why do you shop there?

2 LISTEN

A **PREDICT.** Look at the picture. Where are they?

B ▶ **LISTEN FOR MAIN IDEA.** What are they talking about?

a. a problem with the refrigerator   **b.** food they need to buy

Agnes   Yuka

C ▶ **LISTEN FOR DETAILS.** Check (✓) the things that Agnes will buy.

☐ milk
☐ butter
☐ two tomatoes
☐ a can of tomatoes
☐ two onions
☐ a dozen eggs

D ▶ **EXPAND.** Listen to the whole conversation. What does Agnes need to do?

a. take more money   **b.** get a bigger refrigerator   **c.** write the things down

Listening and Speaking

3 CONVERSATION

A ▶ **LISTEN AND READ. Then listen and repeat.**

A: Hi, Yuka. I'm going to the grocery store for some milk.
Do you need anything?
B: Uh, let me see. Could you get a can of tomatoes?
A: A can of tomatoes? Sure, no problem.
B: Oh, and I need some onions.
A: How many onions?
B: Two.
A: All right. A can of tomatoes and two onions.
I'll be back in a little while.

B **WORK TOGETHER. Practice the conversation in Exercise A.**

C **CREATE. Make new conversations. Use the
pictures of food in the boxes.**

A: I'm going to the grocery store for some
_____. Do you need anything?
B: Uh, let me see. Could you get a can
of _____?
A: A can of _____? Sure, no problem.
B: Oh, and I need some _____.
A: How many _____?
B: Two.
A: All right. A can of _____ and
two _____. I'll be back in a
little while.

D **ROLE-PLAY. Make your own conversations.**

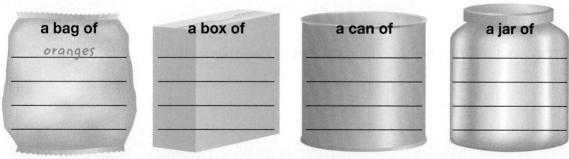

a bag of	a box of	a can of	a jar of
oranges			

I can ask for quantities of food. ■   I need more practice. ■

Lesson 3

Count nouns / Non-count nouns and *How much / How many*

Count nouns/Non-count nouns		
Singular count nouns	**Plural count nouns**	**Non-count nouns**
an onion a sandwich	two onions some sandwiches	bread milk fish rice

Yes/No questions			Affirmative answers			Negative answers		
Are	there **any**	onions?	**Yes**, there	is	**some**.	**No**, there	isn't	**any**.
Is		milk?		are			aren't	

A **COMPLETE.** Use the correct forms of *there is / there are* to make questions and answers.

Grammar Watch

- *There is = There's*
- See page 260 for spelling rules for plurals.
- See page 261 for more examples of non-count nouns.

1. **A:** _____Is there any_____ bread?

   B: Yes, _____there's_____ some on the counter.

2. **A:** _____ tomatoes?

   B: No, _____ any.

3. **A:** _____ coffee?

   B: Yes, _____ some in the breakroom.

4. **A:** _____ carrots?

   B: Yes, _____ some in the refrigerator.

5. **A:** _____ butter?

   B: No, _____, but we have jelly.

6. **A:** _____ bananas in the cafeteria today?

   B: No, _____. I bought the last one.

B **WORK TOGETHER.** Practice the conversations in Exercise A.

Grammar

How much / How many

How	much	bread	do we need?
		milk	
	many	onions	
		cans of soup	

C **IDENTIFY. Cross out the incorrect words.**

A: How ~~much~~ / many potatoes do we have? Do we need more?

B: Yes. I'll get a five-pound bag at the store.

A: OK. Are you going to get **cheese / cheeses**?

B: Yeah. But how **much / many** cheese do we need?

A: Oh, a pound is fine. We need some **fruit / fruits**, too.

B: OK. I'll get a dozen **orange / oranges**. I love them!

A: How **much / many** milk do we have?

B: None. I'll get a half-gallon.

A: Could you get some **sugar / sugars**, too?

B: Sure. How **much / many** sugar do you want?

A: One pound is enough.

Shopping List

5 lbs. of potatoes

_____

_____

_____

_____

_____

_____

D **WRITE. Read the conversation in Exercise C again. Complete the shopping list.**

Show what you know!

1. **THINK ABOUT IT. Plan a company picnic. Decide what food and drinks you want to bring. Write the list of food.**

2. **TALK ABOUT IT. Decide how much food you need. Write how much you need.**

   A: Let's bring some chicken sandwiches.
   B: Good idea. How many do we need?
   I think . . .

3. **WRITE ABOUT IT. Now write five sentences about your picnic. Write where you will go and what you will bring.**

   The company will have a picnic in Central Park. We will bring ten chicken sandwiches and three gallons of orange juice. We'll also take . . .

I can use count and non-count nouns and *how much / how many.* ■

I need more practice. ■

Lesson **4** **Nutrition information**

1 READ FOOD LABELS

A **DISCUSS.** Work with a small group. Do you eat a healthy diet? How do you know the foods you eat are healthy?

B **IDENTIFY.** Read the article. Complete the information below.

What's in My Food?

Carbohydrates, cholesterol, fiber, protein, sodium, and sugar are some of the nutrients in food. All of these nutrients are good for you, but only in the right amounts.

Carbohydrates give you energy for several hours. Foods such as pasta, bread, and potatoes have a lot of carbohydrates.

Cholesterol is only in animal fat. Foods such as butter, mayonnaise, red meat, and eggs have a lot of cholesterol. Too much cholesterol is not good for you.

Fiber is from plants. Foods such as vegetables, fruits, and grains all have lots of fiber. Fiber is good for you. It helps your stomach digest food.

Protein makes your body strong. Foods such as chicken, fish, and beans have a lot of protein.

Sodium is another word for salt. Foods such as potato chips, canned soups, and olives have a lot of sodium. Too much sodium is not good for you.

Sugar gives you quick energy. Candy, cookies, and soda have a lot of sugar. Too much sugar is not good for you. Watch out! Sometimes sugar has a different name, such as high-maltose corn syrup or high-fructose corn syrup.

How do you find out what's in your food?

Read the ingredient and nutrition labels on your food packages. An ingredient label lists all the ingredients in the food. The ingredients are listed in the order of amount. The first ingredient on the list is the main (or largest) ingredient. The last ingredient is the smallest one. A nutrient label lists the amount of each nutrient in one serving of the food. To eat a healthy diet, you need to ask, "What's in my food?" and make sure you eat the right amount of each nutrient.

1. **carbohydrates:** bread, potatoes, _____*pasta*_____
2. **cholesterol:** butter, mayonnaise, red meat, _____
3. **fiber:** vegetables, grains, _____
4. **protein:** chicken, beans, _____
5. **sodium:** potato chips, olives, _____
6. **sugar:** candy, soda, _____

C **INTERPRET.** Read the sentences. Circle *True* or *False*. Correct the false statements.

1. To find out what is in your food, you need to read the nutrition label.	True	False
2. The ingredients are listed in alphabetical order.	True	False
3. The main ingredient of the food is listed first.	True	False
4. The label lists the amount of nutrients in one container.	True	False

Workplace, Life, and Community Skills

D **COMPARE.** Read the nutrition labels. Circle *True* or *False*. Note that *g* = grams and *mg* = milligrams.

1. There are 16 servings in a gallon of milk.   True   False

2. The whole milk has 160 calories per serving.   True   False

3. The whole milk has 8 grams of total fat per gallon.   True   False

4. The non-fat milk has 5 milligrams of cholesterol per serving. True   False

5. The whole milk has 125 milligrams of sodium per serving.   True   False

6. Both kinds of milk have 12 grams of sugar per serving.   True   False

7. The non-fat milk has 12 grams of added sugars per serving.   True   False

8. The non-fat milk has zero grams of protein per serving.   True   False

E **COMPARE.** Look at the two nutrition labels in Exercise D. Which milk do you think is better for your health? Why?

I think whole milk is better because . . .

F **EXAMINE.** Read the labels. Circle the main ingredient. Underline the sugar ingredients. Do you think these foods are good for your health? Why?

G <u>GO ONLINE.</u> Search for the ingredients in a food you like. Are the ingredients good for you? Report your findings.

WHOLE MILK, 1 gallon

Nutrition Facts
16 servings per container

Serving size	1 cup

Amount per serving

Calories   **160**

Total Fat 8g
Cholesterol 35mg
Sodium 125mg
Total Carbohydrate 13g
   Dietary Fiber 0g
     Sugar 12g
       Added sugars 0g
Protein 8g

NON-FAT MILK, 1 gallon

Nutrition Facts
16 servings per container

Serving size	1 cup

Amount per serving

Calories   **90**

Total Fat 0g
Cholesterol 5mg
Sodium 130mg
Total Carbohydrate 13g
   Dietary Fiber 0g
     Sugar 12g
       Added sugars 0g
Protein 8g

PEANUT ENERGY BAR

Ingredients: peanuts, high-maltose corn syrup, sugar, rolled oats, high-fructuse corn syrup.

SUNSHINE ORANGE DRINK

Ingredients: water, high-fructose corn syrup, sugar, 2% or less of each of the following juices — orange, apple, lime, grapefruit.

I can read food labels. ■   I need more practice. ■

Make decisions when shopping for food

1 BEFORE YOU LISTEN

A **READ.** Look at some things that are important to people when they buy food.

Convenience is important to me. I buy food that's easy to prepare.

1.

I buy food that **tastes good**. That's all I care about.

2.

I think about **price**. I get store brands and things on sale.

3.

I buy **healthy** food like low-fat milk and whole wheat bread.

4.

I like **fresh** fruits and vegetables. I don't buy frozen or canned food.

5.

B **MAKE CONNECTIONS.** What's important to *you* when you buy food?

2 LISTEN

A ▶ **LISTEN FOR MAIN IDEA.** What is the commercial for? Circle the answer.

a.

b.

c.

B ▶ **LISTEN FOR DETAILS.** Check (✓) the words you hear.

☐ better taste   ☐ lower price   ☐ fresher
☐ healthier meals   ☐ better for you   ☐ easier to prepare

3 CONVERSATION

A **PREDICT.** Look at the picture. What are they shopping for?

B ▶ **LISTEN.** What are they talking about?

a. a brand of coffee
b. who is going to pay for the coffee
c. how much coffee they need

C ▶ **LISTEN AND READ.** Then listen and repeat.

A: Oh, you buy Franklin brand coffee. Is it good?
B: Yes, it's excellent. I think it's better than all the other brands.
A: Really? Why?
B: It tastes great and it's not expensive.

D **WORK TOGETHER.** Practice the conversation in Exercise C.

E **CREATE.** Make new conversations. Use the words in the boxes.

A: Oh, you buy _____ brand _____. Is it good?
B: Yes, it's excellent. I think it's better than all the other brands.
A: Really? Why?
B: _____ and it's not expensive.

Sunshine	orange juice	It tastes good
Captain Cook	fish	It's always fresh
Dairy Glenn	ice cream	It's low-fat

F **MAKE CONNECTIONS.** Talk about a product you like. Explain why you like it.

I can make decisions when shopping for food. ■   I need more practice. ■

Grammar

Comparative adjectives with *than*

Comparative adjectives with *than*				
This coffee is	fresh.	It's	**fresher**	**than** the other brands.
	tasty.		**tastier**	
	expensive.		**more expensive**	

To form comparative forms of:	
one-syllable adjectives	⟶ Add -*er*
two-syllable adjectives ending in *y*	⟶ change *y* to *i* and add -*er*
adjectives with two or more syllables	⟶ use *more* + an adjective

Grammar Watch

- Some comparative adjectives are irregular. For example: *good* ⟶ *better*.
- See page 261 for more spelling rules.

A **APPLY.** Make comparative forms with -*er* or *more*.

1. fresh   *fresher*
2. fast   _____
3. good   _____
4. delicious   _____
5. sweet   _____
6. expensive   _____
7. healthy   _____
8. fattening   _____
9. salty   _____

B **COMPLETE.** Write the comparative form of the adjective. Add *than*.

1. Bananas are (sweet) ___*sweeter than*___ apples.
2. Jelly is (cheap) _____ butter.
3. Fresh orange juice tastes (good) _____ frozen orange juice.
4. Homemade meals are (tasty) _____ fast food.
5. Fresh fruit is (nutritious) _____ canned fruit.
6. Canned soup is (convenient) _____ homemade soup.
7. Vegetables are (good for you) _____ cookies.
8. Sandwiches are (easy to make) _____ hamburgers.

Grammar

C APPLY. Compare the food in the supermarket ad. Use adjectives from the box or other adjectives.

A small salad is cheaper than a large salad.

cheap
delicious
expensive
fattening
fresh
good
nutritious
salty

D WRITE. Now write six sentences comparing the food in the ad.

Super prices this week!

14" Ready-to-bake pizza $5.99 each 2 for $10.99

Try our salads! $2.99 small large $4.99

Super Salty potato chips 89¢ 12-oz. bag

Hart's fat-free, low-sodium pretzels $1.89 12-oz. box

Show what you know!

1. **THINK ABOUT IT.** Think of a food or drink you like. Complete the information below.

   My product: _____

   Three things I like about this product:

   1. _____
   2. _____
   3. _____

2. **WRITE ABOUT IT.** Now write three sentences comparing it to other brands or products.

   1. _____
   2. _____
   3. _____

3. **PRESENT IT.** Make a presentation about your product. Explain how or why it is better than other brands.

   Happy Cows yogurt is more delicious than other brands. It is . . .

I can use comparative adjectives with *than*. ☐   I need more practice. ☐

Read about the effects of caffeine

1 BEFORE YOU READ

A **MATCH.** Write the letter of the word next to the correct definition.

_____ **1.** = the substance in coffee that makes people feel more awake   **a.** caffeine

_____ **2.** = a change caused by an event or action   **b.** consume

_____ **3.** = something that is made or grown, usually to be sold   **c.** contain

_____ **4.** = have something inside   **d.** effect

_____ **5.** = eat or drink something   **e.** product

B **IDENTIFY.** Which products contain caffeine? Which one has the most caffeine?

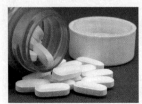   

A pain reliever for headaches   **An energy drink**   **Cola**   **Lemon/lime soda**

2 READ

▶ Listen and read.

Academic Skill: Get Meaning from Context

You can sometimes guess the meaning of a word from its context (the words and sentences around it).

Caffeinated Nation

1 You have a cup of coffee for breakfast. Later, you have a cola with lunch. After work, you take some pain reliever for a headache. You may not know it, but each of these products contains caffeine. About 90 percent of the
5 people in the United States consume caffeine every day. Most of them get it from coffee. Some get it from energy drinks, tea, chocolate, or medicines.

What are the effects of caffeine?

Fifteen minutes after caffeine enters your body, you
10 start to feel changes. Your heart beats faster. You have more energy and feel more awake. You feel happier. These effects can last for several hours. When they go away, you may feel a little tired and sad.

Is caffeine bad for you?

15 For most adults, up to 400 milligrams of caffeine a day is not harmful.* That is the amount in one to four cups of coffee. Small amounts of caffeine may even be good for you. But caffeine affects people in different ways, so it's hard to say how much is the right amount.

20 Too much caffeine can be bad for your health. It can make you feel nervous and irritable. It can give you a headache or an upset stomach. If you consume caffeine too late in the day, you may find it hard to sleep at night.

25 It's a good idea to read the labels on medicines, foods, and beverages. Find out if they contain caffeine and how much.

*Source: The U.S. Food and Drug Administration

Amount of caffeine per cup

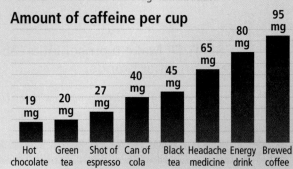

Hot chocolate	Green tea	Shot of espresso	Can of cola	Black tea	Headache medicine	Energy drink	Brewed coffee
19 mg	20 mg	27 mg	40 mg	45 mg	65 mg	80 mg	95 mg

Reading

3 CLOSE READING

A IDENTIFY. What is the main idea?

Most people in the U.S. consume caffeine every day _____.
a. in many different products
b. and it can have both good and bad effects
c. but they don't know how much they're consuming

B CITE EVIDENCE. Complete the sentences. Where is the information? Write the line numbers.

1. Caffeine starts to have effects on the body after _____ minutes.   **Lines**
   a. 5   b. 15   c. 25   _____

2. When the effects of caffeine go away, people _____.
   a. sometimes feel a   b. need to consume   c. often get headaches   _____
      little sad and have   more caffeine
      less energy

3. Up to _____ milligrams of caffeine a day is safe for most adults.
   a. 40   b. 100   c. 400   _____

C INTERPRET. Complete the sentences about the bar graph.

1. Which drink has the highest level of caffeine per cup?
   a. energy drink   b. tea   c. espresso

2. Headache medicine contains _____.
   a. 6.5 mg of caffeine   b. 65 mg of caffeine   c. 85 mg of caffeine
      per cup   per cup   per cup

4 SUMMARIZE

Complete the summary with the words in the box.

amounts	effects	products
consume	health	

Most people in the U.S. (1) _____ caffeine every day. They get it from coffee and
(2) _____ such as tea, cola, chocolate, and some medicines. Caffeine has several
(3) _____ on the body. It affects people in different ways. Small (4) _____
are probably safe and may be good for your (5) _____. Too much caffeine is bad for you.

Show what you know!

1. **THINK ABOUT IT.** List the products you consume that have caffeine. Write how much you consume in a day.

2. **TALK ABOUT IT.** Which products with caffeine do you consume? How does caffeine affect you? Is it ever a problem for you?

3. **WRITE ABOUT IT.** Write about the caffeine you consume and how it affects you.

   I get caffeine from _____. Caffeine makes me feel _____.
   Caffeine (is sometimes / isn't) a problem for me because _____.

I can get meaning from context. ☐   I need more practice. ☐

Order food in a restaurant

1 BEFORE YOU LISTEN

DISCUSS. Look at the menu. Which dishes and drinks do you know? Which look good?

Mom's Café

Main Dishes
Main dishes are served with a house salad and your choice of one side.

All Main Dishes **$9.95**

meatloaf   roast chicken   pork chops

Asian noodles   hamburger   fish sandwich   macaroni and cheese

Sides
coleslaw   French fries
mixed vegetables   onion rings
mashed potatoes

Drinks
soda   bottled water
apple juice   iced tea

2 LISTEN

A **PREDICT.** Look at the picture. Where are they? What is happening?

B ▶ **LISTEN FOR MAIN IDEA.** Which of these sentences do you hear?

- ☐ Are you ready to order?
- ☐ What do you want to eat?
- ☐ And what would you like with that?
- ☐ Would you like something else?

C ▶ **LISTEN FOR DETAILS.** What do they order?

D ▶ **EXPAND.** Listen to the whole conversation. Why is the server surprised?

- **a.** The woman wants to change her order.
- **b.** The man ordered a lot of food.
- **c.** The people decide to leave the restaurant.

Sally

Edgar   Lina

3 PRONUNCIATION

A ▶ **PRACTICE. Listen. Then listen and repeat.**

Are you ready **to** order?
I'd like **the** meatloaf.
A side **of** mixed vegetables.

> **to, the, a, of**
>
> The words *to*, *the*, *a*, and *of* usually have a weak pronunciation. The vowel sound is short and quiet.

B ▶ **APPLY. Listen and complete each sentence with *to*, *the*, *a*, or *of*.**

1. I'd like _____ soda.
2. I'm ready _____ order now.
3. I'll have _____ roast chicken.
4. Could I have a side _____ coleslaw?

4 CONVERSATION

A ▶ **LISTEN AND READ. Then listen and repeat.**

A: Here are your iced teas. Are you ready to order?
B: Yes. I'd like the meatloaf.
A: And what would you like with that?
B: A side of mixed vegetables.
A: OK. Meatloaf with mixed vegetables.
B: And a hamburger with a side of onion rings.
A: A hamburger with onion rings.

B **WORK TOGETHER. Practice the conversation in Exercise A.**

C **ROLE-PLAY. Make your own conversations. Use the menu on page 200 and the suggestions in the boxes. Take turns being a server and a customer.**

Server:	Customer:
Are you ready to order?	I'd like _____
What would you like with that?	I'll have _____.
I'll be right back with your _____.	Could I have _____?

I can order food in a restaurant. ■	I need more practice. ■

Quantifiers with plural and non-count nouns

Quantifiers with plural nouns						
Affirmative			**Negative**			
We have	**a lot of**	apples.	We don't have	**a lot of**	apples.	
	many			**many**		
	some			**any**		
	a few					

Quantifiers with non-count nouns					
Affirmative			**Negative**		
We have	**a lot of**	sugar.	We don't have	**a lot of**	sugar.
	some			**much**	
	a little			**any**	

Grammar Watch

Don't use *much* + a non-count noun in affirmative statements.

Example: *We eat a lot of rice.*

(**Not:** ~~*We eat much rice.*~~)

A IDENTIFY. Cross out the incorrect words.

1. Apple juice has ~~many~~ / **a lot of** sugar.
2. You should eat **some / a few** fruit every day.
3. Vegetables have **a lot of / many** fiber.
4. Athletes eat **much / a lot of** carbohydrates to get energy.
5. There aren't **a few / many** nutrients in a bag of candy.
6. There is usually **a lot of / much** salt and fat in cheese.

B COMPLETE. Use a correct quantifier from the box. Use each word only once.

a few	any	a little	~~a lot of~~	many

1. **A:** Do you eat _____*a lot of*_____ eggs? You know, they have a lot of cholesterol.

   B: No, not really. I only eat _____ eggs a week.

2. **A:** I really like fish. Do you eat a lot of fish?

   B: No, I don't eat _____ fish. I don't like it.

3. **A:** I think we have milk.

   B: We have _____ milk, but it's not enough.

4. **A:** I want to make banana bread. Do we have bananas?

   B: I'm afraid we don't have _____ bananas, only one or two.

I can use quantifiers with plural and non-count nouns. ■   I need more practice. ■

Lesson 10

Write about nutrients in a dish

1 STUDY THE MODEL

READ. Answer the questions.

Badrul Dewan

My Favorite Dish

Rice and beans is a tasty and healthy dish. It has many ingredients like rice, beans, and vegetables. It has healthy nutrients such as protein and fiber. It does not have unhealthy nutrients like cholesterol and sugar.

1. What is Badrul's favorite dish?
2. What ingredients are in the dish?
3. What healthy nutrients does the dish have?
4. What unhealthy nutrients does the dish have?

2 PLAN YOUR WRITING

WORK TOGETHER. Ask and answer the questions.

1. What is a dish you like?
2. What ingredients are in the dish?
3. What healthy nutrients does the dish have?
4. What unhealthy nutrients does the dish have?

Writing Skill: Use *like* and *such as* to introduce examples

Give examples in your writing. Use *like* and *such as* to introduce examples. For example:

It has healthy nutrients such as protein and fiber.

It does not have unhealthy nutrients like cholesterol and sugar.

3 WRITE

Now write about the nutrients in a dish you like. Use the model, the Writing Skill, and your ideas from Exercise 2 to help you.

WRITING CHECKLIST

☐ The paragraph answers the questions in Exercise 2.

☐ There are commas between words in lists.

☐ There are examples of ingredients and nutrients.

4 CHECK YOUR WRITING

WORK TOGETHER. Read the checklist. Read your writing aloud. Revise your writing.

I can use *like* and *such as* to introduce examples. ■   I need more practice. ■

Ask for help

1 MEET ANH

Read about one of her workplace skills.

I know when to ask for help. For example, when a customer asks a question and I don't know the answer, I ask my co-workers.

2 ANH'S PROBLEM

READ. Circle *True* or *False*.

Anh works in a bakery. She sells baked goods to customers. A customer points at a pie. She says, "That pie looks delicious, but I can't eat eggs. Does it have eggs in it?" Anh doesn't know the answer to the question.

1. Anh bakes food at a bakery.	True	False
2. Maybe the customer will buy the pie.	True	False
3. Anh knows the ingredients in the pie.	True	False

3 ANH'S SOLUTION

A **WORK TOGETHER.** Anh knows when to ask for help. What does she say? Explain your answer.

1. Anh says, "Don't worry. There aren't any eggs in it."
2. Anh says, "I don't know, but let me ask. I'll be right back."
3. Anh says, "I'm not sure. it probably doesn't have eggs."
4. Anh says _____.

B **ROLE-PLAY.** Look at your answer to 3A. Role-play Anh's conversation.

Show what you know!

1. **TALK ABOUT IT.** Do you know when to ask for help? How do you ask for help in class? At work? At home? Give examples.

2. **WRITE ABOUT IT.** Write an example in your Skills Log.

    I can ask for help in class. When I don't know the meaning of an English word, I ask the teacher.

I can give an example of how I ask for help. ■

Unit Review: Go back to page 185. Which unit goals can you check off?

11 Call 911!

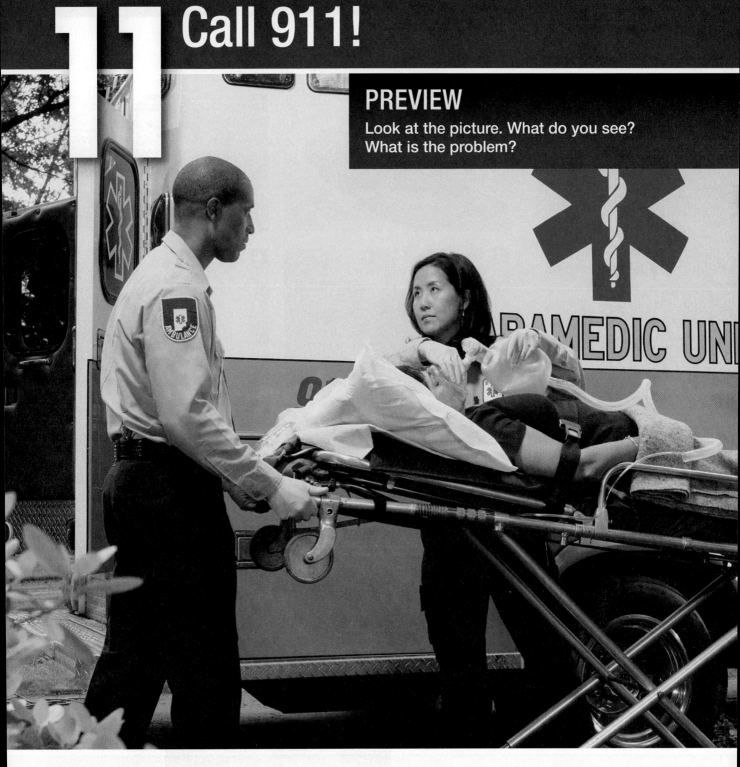

PREVIEW
Look at the picture. What do you see?
What is the problem?

UNIT GOALS

- [ ] Describe medical emergencies
- [ ] Call 911
- [ ] Identify fire hazards
- [ ] Understand fire safety procedures
- [ ] Describe an emergency
- [ ] Respond to police instructions

- [ ] **Academic skill:** Identify supporting details
- [ ] **Writing skill:** Answer *wh-* questions to give information
- [ ] **Workplace soft skill:** Show how you follow safety procedures

Vocabulary

Lesson 1

Medical emergencies

A PREDICT. Look at the pictures. What do you see? Which medical emergencies do you know?

B ▶ LISTEN AND POINT. Listen again and repeat.

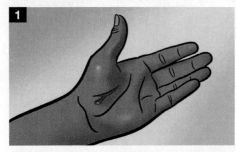

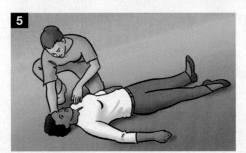

Vocabulary

Medical emergencies

1. She's bleeding.
2. He's choking.
3. She's having trouble breathing.
4. He's having a heart attack.
5. She's unconscious.
6. He's having an allergic reaction.
7. He swallowed poison.
8. She burned herself.
9. He fell.

C **IDENTIFY.** Student A, point to a picture and ask about the emergency. Student B, say the emergency.

Student A points to picture 5.
A: What's the emergency?
B: She's unconscious.

Study Tip

Self-test your pronunciation
Record yourself. Read each sentence aloud. Listen. If you don't like your pronunciation, record the sentence again.

D **ANALYZE.** Look at the list of medical emergencies in Exercise B. Underline the verbs. Then write the sentences in the correct column below.

happened in the past	happening right now
He swallowed poison.	

Show what you know!

1. **THINK ABOUT IT.** Look at the medical emergencies. Check (✓) the most serious emergencies.

2. **TALK ABOUT IT.** 911 is a special phone number for medical emergencies. Compare your serious emergencies. Do you call 911 in these emergencies?

   A: Call 911 when a person is choking.
   B: Call 911 when a person is having a heart attack.

3. **WRITE ABOUT IT.** Write a list of medical emergencies for 911.

   Call 911
   The person is choking.
   The person is having a heart attack.

I can describe medical emergencies. ■   I need more practice. ■

Listening and Speaking

Call 911 to report a medical emergency

1 BEFORE YOU LISTEN

A **MATCH.** Write the words under the pictures.

| heart attack | hurt knee | poison | sinus infection |

1. _____
2. _____
3. _____
4. _____

B **IDENTIFY.** Call 911 for free from any phone when there is an emergency. Circle the pictures that show an emergency.

2 LISTEN

A **PREDICT.** Look at the picture. Who is the woman calling?

B ▶ **LISTEN.** What is the woman doing?

a. reporting an emergency
b. checking in to a hospital
c. ordering a taxi

C ▶ **LISTEN FOR DETAILS.** What does the 911 operator ask? Check the questions.

☐ What's your emergency?
☐ Where are you?
☐ What's the location of the emergency?
☐ What are the cross streets?
☐ What are you doing?
☐ What's your name?

D ▶ **EXPAND.** Listen to the whole conversation. What will happen next?

a. An ambulance will come for the man.   b. The woman will drive to the hospital.

3 PRONUNCIATION

A ▶ **PRACTICE.** Listen to the words. Then listen and repeat.

    al·ler·gic   lo·ca·tion   sit·u·a·tion   am·bu·lance   e·mer·gen·cy

B ▶ **APPLY.** Listen. Mark (•) the stressed syllable.

1. e·lec·tric
2. re·ac·tion
3. con·ver·sa·tion
4. un·con·scious

Stressed Syllables

Many words in English have more than one syllable. In these words, one syllable is stressed. It is longer and louder than the other syllables.

4 CONVERSATION

A ▶ **LISTEN AND READ.** Then listen and repeat.

A: 9-1-1. What's your emergency?
B: I think a man is having a heart attack.
A: OK. What's the location of the emergency?
B: Dave's Sports Shop at 103 Elm Street.
A: What are the cross streets?
B: 17th and 18th Avenues.
A: All right. What's your name?
B: Olivia Ramos.

B **WORK TOGETHER.** Practice the conversation in Exercise A.

C **CREATE.** Make new conversations. Use different emergencies and locations.

A: 9-1-1. What's your emergency?
B: ▭
A: OK. What is the location of the emergency?
B: ▭
A: What are the cross streets?
B: ▭
A: All right. What's your name?
B: _____.

A woman is having trouble breathing.	Fresh Supermarket on Coral Way.	42nd and 43rd Avenues.
A man is unconscious.	S & S Pharmacy on Route 1.	36th and 37th Streets.
Someone is hurt and is bleeding a lot.	All-Day Café on Palm Street.	Oak and Maple Avenues.

D **ROLE-PLAY.** Make your own conversations.

I can call 911 to report a medical emergency. ▢   I need more practice. ▢

Present continuous: Statements and questions

Present continuous: Statements and questions

Statements

The man	is	having	a heart attack.
	is not		

Yes / No questions

Is	he	bleeding?

Short answers

Yes,	he	is.
No,		isn't.

Information questions

What	are	they	doing?
	is	happening?	

Where	are	you	going?
	is	he	

Who	is	calling 911?

Answers

They	're	talking to the police.
The driver	is	

I	'm	going to the hospital.
He	's	

The driver	is	calling.

Grammar Watch

- You can use contractions in the present continuous.
- See page 258 for spelling rules for *-ing* verbs.

A **COMPLETE.** Use the present continuous and the verbs in parentheses.

1. Help! My co-worker _____is choking_____!
   (choke)

2. A man just fell down in the parking lot. He _____.
   (not breathe)

3. _____ you _____ to the 911 operator now?
   (talk)

4. A woman _____ on the ground. She's unconscious.
   (lie)

5. They are taking Frank to the hospital. Who _____
   (go)
   with him?

6. The police _____. Where _____
   (leave)
   they _____?
   (go)

7. What _____? There are a lot of fire trucks.
   (happen)

8. I cut my finger. It hurts, but it _____ a lot.
   (not bleed)

9. Mike _____ an allergic reaction. I _____ him
   (have)   (take)
   to the emergency room.

Grammar

B **COMPLETE.** Use the present continuous and the verbs in parentheses.

A: You won't believe this. There is an accident in front of my house!

B: Oh, no! What's _____happening_____?
1. (happen)

A: Well, one man _____ 911. Wait . . . Now I see an ambulance. It
2. (call)

_____ down the street. And a fire truck.
3. (come)

B: Is anyone hurt?

A: I'm not sure. A man _____ a woman. He _____ to
4. (help)   5. (talk)

her and she _____ her head. I think she _____.
6. (hold)   7. (bleed)

Show what you know!

1. **THINK ABOUT IT.** Look at the picture. What are the people doing?

2. **TALK ABOUT IT.** Ask and answer questions about what each person is doing. Take turns.

   A: What is the baby doing?
   B: The baby is crying.

3. **WRITE ABOUT IT.** Now write five sentences about what people are doing.

   The woman is _____.

   _____

   _____

   _____

   _____

I can use present continuous in statements and questions. ☐   I need more practice. ☐

Lesson 4

Fire hazards and safety procedures

1 IDENTIFY FIRE HAZARDS

A **DESCRIBE.** Look at the picture. Match the fire hazards to their descriptions.

1. _____ a heater close to paper files
2. _____ no window exit
3. _____ an electrical cord under a rug
4. _____ cloth on a lamp
5. _____ too many plugs in an electrical outlet

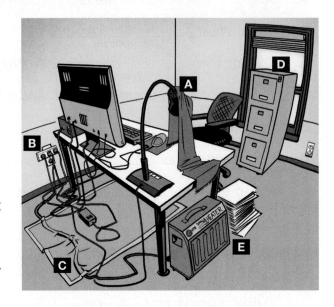

B **WORK TOGETHER.** What are other fire hazards? What can people do to make their workplaces safe?

2 UNDERSTAND FIRE SAFETY PROCEDURES

A **LABEL.** Match each picture with a word or phrase from the box.

| an escape plan | exit | a fire escape | a fire extinguisher | a smoke alarm |

 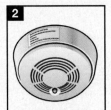 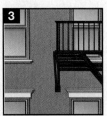 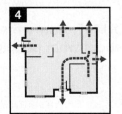 

1. a fire extinguisher

2. _____

3. _____

4. _____

5. _____

B ▶ **SELF-ASSESS.** Listen and check your answers. Then listen and repeat.

I can identify fire hazards. ◼   I need more practice. ◼

C ▶ **LISTEN.** Then listen again and complete the tips below.

Fire Safety Tips for the Workplace

**GET OUT
STAY OUT
CALL 911**

1. Leave your _____ immediately. Do not take anything with you, but alert your co-workers.
2. Don't stop to call _____. Call from a safe location outside of the building.
3. Don't use an _____ to exit the building. Use the stairs.
4. Close any open doors. This will _____ the fire from spreading quickly.
5. Feel every closed _____ before opening it. Don't open a door that is hot. Try to find another exit.
6. If you smell _____, stay close to the floor. Cover your mouth and nose with a wet cloth.
7. When you get outside, do not go back to your workplace for any reason. Tell _____ about anyone still inside the building.

D **DETERMINE.** Read about Carmen. Which of the fire safety tips from Exercise C did she follow? Did she make any mistakes?

> Yesterday afternoon, there was a fire at Carmen's workplace. First, she called 911. Then, she got her wallet and keys from her desk. She touched the door to her office, but it was not hot. She opened the door. She saw a few other open doors. She took the stairs to the first floor. There was a lot of smoke on the first floor. She continued to walk towards the exit. She waited across the street with a few of her co-workers.

E **INTERPRET.** Look at the fire escape plan for Carmen's workplace. Answer the questions.

1. How many offices are there?
2. How many exits are there?
3. If you are in office 403, where should you exit?
4. If you are in office 406, where should you exit?
5. If you are in the Meeting Room, where should you exit?
6. Where should you wait for help in case of emergency?

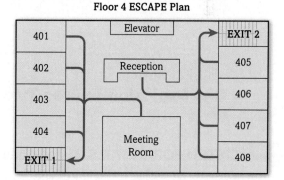

Floor 4 ESCAPE Plan

MEETING PLACE: parking lot across the street

F GO ONLINE. Search for workplace fire-escape plans or your own workplace's fire-escape plan. Select one image. Describe the escape procedure to a classmate.

I can understand fire safety procedures. ■   I need more practice. ■

Describe an emergency

1 BEFORE YOU LISTEN

MATCH. Write the words under the pictures.

| a car accident | a construction accident | an explosion | a robbery |

1. _____ 2. _____ 3. _____ 4. _____

2 LISTEN

A **PREDICT.** Look at the picture. What are they talking about?

a. bad traffic   **b.** bad news   **c.** bad weather

B ▶ **LISTEN.** Which story are they talking about?

a.
City Herald   HEADLINES | WEATHER
Fire Destroys Hotel, No Injuries Reported
Lorem ipsum dolor sit amet, consectetuer adipiscing

b.
Greenville Times   🔍
Route 52 Car Accident Leaves Two Hospitalized
Lorem ipsum dolor sit amet, consectetuer adipiscing

c.
Village News   LOCAL | SPORTS
Gas Explosion Injures Two
Lorem ipsum dolor sit amet, consectetuer adipiscing

d.
Journal News
First Federal Bank Robbed, No One Hurt
Lorem ipsum dolor sit amet, consectetuer adipiscing

C ▶ **LISTEN FOR DETAILS.** Listen again. What happened to two people?

a. They called 911.   **b.** They went to the hospital.   **c.** They had a car accident.

D ▶ **EXPAND.** Listen to the whole conversation. What happened after the emergency situation?

a. Some streets were closed.   **b.** The hospital was full.   **c.** There was a car accident.

Listening and Speaking

3 PRONUNCIATION

A ▶ **PRACTICE. Listen to the words. Notice the sound /h/ at the beginning of the second word in each pair. Then listen and repeat.**

<table>
<tr><td>**1.** ear</td><td>hear</td><td>**3.** art</td><td>heart</td></tr>
<tr><td>**2.** I</td><td>high</td><td>**4.** ow</td><td>how</td></tr>
</table>

> **H sound**
>
> The 'h' sound is an unvoiced sound. At the beginning of words, it makes a quiet sound, with a puff of air.

B ▶ **APPLY. Listen to each pair of words. Are the two words the same (S) or different (D)? Write S or D.**

1. ____   **2.** ____   **3.** ____   **4.** ____   **5.** ____   **6.** ____

4 CONVERSATION

A ▶ **LISTEN AND READ. Then listen and repeat.**

A: Did you hear what happened yesterday?
B: No. What happened?
A: There was a gas explosion downtown.
B: Oh my gosh. That's terrible. Was anybody hurt?
A: Yes. Two people went to the hospital.

B **WORK TOGETHER. Practice the conversation in Exercise A.**

C **CREATE. Make new conversations. Use the words in the boxes.**

A: Did you hear what happened yesterday?
B: No. What happened?
A: There was a ▢▢▢▢▢ downtown.
B: Oh my gosh. That's terrible. Was anybody hurt?
A: ▢▢▢▢

robbery	No one was hurt.
car accident	There were no injuries.
construction accident	Four people were hurt.

D **ROLE-PLAY. Make your own conversations.**

I can describe an emergency. ▢	I need more practice. ▢

Grammar

There was / There were

There was / There were						
Affirmative				**Negative**		
There	**was**	a gas explosion	yesterday.	**There**	**wasn't a** / **was no**	fire.
	were	two car accidents			**weren't any** / **were no**	injuries.

Yes / No questions		Short answers		
Was	a fire?	Yes,	**there**	**was.**
there				**were.**
Were	any injuries?	No,		**wasn't.**
				weren't.

A **COMPLETE.** Use *there was*, *there were*, *was there*, or *were there*.

1. **A:** What happened downtown last night?
   B: _____There was_____ a robbery at the jewelry store.
   A: _____ any customers there?
   B: Yes, _____. But no one was hurt.

2. **A:** _____ a problem at the high school last night.
   B: I know. _____ a fight after the basketball game.
   A: Wow! Did the police come?
   B: Yes, _____ five police cars in the parking lot.

3. **A:** _____ an explosion at the factory yesterday.
   B: Was anybody hurt?
   A: No, luckily _____ no injuries.

4. **A:** _____ an accident on Main Street this morning?
   B: Yes, _____. I heard about it on the radio.
   A: I thought so. _____ a lot of traffic, and I was late to work.

Grammar

B WRITE. Use *there was* or *there were* and words from the box. Write two sentences to describe each emergency situation.

a crowd of people

a lot of smoke

lots of police

a traffic jam

1. _____

_____

2. _____

_____

3. _____

_____

4. _____

_____

C WORK TOGETHER. Ask and answer questions about the situations in Exercise B.

A: *What happened last night?*
B: *There was a fire. There was a lot of smoke.*

Show what you know!

1. **THINK ABOUT IT.** Think about an emergency situation you have heard about.

2. **WRITE ABOUT IT.** Write three sentences about one of the emergency situations.

   There was a fire last night. There was a lot of smoke.
   There was a fire on Center Street yesterday. Some people went to the hospital.

3. **PRESENT IT.** Give a short presentation about an emergency situation you had or you heard about.

   I watched the news on TV last night. There was a fire on Center Street. Some people went to the hospital.

I can use *there was / there were.* ■   I need more practice. ■

Read about being safe at work

1 BEFORE YOU READ

A MATCH. Complete the sentences with words from the box.

| safety gear | a safety hazard | toxic chemicals |

1. _____ are dangerous.

2. Some workers need to wear _____.

3. A wet floor is _____.

B BRAINSTORM. Accidents sometimes happen at work. What are some ways that workers can get hurt?

2 READ

▶ Listen and read.

> **Academic Skill: Identify Supporting Details**
>
> Authors use supporting details to help explain the main ideas. Supporting details can be reasons, examples, or steps.

1 **What is OSHA?**
OSHA is the Occupational Safety and Health Administration. It's part of the U.S. government. Its job is to help workers avoid getting hurt or
5 sick at work.

What does OSHA do?
OSHA tries to make sure workers stay safe and healthy. It sets safety and health standards for workplaces. Employers must obey these rules.
10 OSHA also provides information and training. OSHA inspectors often visit workplaces. They look for health and safety hazards.

Do workers in the U.S. have the right to a safe workplace?
15 Yes, they do.

What are some other rights that workers have?
Workers have the right to:
• get job training in a language they understand
20 • receive the safety gear they need
• be protected from toxic chemicals
• report a work-related injury or illness
• see records of injuries in the workplace

Tests are sometimes done to find hazards in the
25 workplace. Workers have the right to see test results.

What can workers do if they are afraid for their health or safety?
They can talk about health or safety hazards with
30 their employer. They have the right to ask questions without fear. They have the right to ask for an OSHA inspection. If they want, they can speak to the inspector.

How can workers contact OSHA?
35 They can call OSHA. They can also visit an OSHA office. Every state has OSHA offices. Workers can also e-mail OSHA from the OSHA website.

Source: https://www.osha.gov/workers/index.html

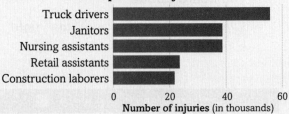

Occupational Injuries

Number of injuries (in thousands)

Reading

3 CLOSE READING

A IDENTIFY. What is the main idea?

OSHA is a part of the U.S. government that _____.
a. helps people who lose their job
b. takes care of people with injuries or illnesses
c. protects people from health and safety hazards at work

B CITE EVIDENCE. Complete the sentences. Where is the information? Write the line numbers.

Lines

1. OSHA is responsible for helping workers avoid _____.
   a. working
   b. getting hurt or sick at work
   c. inspections in their workplace
   _____

2. Employers have to give their workers _____ when the workers need it.
   a. a hazard
   b. a rule
   c. safety gear
   _____

3. Employers have to protect workers from _____.
   a. toxic chemicals
   b. records of workplace injuries
   c. OSHA inspectors
   _____

C INTERPRET. Complete the sentences about the bar graph.

1. Almost _____ injuries take place among janitors.
   a. 50,000
   b. 30,000
   c. 40,000

2. The most hazardous occupation is _____.
   a. a retail assistant
   b. a construction laborer
   c. a truck driver

4 SUMMARIZE

Complete the summary with the words in the box.

contact	employers	hazards	inspectors	right

OSHA is a part of the U.S. government. It makes rules about health and safety in the workplace. (1) _____ have to follow these rules. Workers have the (2) _____ to a safe workplace. OSHA (3) _____ sometimes check for (4) _____ in the workplace. Workers can (5) _____ OSHA to learn more.

Show what you know!

1. TALK ABOUT IT. What rights do you have in the workplace to help you stay safe and healthy? Talk with your class.

2. WRITE ABOUT IT. Write about your rights in the workplace.

   At work, I have the right to _____.

I can identify supporting details. ■   I need more practice. ■

1 BEFORE YOU LISTEN

A MATCH. Write the words under the pictures. Do you know any other traffic violations?

distracted driving   not wearing a seat belt   running a red light   speeding   tailgating

1. _____   2. _____   3. _____   4. _____   5. _____

B DISCUSS. Do you know what to do if you are pulled over by the police?

C CHOOSE. Take the quiz. Check *True* or *False*.

Do you know what to do if you get pulled over?

1. Always pull over to the left.   ☐ True   ☐ False

2. After you pull over, get out of your car.   ☐ True   ☐ False

3. Keep your hands on the steering wheel.   ☐ True   ☐ False

4. Give the officer your driver's license, registration, and proof of insurance.   ☐ True   ☐ False

5. Don't argue with the police officer.   ☐ True   ☐ False

6. If a police officer gives you a ticket, you need to pay immediately.   ☐ True   ☐ False

Listening and Speaking

2 LISTEN

A ▶ **SELF-ASSESS.** Listen. Check your answers on the quiz.

B ▶ **LISTEN FOR DETAILS.** Listen again. Correct the false sentences in the quiz.

C ▶ **EXPAND.** Listen to the whole conversation. When is it OK to leave?

    a. after the officer gives you a ticket
    b. after the officer gives you permission to go
    c. after the officer leaves

3 CONVERSATION

A ▶ **LISTEN AND READ.** Then listen and repeat.

A: I need to see your license, registration, and proof of insurance.
B: OK. My license is in my pocket. The other things are in the glove compartment.
A: That's fine. You can get them.
B: Here you go.
A: I'll be back in a moment. Please turn off your engine and stay in your car.

[a few minutes later]

A: Do you know why I pulled you over?
B: I'm not sure.
A: I pulled you over for speeding.
B: I see.

B **WORK TOGETHER.** Practice the conversation in Exercise A.

C **ROLE-PLAY.** Make new conversations. Use different traffic violations.

I can respond to a police officer's instructions. ■   I need more practice. ■

Compound imperatives				
Affirmative				
Turn off	your engine	**and**	**stay**	in your car.
Negative				
Don't get out	of your car	**or**	**take off**	your seat belt.

Grammar Watch

- Connect two affirmative imperatives with *and*.
- Connect two negative imperatives with *or*.

A **APPLY.** Write *and* or *or*.

1. Drive carefully ___and___ follow all traffic laws.
2. Wear your seat belt _____ use car seats for children.
3. Don't text _____ use your phone while driving.
4. Drive more slowly _____ leave extra room between cars in bad weather.
5. Don't tailgate _____ change lanes without signaling.

B **WRITE.** Rewrite each pair of sentences as two imperatives with *and*.

What to do during a traffic stop:

1. You should use your turn signal. You should pull over to a safe spot.
   Use your turn signal and pull over to a safe spot.

2. You should wait for the police officer. You should roll down your window.
   _____

3. You should be polite. You should follow the officer's instructions.
   _____

4. You should not argue with the officer. You should not offer money to the officer.
   _____

5. You should not start your car. You should not leave until the officer gives you permission to go.
   _____

I can use compound imperatives. ■   I need more practice. ■

Writing

Write about an emergency

1 STUDY THE MODEL

READ. Answer the questions.

Ivan Popov

My Neighbor's Emergency

My neighbor had an emergency last week. She had a car accident on Main Street. She had a heart attack and hit a parked car. There was a big crowd of people and everyone was worried. My neighbor went to the hospital, but now she's feeling much better.

1. Who had the emergency?
2. When did it happen?
3. Where did it happen?
4. Why did it happen?
5. What happened?
6. How is the person now?

2 PLAN YOUR WRITING

WORK TOGETHER. Ask and answer the questions.

1. Think of an emergency. Who had the emergency?
2. When did it happen?
3. Where did it happen?
4. Why did it happen?
5. What happened?
6. How is the person now?

Writing Skill: Answer wh- questions to give information

Wh- questions begin with words like who, what, when, where, why, and how.

Answer wh- questions to give information about an event. For example:

Who had the emergency?

3 WRITE

Write about an emergency. Use the model, the Writing Skill, and your ideas from Exercise 2 to help you.

WRITING CHECKLIST

☐ The paragraph answers the questions in Exercise 2.

☐ The paragraph answers wh- questions.

☐ The paragraph includes details about time, people, and places.

4 CHECK YOUR WRITING

WORK TOGETHER. Read your writing with a partner.

I can answer wh- questions to give information. ■   I need more practice. ■

Follow safety procedures

1 MEET LUIS

Read about one of his workplace skills.

> I follow safety procedures. For example, when I have an accident at work, I report it. That way, I can stop more accidents from happening and make the workplace safer for everyone.

2 LUIS'S PROBLEM

READ. Circle *True* or *False*.

Luis just had an accident at work. He had to get a box from a high shelf. He climbed to the top of a ladder, but the shelf was too high. He couldn't reach the box. He fell off the ladder and hurt his leg. Workers are supposed to report accidents, but that takes time. Luis is busy today. He's not sure what to do.

1. Luis reached for a box and it fell on him.	True	False
2. Luis hurt his hand when he reached for a box.	True	False
3. Luis has to complete a report about his accident.	True	False

3 LUIS'S SOLUTION

WORK TOGETHER. Luis follows safety procedures. What does he do? Explain your answer.

1. Luis keeps working. He doesn't report the accident.
2. Luis tells his supervisor about the accident.
3. Luis tells his co-workers about the accident.
4. Luis should _____.

Show what you know!

1. **TALK ABOUT IT.** Do you follow safety procedures? How do you follow safety procedures in class? At work? At home? Give examples.

2. **WRITE ABOUT IT.** Write an example in your Skills Log.

   I follow safety procedures in class. When the fire alarm rings, I always follow the rules. I go outside until the fire alarm stops.

I can give an example of how I follow safety procedures. ■

Unit Review: Go back to page 205. Which unit goals can you check off?

12 The World of Work

PREVIEW
Look at the picture.
What do you see?

UNIT GOALS

- [ ] Identify job responsibilities
- [ ] Ask about policies at work
- [ ] Read a pay stub
- [ ] Understand payroll deductions and overtime
- [ ] Ask a co-worker to cover hours
- [ ] Request a schedule change
- [ ] **Academic skill:** Think about what you know
- [ ] **Writing skill:** Give details to support an idea
- [ ] **Workplace soft skill:** Show how you are a team player

Vocabulary

Lesson 1

Job Responsibilities

A PREDICT. Look at the pictures. What do you see? Which job responsibilities do you know?

B ▶ LISTEN AND POINT. Listen again and repeat.

Vocabulary

Job responsibilities

1. clock in/out
2. call in late
3. follow directions
4. ask questions
5. report problems with the equipment
6. work as a team
7. wear a uniform
8. wear safety gear
9. wash hands
10. wear gloves
11. maintain the equipment
12. store the equipment

C **DISCUSS. Look at the job titles. What are the responsibilities for each job?**

nursing assistant   sales associate
computer system administrator   warehouse worker

A: *What are the responsibilities of a nursing assistant?*
B: *A nursing assistant has to wash hands, wear gloves . . .*

D **GIVE EXAMPLES. Complete the chart with examples.
There may be more than one correct answer.**

Study Tip

Study words that go together
Choose six job responsibilities. Make cards. Write the verb on the front of the card and the other words on the back.
wear / a uniform
wash / hands

An employee has to . . .	EXAMPLE
dress appropriately	*wear a uniform*
follow health and safety rules	
be on time	
communicate well with others	
treat equipment correctly	

Show what you know!

1. **THINK ABOUT IT.** Think of a job you have or want to have. List the responsibilities for that job.

   warehouse worker — clock in and clock out .

2. **TALK ABOUT IT.** Tell your classmates about the job and the responsibilities.

   A: *I am a warehouse worker. I have to clock in every day.*
   B: *I want to be a computer systems administrator. A computer systems administrator has to maintain the computer equipment.*

3. **WRITE ABOUT IT.** Write three sentences about a job and its responsibilities.

I can identify job responsibilities. ■   I need more practice. ■

1 BEFORE YOU LISTEN

A **INTERPRET.** Look at the picture of a hotel guest and an employee of the hotel. What is the employee doing wrong?

A **DISCUSS.** What other things are employees often not allowed to do at work?

2 LISTEN

A **PREDICT.** Look at the picture. Who is Michelle? Who are the other people?

B ▶ **LISTEN FOR MAIN IDEA.** Check (✓) the topics that Michelle talks about.

☐ wearing the right clothing
☐ wearing safety gear
☐ being on time
☐ working as a team

C ▶ **LISTEN FOR DETAILS.** Listen again. Complete the sentences.

1. You must wear your _____ during your work shift.
   a. name tag   **b.** employee ID badge   **c.** safety gear

2. Employees in housekeeping and food service must wear _____.
   a. a uniform   **b.** latex gloves   **c.** boots

3. During your 6-hour shift you must _____.
   a. not take a break   **b.** take a 15-minute break   **c.** take a 30-minute break

4. You must not _____ for another employee.
   a. clock in or clock out   **b.** call in late   **c.** ask questions

D ▶ **EXPAND.** Listen to the whole conversation. Next, Michelle will talk about the company's _____.
   a. vacation-time policy   **b.** sick-day policy   **c.** policy for calling in late

Listening and Speaking

3 PRONUNCIATION

A ▶ **PRACTICE. Listen. Then listen and repeat.**

Intonation in *yes/no* questions

In *yes/no* questions, the voice usually goes up at the end.

Can I ask you a few questions?

Do we have to clock out?

Are we allowed to wear sneakers?

B ▶ **APPLY. Listen. Use an arrow to mark where the voice goes up.**

1. Do we need to wear gloves?

2. Did you clock in?

3. Can I report a problem?

4 CONVERSATION

A ▶ **LISTEN AND READ. Then listen and repeat.**

Employee: Hi, Michelle. Can I ask you a question?
Trainer: Sure. What do you want to know?
Employee: Am I allowed to wear sneakers?
Trainer: No, you aren't. You have to wear boots.
Employee: OK. Thanks. I'm glad I asked.

B **WORK TOGETHER. Practice the conversation in Exercise A.**

C **CREATE. Make new conversations. Use the words in the boxes.**

A: Hi, _____. Can I ask you a question?
B: Sure. What do you want to know?
A: Am I allowed to _____?
B: No, you aren't. You have to _____.
A: OK. Thanks. I'm glad I asked.

eat in front of customers	eat in the break room
park anywhere	park in the back
trade shifts	talk to a manager

D **ROLE-PLAY. Make your own conversations.**

I can ask about policies at work. ☐   I need more practice. ☐

Grammar

Expressions of necessity and prohibition

Expressions of necessity: *must / have to*

You	have to		
	must	wear	boots.
He	has to		
	must		

Use *have to* for questions (not *must*).
Do you have to wear a uniform?
Where do we have to clock in?

Expressions of prohibition: *must not / can't*

| You | must not | wear | sneakers. |
| | can't | | |

A COMPLETE. Use *must*, *must not*, *have to*, or *can't* and the verbs in parentheses. There may be more than one correct answer.

1. **A:** _Do I have to go_ (I / go) to the orientation meeting today?
   B: Yes. All new employees _____ (go) to the meeting.

2. **A:** Can we smoke in the breakroom?
   B: No, you _____ (smoke) anywhere in the building. You _____ (go) outside to the designated smoking area.

3. **A:** What's the uniform for supervisors?
   B: Supervisors _____ (wear) dark suits and black shoes.

4. **A:** I need to take a sick day. Who do I have to tell?
   B: You _____ (call) your manager at least 30 minutes before the start of your shift.

5. **A:** I'm going to eat lunch at my desk.
   B: Sorry, it's not allowed. You _____ (eat) at your desk. You _____ (eat) in the break room.

Grammar

B **READ.** The e-mail is about responsibilities. Who is the information for?

C **COMPLETE.** Read the e-mail again. Use the correct form of *have to*, *must*, *must not*, or *can't* to complete the statements. There may be more than one correct answer.

1. The employee _has to be_ on time for work.

2. He _____ if he's going to be late.

3. He _____ his breaks on time.

4. He _____ in and out.

5. He _____ in and out for other employees.

6. He _____ personal calls at work.

To: All new employees
From: HR department
Subject: Your Duties as an Employee

Hello, and welcome again to B.T. Corporation.

To make your work more successful, here is a list of reminders:
- Be on time. This is very important.
- Call your supervisor if you are going to be late.
- Begin and end your breaks at the scheduled times.
- Don't forget to clock in and out.
- Don't clock in or out for other employees.
- Don't make personal calls at work.

Show what you know!

1. **THINK ABOUT IT.** Think about one role you have (for example, an employee, a parent, or a student). Write it on the line. Check the responsibilities you have in that role. Add other responsibilities that you have.

2. **TALK ABOUT IT.** Tell your partner what your role is. Tell about your responsibilities in that role. Take turns.

   A: I'm a parent. I have to work a lot of hours.
   B: I'm a student. I have to work a lot of hours, too!

Responsibilities of a/an _____
- ☐ work a lot of hours
- ☐ not be late
- ☐ supervise people
- ☐ communicate in English
- ☐ _____
- ☐ _____

3. **WRITE ABOUT IT.** Now write six sentences about your responsibilities.

I'm a _____. I have to _____.

_____

I can use expressions of necessity and prohibition. ■   I need more practice. ■

Lesson 4 — Pay stubs, payroll deductions, and overtime hours

1 READ A PAY STUB

A INTERPRET. Look at Kim's pay stub. How much money did she earn? How much money did she get?

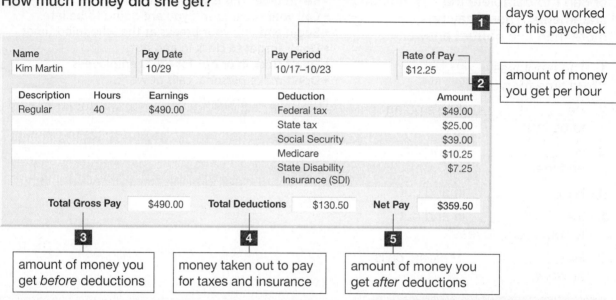

					1 days you worked for this paycheck

Name	Pay Date		Pay Period		Rate of Pay —
Kim Martin	10/29		10/17–10/23		$12.25

2 amount of money you get per hour

Description	Hours	Earnings		Deduction	Amount
Regular	40	$490.00		Federal tax	$49.00
				State tax	$25.00
				Social Security	$39.00
				Medicare	$10.25
				State Disability Insurance (SDI)	$7.25

Total Gross Pay	$490.00	Total Deductions	$130.50	Net Pay	$359.50

3 amount of money you get *before* deductions

4 money taken out to pay for taxes and insurance

5 amount of money you get *after* deductions

B DETERMINE. Look at the pay stub again. Correct the incorrect statements.

1. The pay stub is for ~~two weeks~~ *one week* of work.

2. The pay stub includes Kim's job title.

3. The company paid her on 10/23 for this pay period.

4. She gets paid $40 per hour.

5. Kim gets paid for 50 hours of work.

6. Kim's gross pay is $359.50.

I can read a pay stub. ■   I need more practice. ■

Workplace, Life, and Community Skills

2 UNDERSTAND PAYROLL DEDUCTIONS AND OVERTIME HOURS

A **MATCH.** Look at the pay stub again. Match the deductions with the definitions.

1. _____ Federal tax
2. _____ State tax
3. _____ Social Security
4. _____ Medicare
5. _____ State Disability Insurance (SDI)

a. tax you pay the state government
b. money for older people not working now
c. money for workers who are disabled and can't work
d. money for health care for older people
e. tax you pay the U.S. government

B **INTERPRET.** Read the excerpt from the employee handbook. Answer the questions.

1. When does an employee get overtime pay?
2. How many hours are in a standard work week?
3. What is the pay rate for overtime pay?

> **Overtime Policy**
> When you are approved to work more than 40 hours a week, you earn overtime pay. Overtime pay is paid at one and a half times your regular hourly rate.

C **DETERMINE.** Read Alex's pay stub. Answer the questions.

Name	Pay Date	Pay Period	Rate of Pay
Alex Smith	12/22	12/02–12/16	$12.00

Description	Hours	Earnings	Deduction		Amount
Regular	80	$960.00	Federal tax		$114.00
Overtime	10	$180.00	State tax		$57.00
			FICA	Social Security	$85.50
				Medicare	$20.50

Total Gross Pay	$1,140.00	**Total Deductions**	$277.00	**Net Pay**	$863.00

1. How many deductions were taken out of Alex's pay stub? _____
2. Which deduction totaled $114? _____
3. How many overtime hours did he work? _____
4. What two deductions are a part of FICA? _____
5. How much money was taken out in deductions? _____
6. How much money did he get after deductions? _____

D **IDENTIFY.** Look at Alex's pay stub. How much was Alex paid per hour for overtime?

E <u>GO ONLINE.</u> Search for other common deductions that can appear on a pay stub. Have you seen any of them before? Choose one deduction and explain it to your partner.

I can understand payroll deductions and overtime hours. ■   I need more practice. ■

1 BEFORE YOU LISTEN

DISCUSS. What should employees do if they are going to miss work?

2 LISTEN

A **PREDICT.** Look at the picture. What are they talking about?

B ▶ **LISTEN FOR MAIN IDEA.** What does Cam ask Rachel to do?

a. work on the weekend
b. take a test
c. take his shift

C ▶ **LISTEN FOR DETAILS.** Listen again. Complete the sentences.

1. Cam _____ work on Monday.
   a. wants to   b. can't   c. doesn't have to

2. Rachel _____ take Cam's shift.
   a. is going to   b. can't   c. must not

D ▶ **EXPAND.** Listen to the whole conversation. Complete the sentences.

1. Cam and Rachel check the schedule to see _____.
   a. who is working that day
   b. what time the shift starts
   c. what time the shift ends

2. Rachel _____ work with Tim.
   a. doesn't want to   b. likes to   c. doesn't like to

3 PRONUNCIATION

A ▶ **PRACTICE.** Listen. Then listen and repeat.

What's up?   What time do you start?

I have to study.   I start at 9:30.

B ▶ **APPLY.** Listen. Use an arrow to mark where the voice goes down.

1. What's the favor?
2. I can take your shift.
3. I have to work.
4. Who is on the schedule?

4 CONVERSATION

A ▶ **LISTEN AND READ.** Then listen and repeat.

A: Hi, Rachel. Can I ask you a favor?
B: Sure. What is it?
A: I'm on the schedule for Monday, but I can't come in.
B: Oh, what's up?
A: I have to study for a test. Can you take my shift for me?
B: What time do you start?
A: 9:30.
B: No problem.

B **WORK TOGETHER.** Practice the conversation in Exercise A.

C **CREATE.** Make new conversations. Use the words in the boxes.

A: Hi, _____. Can I ask you a favor?
B: Sure. What is it?
A: I'm on the schedule for Monday, but I can't come in.
B: Oh.
A: I have to _____. Can you take my shift for me?
B: What time do you start?
A: 9:30.
B: No problem.

What's going on?	babysit my niece
What's happening?	go to the dentist
Why not?	pick up my in-laws at the airport

D **ROLE-PLAY.** Make your own conversations.

I can ask a co-worker to cover my hours. ■   I need more practice. ■

6
Lesson

Information questions with *Who / What / Which / When / Where*

Information questions with *Who*				Grammar Watch

Who = subject			Answer
Who	**works** **collects**	on Monday? the timesheets?	**Cam** works on Monday. **Your supervisor** collects the timesheets.

Who = object			Answer
Who	**does** **do**	Cam I	**work** with? **give** my timesheet to?	Cam works with **Rachel**. You give it to **your supervisor**.

Grammar Watch

- To ask about the subject, use *Who* + a verb.
- To ask about the object, use *Who* + a helping verb + a subject + a verb.

A **APPLY.** Put the words in order and write the questions. Capitalize the first word.

1. who / extra hours / needs   *Who needs extra hours?* _____
2. I / ask / who / do / about sick time _____
3. the schedule / makes up / who _____
4. I / call / do / who / about trading shifts _____
5. goes / on break / who / at 10:45 A.M. _____

B **WRITE.** Read the answer. Then write questions with *Who* to ask for the underlined information.

1. **A:** *Who needs a favor?* _____
   B: Your co-worker needs a favor.

2. **A:** _____
   B: I usually work with another associate.

3. **A:** _____
   B: The supervisor wants to talk to Jim.

4. **A:** _____
   B: They need to see their manager.

5. **A:** _____
   B: Someone in the warehouse usually helps me.

Grammar

Information questions with *What / Which / When / Where*

Questions				Answers
What time		my shift	**begin**?	At 3:00 p.m.
Which days	**do**	I	**have** off?	Monday and Friday.
When	**does**	you	**start** your break?	In five minutes.
Where		he	**work**?	In a warehouse.

C WRITE. Make information questions. Use *What time, Which, When, Where* and the words in parentheses.

1. **A:** (day / you / have off) *Which day do you have off?*

   B: Tuesday.

2. **A:** (your shift / start) _____

   B: At 3:00 P.M.

3. **A:** (I / get / a vacation) _____

   B: After six months on the job.

4. **A:** (I / clock in) _____

   B: Outside the employee break room. The time clock is on the wall.

5. **A:** (we / get / breaks) _____

   B: At 10:15 A.M. and 2:30 P.M.

Show what you know!

1. **TALK ABOUT IT.** Look at the employee work schedule. Take turns. Ask and answer questions. Use *What, Which, What time,* and *When.*

   A: *What does Marco do?*
   B: *He's a cashier.*
   A: *What time does he start work?*
   B: *At 8:00.*

2. **WRITE ABOUT IT.** Now write three questions that you asked.

	Mon.	Tues.	Wed.	Thu.	Fri.	Sat.	Sun.
Eduardo, stock clerk	OFF	OFF	6–2 Break: 11–11:30	6–2 Break: 11–11:30	6–2 Break: 11–11:30	6–2 Break: 11–11:30	6–2 Break: 11–11:30
Stan, stock clerk	OFF	OFF	6–1 Break: 11–11:30	6–1 Break: 11–11:30	6–1 Break: 11–11:30	6–2 Break: 11–11:30	6–2 Break: 11–11:30
Deng, stock clerk	6–2 Break: 12–12:30	6–2 Break: 12–12:30	6–1 Break: 12–12:30	6–1 Break: 12–12:30	OFF	OFF	6–2 Break: 12–12:30
Ivan, cashier	OFF	OFF	8–2 Break: 11–11:30	8–2 Break: 11–11:30	8–2 Break: 11–11:30	8–2 Break: 11–11:30	8–2 Break: 11–11:30
Marco, cashier	8–2 Break: 12–12:30	8–2 Break: 12–12:30	8–2 Break: 12–12:30	8–2 Break: 12–12:30	OFF	OFF	8–2 Break: 12–12:30
Will, cashier	OFF	9–2 Break: 12–12:30	9–2 Break: 12–12:30	9–2 Break: 12–12:30	9–2 Break: 12–12:30	OFF	9–2 Break: 12–12:30

I can make information questions with *who / what / which / when / where.* ■   I need more practice. ■

1 BEFORE YOU READ

A COMPLETE. Use the words in the box to complete the sentences.

| disabled | earnings | qualify | retired | spouse |

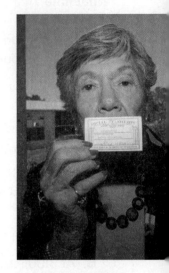

1. Your husband or wife is your _____.
2. Ann stopped working at age 66. Now she's _____.
3. Ed was in a car accident. Now he can't walk. He's _____.
4. The money you get for the work you do is your _____.
5. If you _____ for something (like a bank loan or free health insurance), then you can get it.

B MAKE CONNECTIONS. What is Social Security? Who can have a Social Security card?

2 READ

▶ Listen and read.

> **Academic Skill: Think about what you know**
>
> Before you read, think about what you already know about the topic.

Social Security Fact Sheet HOME | CONTACT US | HELP   🔍 Search

1 **What is Social Security?**
Social Security is a U.S. government program. It pays money, called *benefits*, to people. There are several ways a person can qualify for benefits. Most of the people who get them are age 62 or older. Often, they are retired. Some of the people are
5 disabled and can't work. Some are family members of workers who died.

How did it start?
The U.S. government created Social Security in 1935. It was during the Great Depression. Many people couldn't find jobs. Many were poor. Life was very hard for many older people. Social Security was created to help.

How does Social Security work?
10 Workers pay a Social Security tax. Employers take the money out of workers' paychecks and send it to the government. The government uses the money to pay benefits.

How much tax do people pay?
Workers pay 6.2 percent of their earnings. Their employers pay another 6.2 percent. Self-employed workers pay 12.4 percent of their earnings.

15 **Can everyone get Social Security benefits when they retire?**
No. You, or your spouse, have to work and pay Social Security taxes for ten years. Then you qualify to get retirement benefits.

Can a noncitizen get retirement benefits?
Yes. Any person who works legally in the U.S. and pays Social Security taxes for ten years can get them.

Does everyone get the same amount?
20 No. Some people pay more Social Security taxes than others. That's because they work longer or make more money. So they qualify for more money when they retire. The average benefit for a retired worker is now over $1,400 a month.

Reading

3 CLOSE READING

A IDENTIFY. What is the main idea?

Social Security is a U.S. government program that _____.
a. helps Americans who lose their jobs
b. takes money out of workers' paychecks
c. uses tax dollars to support retired or disabled people

B CITE EVIDENCE. Complete the statements. Where is the information? Write the line numbers.

Lines

1. The only way you can get Social Security benefits is to _____.
   a. be over age 62   b. be disabled   c. qualify   _____

2. If a worker dies, his or her young children _____ Social Security benefits.
   a. can get   b. cannot get   c. have to pay for   _____

3. Workers pay Social Security tax _____.
   a. in some states   b. out of every   c. on April 15   _____
      but not others   paycheck   ("Tax Day")

4. To qualify for retirement benefits, you (or your spouse) have to pay Social
   Security taxes for _____ years.
   a. ten   b. twenty   c. forty   _____

5. You _____ a U.S. citizen to get retirement benefits from Social Security.
   a. must be   b. don't have to be   c. can't be   _____

6. Some retired people get a bigger Social Security check than others
   because _____.
   a. they need more   b. they paid the   c. they worked   _____
      money to live on   higher 12.4% tax   longer

4 SUMMARIZE

Complete the summary with the words in the box.

benefits	disabled	retired	tax

Social Security is a U.S. government program that makes payments called

(1) _____ to people who qualify. Some of these people can't work because

they're (2) _____. Most of them are (3) _____. The money to pay

benefits comes from a (4) _____ on workers' earnings.

Show what you know!

1. **THINK ABOUT IT.** In your native country, what do older people do when they
   cannot work? Is there a program like Social Security?

2. **WRITE ABOUT IT.** Write your opinion of the Social Security program.

   In my opinion, Social Security is helpful because _____.

3. **PRESENT IT.** Compare retirement in your native country with retirement in the United
   States. Make a short presentation about government programs to support retired people.

I can think about what I know before reading. ■   I need more practice. ■

1 BEFORE YOU LISTEN

A READ. Look at some reasons that people change their work schedules.

My son is starting school.

I'm taking classes now.

My wife needs the car during the day.

My husband's work schedule changed.

B DISCUSS. What are some other reasons?

2 LISTEN

A PREDICT. Look at the picture. Who is Ron?

a. Linda's manager
b. Linda's customer
c. Linda's friend

Ron   Linda

B ▶ LISTEN FOR MAIN IDEA. What does Linda want to do?

a. work fewer hours
b. change her schedule
c. work in the morning

C ▶ LISTEN FOR DETAILS. Listen again. Answer the questions.

1. When does Linda work now?
   a. mornings   b. afternoons   c. evenings

2. Why does she ask for a schedule change?
   a. She wants to take classes.
   b. Her husband is taking classes.
   c. Her son's classes are in the mornings.

D ▶ EXPAND. Listen to the whole conversation. What kind of classes is Linda planning to take?

3 CONVERSATION

A ▶ **LISTEN AND READ.** Then listen and repeat.

A: Excuse me, Ron. Can I speak to you for a minute?
B: Sure, Linda. What's up?
A: I need to talk to you about my schedule.
B: OK. Right now you work in the mornings, right?
A: Yes. But I'm planning to take classes now. Could I change to evenings?
B: Well, let me look at the schedule. I'll get back to you.
A: OK. Thanks.

B **WORK TOGETHER.** Practice the conversation in Exercise A.

C **CREATE.** Make new conversations. Use the words in the boxes.

A: Excuse me, _____. Can I speak to you for a minute?
B: Sure, _____. What's up?
A: I need to talk to you about my schedule.
B: OK. Right now you work _____, right?
A: Yes. But _____. Could I change to _____?
B: Well, let me look at the schedule. I'll get back to you.
A: OK. Thanks.

> the second shift
> Tuesdays and Thursdays
> full-time

> my daughter is starting school
> my hours changed at my other job
> my mom can't take care of my son anymore

> the first shift
> Mondays and Wednesdays
> part-time

D **ROLE-PLAY.** Make your own conversations.

| I can request a schedule change. ■ | I need more practice. ■ |

Lesson 9

Can / Could to ask permission

Can / Could to ask permission			Answers
Questions			
Can Could	I	**speak** to you?	Sure. Of course. Yes, you **can**.
		change to evenings?	
		have Friday off?	

Grammar Watch

- *Could* is more formal than *can* to ask permission.
- Use *can* to answer questions. Do not use *could* in answers.

A **WRITE. Complete the conversations. Write questions with *can* or *could*.**

1. **A:** <u>Can I take a break now?</u> _____
   B: Sure, you can take a break. But please wait till Mara comes back.

2. **A:** _____
   B: Sure. No problem. We can trade shifts on Friday.

3. **A:** _____
   B: I'm sorry, but you can't have Friday off. We need you on Friday.

4. **A:** _____
   B: Yes, we can talk about the schedule. Come into my office.

5. **A:** _____
   B: Sorry, I can't cover your hours tomorrow. I have plans.

6. **A:** _____
   B: Go ahead. You can leave a little early tonight. We're not that busy.

7. **A:** _____
   B: OK. I think I can give you more hours next week. I'll see what I can do.

B **ROLE-PLAY. Ask permission to do something. Use the ideas in the box. Take turns.**

| borrow your pen | copy your notes | have a piece of paper | use your dictionary |

A: Could I use your dictionary, please?
B: Sure.

I can use *can / could* to ask permission. ☐   I need more practice. ☐

1 STUDY THE MODEL

READ. Answer the questions.

> Ardita Gega
>
> ### Food Service Job Responsibilities
>
> Food service workers have many responsibilities. For one thing, they need to wear the right clothing. That is, they have to wear clean uniforms. They also must follow health and safety rules. This means they have to wear latex gloves. Finally, they have to communicate well with co-workers. That is, they need to work as a team.

1. What job does Ardita know about?
2. What clothing do the workers need to wear?
3. What health and safety rule do they need to follow?
4. Who do they have to communicate with?

2 PLAN YOUR WRITING

WORK TOGETHER. Ask and answer the questions.

1. What job do you know a lot about?
2. Do the workers need to wear the right clothing? Explain.
3. Do they need to follow rules? Explain.
4. Who do they need to communicate with?

3 WRITE

Now write about a job you know about. Use the model, the Writing Skill, and your ideas from Exercise 2 to help you.

4 CHECK YOUR WRITING

WORK TOGETHER. Read the checklist. Read your writing aloud. Revise your writing.

Writing Skill: Give details to support an idea

Give details to support each idea. Introduce the details with *This means* or *That is*.

For example:

For one thing, they need to wear the right clothing. That is, they have to wear clean uniforms.

WRITING CHECKLIST

☐ The paragraph answers the questions in Exercise 2.

☐ There is a topic sentence.

☐ There are supporting details introduced with the words *This means* or *That is*.

I can give details to support an idea. ■	I need more practice. ■

Lesson 11

Be a team player

1 MEET YURI

Read about one of his workplace skills.

I am a team player. When my co-workers can't finish important work, I help them. Sometimes that means I have to give up my personal time.

2 YURI'S PROBLEM

READ. Circle *True* or *False*.

Yuri is a mechanic. He had a busy workday today. He's tired and ready to go home. He says, "See you tomorrow!" His co-worker says, "Hey, Yuri, my customer needs his car today. I need to work on it for one more hour, but I have to leave. It's my mother's 70th birthday, and her party starts in 15 minutes. Can you help me out?"

1. Yuri just started work.   True   False
2. His co-worker wants to go to a party.   True   False
3. His co-worker wants Yuri to fix a car for him.   True   False

3 YURI'S SOLUTION

Ⓐ **WORK TOGETHER.** Yuri is a team player. What does he say to Sam? Explain your answer.

1. Yuri says, "Sure. No problem."
2. Yuri says, "Sorry, no. That's your job."
3. Yuri says, "Maybe one of the other guys can help you."
4. Yuri says _____.

Ⓑ **ROLE-PLAY.** Look at your answer to 3A. Role-play Yuri's conversation.

Show what you know!

1. **THINK ABOUT IT.** Are you a team player? Are you a team player in class? At work? At home? Give examples.

2. **WRITE ABOUT IT.** Write an example in your Skills Log.

   I'm a team player in class. When I do a group project with other students, I always help my partners.

I can give an example of how I am a team player. ▪

Unit Review: Go back to page 225. Which unit goals can you check off?

MY SOFT SKILLS LOG

This is a list of my soft skills. They are skills I use every day. They are important for work, school, and home. In a job interview, I can talk about my soft skills. I can give these examples from my life.

Unit 1: I am inclusive.

For example, _____

_____

_____

_____

Unit 2: I separate work life from home life.

For example, _____

_____

_____

_____

Unit 3: I'm a good listener.

For example, _____

_____

_____

_____

Unit 4: I am professional.

For example, _____

_____

_____

_____

Unit 5: I take initiative.

For example, _____

_____

_____

_____

Unit 6: I am dependable.

For example, _____

_____

_____

_____

Unit 7: I show respect for others.

For example, _____

_____

_____

_____

Unit 8: I am honest.

For example, _____

_____

_____

_____

Unit 9: I plan well.

For example, _____

_____

_____

_____

Unit 10: I know when to ask for help.

For example, _____

_____

_____

_____

Unit 11: I follow safety procedures.

For example, _____

_____

_____

_____

Unit 12: I am a team player.

For example, _____

_____

_____

_____

GRAMMAR REVIEW

UNIT 1 GRAMMAR REVIEW

A COMPLETE. Use the correct forms of the words in parentheses.

1. **A:** Excuse me. _____Are you_____ Tony Jones?
   (you / be)

   B: No, I _____. Tony _____ the tall guy over there. He
   (not / be)   (be)

   _____ short, dark hair and a goatee.
   (have)

   A: Oh, I see him. Thanks.

2. **A:** You look familiar. _____ an employee at the county hospital?
   (you / be)

   B: Yes, I _____. I _____ a technician in the radiology
   (be)   (be)

   department.

3. **A:** _____ your manager's name?
   (what / be)

   B: Ted Chen. He _____ a really good supervisor.
   (be)

B IDENTIFY. Cross out the incorrect words.

My name **has / is** Ellen. **I'm / I have**
21 years old. This is my sister, Isabel.
We're twins. As you can see, we
look alike. My hair **is / am** long and
brown, **and / but** my sister's hair is
similar. We both **have / are** brown
eyes. **I'm / I have** not tall, **but / and**
my sister is short.

We are very similar, **and / but** we're
not alike in every way. My sister
is / has talkative, **but / and** I'm quiet.
My sister **has / is** outgoing, **but / and** I'm shy. My sister is always cheerful, **and / but** I am
sometimes moody. Oh, and one more difference: I **am / are** laid-back, **but / and** my sister **is
/ are** bossy. Don't tell my sister I wrote that!

GRAMMAR REVIEW

UNIT 2 GRAMMAR REVIEW

A COMPLETE. Write questions. Use the simple present and the verbs in parentheses.

1. _____*Does*_____ Rohan _____*have*_____ kids? (have)

2. Where _____*does*_____ Ned _____*work*_____? (work)

3. What _____ Ned and Lan _____ in common? (have)

4. _____ Artur _____ a child? (have)

5. Where _____ Aki _____? (live)

6. How many children _____ Lan _____? (have)

7. Where _____ Rohan and Lan _____? (work)

8. _____ Lan and Aya _____ something in common? (have)

9. What _____ Aki, Artur, and Aya _____ in common? (have)

10. _____ Rohan and Ned _____ at the same place? (work)

B EXAMINE. Look at the chart. Answer the questions in Exercise A.

	Ned	Aki	Artur	Rohan	Lan	Aya
work	at a hospital	in a restaurant	in his uncle's store	in an office	in an office	at a hospital
live	at his brother-in-law's house	in an apartment	in an apartment	in a house	at her brother-in-law's house	in an apartment
children	1	2	0	3	2	2

UNIT 3 GRAMMAR REVIEW

A COMPLETE. Use the correct forms of the verbs. Use contractions if possible.

A: I'm going to run _____ some errands this afternoon.

    1. (be going to / run)

B: Oh. What do you need to do?

A: First I _____ at the bank. Then I _____

              2. (need / stop)   3. (be going to / buy)

sweatpants. And you—what are your plans for today?

B: Well, I _____ at the swimming pool.

              4. (be going to / relax)

A: That sounds great. I _____, too. Can I go with you? Maybe I really

                                    5. (want / relax)

_____ any errands today after all!

    6. (not need / run)

B WRITE. Look at the picture. Write the reason for each return.

1. It's too tight.   4. _____

2. _____   5. _____

3. _____   6. _____

GRAMMAR REVIEW

UNIT 4 GRAMMAR REVIEW

A **IDENTIFY.** Cross out the incorrect words.

A: Do you want to come over to watch the game?

B: Sorry, I can't. I ~~have~~ / **have to** go to the supermarket.
My sister is coming over tonight. I **like to / like** cook
a good dinner for her, so I **have to / have** get food.

A: OK. Maybe next week.

B: Sure. You know I love **watch / to watch** the games
on your big-screen TV.

A: Great. Make sure you **don't have / don't have to** run any errands next Saturday!

B **COMPLETE.** Write the sentences with adverbs.

1. I go to work on the weekends.
   (sometimes) <u>I sometimes go to work on the weekends.</u>

2. Dave works on Tuesday and Thursday mornings.
   (usually) _____

3. Ted is late for meetings.
   (always) _____

4. Our supervisor brings coffee and doughnuts on Fridays.
   (often) _____

5. Ralph eats meat or fish.
   (never) _____

6. We are at home during the week.
   (hardly ever) _____

UNIT 5 GRAMMAR REVIEW

A **COMPLETE.** Use the present continuous and the verbs in parentheses.

A: I <u>'m looking for</u> Jon. Is he here today?
1. (look for)

B: Yes, he _____ the light in the lunchroom. It _____, and he
2. (look at) 3. (not work)

_____ to fix it. Bob is in there, too, and they _____ it together.
4. (try) 5. (work on)

That's why May is on the phone right now. She _____ an electrician!
6. (call)

B COMPLETE. Write questions and answers. Use *there is* and *there are*.

1. **A:** _____*Are there*_____ any restaurants nearby?

   B: Yes, _____.

2. **A:** _____ a laundromat nearby?

   B: No, _____.

3. **A:** _____ any stores nearby?

   B: No, _____.

C COMPLETE. Use the words in the box.

Take	Don't use	Don't try	Tell	Call

1. There's no hot water. _____ the building manager.

2. The sink is clogged. _____ to fix it. _____ the landlord.

3. The washer is broken. _____ it. _____ the clothes to the laundromat.

UNIT 6 GRAMMAR REVIEW

A PRACTICE. Read the answers. Write questions about the underlined words.

1. **A:** _Did you work at Global Trading Company?_

   B: <u>Yes</u>, I did. I worked there for two years.

2. **A:** _When did Bo and Fang get married?_

   B: Bo and Fang got married <u>last year</u>.

3. **A:** _____

   B: Victor grew up <u>in Mexico</u>.

4. **A:** _____

   B: We moved <u>because we needed better jobs</u>.

5. **A:** _____

   B: <u>No, we didn't</u>. We didn't know about the software problem.

6. **A:** _____

   B: Todd got that job <u>last year</u>.

GRAMMAR REVIEW

B **COMPLETE. Use the correct past forms of the verbs in parentheses.**

A: _____Why did you decide_____ to become a nurse?
   1. (why / you / decide)

B: My grandmother _____ .
                        2. (come)

to live with us when I was young. When

she _____ older, she
        3. (get)

_____ some health problems.
        4. (have)

My mom and dad both _____ ,
                            5. (work)

and they _____ enough time
              6. (not have)

to do everything. So I _____
                            7. (take)

care of my grandmother for many years, and I _____ it. I
                                                    8. (like)

_____ to help other people, too. So I _____
        9. (want)   **10. (go)**

to nursing school.

A: _____ the right decision?
      11. (you / make)

B: Yes, I _____ . I _____ to love nursing more
            12. (do)   **13. (grow)**

and more.

UNIT 7 GRAMMAR REVIEW

A **COMPLETE. Use the simple past of a verb from the box.**

break	cut	fall	get	~~have~~

1. I _____had_____ a cold for three weeks, but now I feel fine.
2. She _____ down the stairs and hurt her back.
3. He had an accident at work and _____ a bone in his foot.
4. Be careful with that knife. Jim _____ his hand with it yesterday.
5. I went to the doctor's office, and I _____ a prescription.

B DECIDE. Complete the conversations with the words in the boxes.

at	by	for	~~on~~

1. **A:** What are you doing _____ _on_ _____ Wednesday afternoon?
   B: I'm going _____ a checkup.
   A: When is your appointment?
   B: It's _____ 4:30, but I need to go early. They want me to be there _____ 4:15.

at	because	by	from	in	to

2. **A:** I need to see a doctor _____ I think I have an infection.
   B: Can you be here _____ an hour?
   A: I'm sorry, I can't. I work _____ 3:00 _____ 11:00.
   B: How about tomorrow? We have an opening _____ 9:00.
   A: That's fine. Thank you.
   B: OK. Please be here _____ 8:45.

UNIT 8 GRAMMAR REVIEW

A COMPLETE. Use *can* and *can't* and the words in parentheses.

Manager: ___Can you use___ a cash register?
                1. (you / use)

Terry: No, I _____, but _____.
                2.   **3. (I / learn)**

Manager: OK, well, maybe _____ shelves at first.
                          4. (you / stock)

Terry: Sure. _____ that.
              5. (I / do)

Manager: Do you prefer afternoons or evenings?

Terry: _____ in the afternoon or in the evening. I'm flexible.
              6. (I / work)

Manager: _____ on weekends?
              7. (you / work)

Terry: Sure. On the weekend, _____ mornings, afternoons, or evenings.
                            8. (I / work)

Manager: _____ tomorrow?
              9. (you / start)

Terry: Yes, _____.
              10.

GRAMMAR REVIEW

B DECIDE. Write *ago, and, in, last, later,* and *or.*

Ali Osman came to the U.S. _____in_____ 2015. One month _____,

he started school. He got his first job _____ 2016. It was in a hospital, and he

worked nights. Ali didn't like his work schedule. A few weeks _____, his boss

asked, "Ali, do you prefer days _____ nights?" Ali said, "I prefer days." A week

_____, he changed his hours.

Ali continued to go to school. _____ year, he had classes three nights a

week: on Monday, Tuesday, _____ Thursday. This year, he's going to school

_____ the morning. He changed jobs a few weeks _____. He has a

better job at a different hospital. But now he works from 12:00 P.M. to 8:00 P.M., so he can't

go to class in the afternoon _____ the evening.

UNIT 9 GRAMMAR REVIEW

A COMPLETE. Use *will* and the words in parentheses to talk about the future.

MARCH EVENTS
OAK GROVE MIDDLE SCHOOL

Bake Sale

The fourth grade _will have_ a bake sale
1. (have)
on March 6 at 12:30 p.m. in the cafeteria.

Students _____ cookies, cupcakes,
2. (sell)
and other baked goods.

PTO Meeting

The Oak Grove PTO _____
3. (meet)
on March 9. Members _____
4. (discuss)
new school programs for this year.

Please join us!

B APPLY. Write the possessive forms of the nouns. Change the adjectives to adverbs of manner.

1. **A:** How are my (son) _____son's_____ grades in math?
   B: Fine. He's doing very (good) _____well_____.

2. **A:** How were the (children) _____ grades?
   B: Great! They're working (hard) _____ in school.

3. A: I didn't hear the (woman) _____ name.

    B: I think she said, "Mimi." She speaks (quiet) _____.

4. A: I can't read the (student) _____ handwriting.

    B: I know. He writes (sloppy) _____.

C **DECIDE. Cross out the underlined nouns and write object pronouns.**

1. Do you know Mr. Jones? I like ~~Mr. Jones~~ *him* a lot.

2. My daughter Eliza is having a hard time. Can you help <u>Eliza</u>?

3. Brad's homework is hard. He doesn't understand <u>his homework</u>.

4. Asha's schoolbooks are heavy. It's hard for her to carry <u>her schoolbooks</u>.

5. I want to meet my children's teachers. I want to talk to <u>the teachers</u>.

UNIT 10 GRAMMAR REVIEW

A **IDENTIFY. Cross out the incorrect words.**

Cook: Do we have enough **meat / ~~meats~~** for tomorrow?

Assistant: I think so. There's **much / a lot of** meat in the refrigerator. But there isn't **much / many** fish.

Cook: OK. Put it on the list. What about vegetables? Are there **much / any** potatoes?

Assistant: About 100 pounds. But there are only **a little / a few** carrots.

Cook: How **much / many** onions?

Assistant: Onions? There aren't **any / some**.

Cook: OK. Then we need **any / some** carrots and onions. Put **rice / rices** on the list, too.

Assistant: OK. How **much / many** pounds of rice?

Cook: Fifty. And please get **some / any** fruit. I need **much / a lot of** apples for tomorrow's apple pies.

Assistant: I'll put them on the list. We have **some / any**, but only **a little / a few**. I think we need some **sugar / sugars** for the pies, too.

GRAMMAR REVIEW

B **WRITE.** Compare two food products. Make four sentences. Use the comparative forms of adjectives from the box or other adjectives.

delicious	easy to cook	fattening	good for you	sweet	tasty

Apples are better for you than candy bars.

1. _____

2. _____

3. _____

4. _____

UNIT 11 GRAMMAR REVIEW

A **COMPLETE.** Use the correct present continuous form of the verb in parentheses, or the correct form of *there be* in the past.

1. A: Hi, I <u>'m calling</u> because I'm going to be late. I _____ in my car.
              (call)   (sit)

    I'm stuck in a traffic jam. _____ an accident near Lakeland.
                                         (there be)

B: Oh, no! Was anyone hurt?

A: I'm not sure. _____ an ambulance here a few minutes ago.
                       (there be)

B: _____ you _____?
                               (move)

A: Actually, a police officer _____ traffic now. Got to go. I'll see you soon.
                                       (direct)

2. A: Hi, Rita. I hope I _____ at a bad time?
                        (not call)

B: No, I _____ today. The factory is closed. _____ an explosion
          (not work)   (there be)
    yesterday.

A: You're kidding!

B: No, it's true. Luckily, _____ no injuries.
                            (there be)

A: That's amazing. _____ a fire?
                        (there be)

B: Yeah, a big one. _____ ten or twelve fire trucks there.
                        (there be)

A: Wow.

UNIT 12 GRAMMAR REVIEW

A **APPLY. Use *have to, can, can't,* and *could* to complete the conversation. There may be more than one possible answer.**

> **Safety Reminder**
> All employees must wear work boots. No sneakers or sandals allowed!

A: Excuse me. This is my first day. _____ Can _____ I ask you something?

B: Sure. What do you want to know?

A: Well, do we have to wear these uniforms?

B: No, we don't. We _____ wear our own shirts and pants if we want. But we _____ wear work boots. No sneakers or sandals. It's for safety.

A: OK. One more thing. _____ I ask you a favor?

B: What is it?

A: I'm supposed to work Monday, but I _____. You're not on the schedule for Monday. _____ you take my shift?

B: Sure. But ask the supervisor first. We _____ get permission.

B **WRITE. Make information questions. Use the words in parentheses.**

1. **A:** (who) _Who do I give my vacation request form to?_____
   B: Give your vacation request form to your supervisor.

2. **A:** (what time) _____
   B: Kevin can take his break at 12:30.

3. **A:** (where) _____
   B: You store the floor cleaning equipment in the hall closet.

4. **A:** (which days) _____
   B: Tam works on Thursday, Friday, and Saturday this week.

5. **A:** (when) _____
   B: I worked overtime on Thursday and Saturday.

GRAMMAR REFERENCE

UNIT 1, Lesson 3, page 10 and Lesson 9, page 22; UNIT 2, Lesson 3, page 30; UNIT 3, Lesson 6, page 56; UNIT 5, Lesson 3, page 90

Contractions are short forms. Contractions join two words together. In a contraction, an apostrophe (') replaces a letter. Use contractions in speaking and informal writing.

Contractions with *be*

Affirmative

I am	= I'm
you are	= you're
he is	= he's
she is	= she's
it is	= it's
we are	= we're
they are	= they're

Negative

I am not	= I'm not
you are not	= you're not / you aren't
he is not	= he's not / he isn't
she is not	= she's not / she isn't
it is not	= it's not / it isn't
we are not	= we're not / we aren't
they are not	= they're not / they aren't

Negative contractions with *do*

I do not	= I don't
you do not	= you don't
he does not	= he doesn't
she does not	= she doesn't
it does not	= it doesn't
we do not	= we don't
they do not	= they don't

UNIT 5, Lesson 3, page 90

Spelling rules for *-ing* verbs

For most verbs, add *-ing* to the base form of the verb. For example:
work	→	working
do	→	doing

For verbs that end in *e,* drop the *e* and add *-ing.* For example:
change	→	changing
leave	→	leaving
make	→	making

If the base form of a one-syllable verb ends with consonant, vowel, consonant, double the final consonant and add *-ing.* For example:
shop	→	shopping
run	→	running
cut	→	cutting
begin	→	beginning

UNIT 6, Lesson 6, page 116 and UNIT 7, Lesson 6, page 136

Simple past: irregular verbs

Base form	Past-tense form	Base form	Past-tense form	Base form	Past-tense form
be	was/were	get	got	run	ran
begin	began	give	gave	say	said
bleed	bled	go	went	see	saw
break	broke	grow	grew	send	sent
bring	brought	have	had	sing	sang
buy	bought	hurt	hurt	sit	sat
come	came	keep	keep	sleep	slept
cost	cost	know	knew	speak	spoke
cut	cut	leave	left	spend	spent
do	did	lose	lost	swim	swam
drink	drank	make	made	take	took
drive	drove	meet	met	teach	taught
eat	ate	oversleep	overslept	tell	told
fall	fell	pay	paid	think	thought
feel	felt	put	put	understand	understood
find	found	quit	quit	wake up	woke up
forget	forgot	read	read	write	wrote

UNIT 9, Lesson 6, page 176

Spelling rules for adverbs of manner

We can make many adverbs of manner from adjectives.

For most adverbs of manner, add -*ly* to an adjective. For example:

nice	→	nicely
quiet	→	quietly
normal	→	normally

If an adjective ends in *y,* change *y* to *i* and add -*ly.* For example:

happy	→	happily
noisy	→	noisily
angry	→	angrily

UNIT 9, Lesson 9, page 182

Spelling rules for possessive nouns

A possessive noun shows that a person or thing owns something.
Add *'s* to most singular nouns and names. For example:

student	→	student's
girl	→	girl's
Ming	→	Ming's

Add *'s* to singular nouns and names that end in *-s*. For example:

boss	→	boss's
Mr. Jones	→	Mr. Jones's
James	→	James's

Add *'* to plural nouns that end in *-s*. For example:

parents	→	parents'
classmates	→	classmates'
boys	→	boys'

Add *'s* to plural nouns that do not end in *-s*. For example:

children	→	children's
people	→	people's
women	→	women's

UNIT 10, Lesson 3, page 190

Spelling rules for plurals and irregular nouns

Add *-s* to make most nouns plural. For example:

1 student	→	2 students
1 pencil	→	5 pencils
1 house	→	10 houses

Add *-es* to nouns that end with *s, z, x, sh,* or *ch*. For example:

1 sandwich	→	3 sandwiches
1 bus	→	4 buses
1 dish	→	5 dishes

For most nouns that end in *o*, just add *-s*. For example:

1 avocado	→	2 avocados
1 radio	→	2 radios

For some nouns that end in a consonant and *o*, add *-es*. For example:

1 potato	→	2 potatoes
1 tomato	→	8 tomatoes
1 hero	→	4 heroes

When a noun ends in a consonant + *y*, change *y* to *i* and add *-es*. For example:

1 baby	→	3 babies
1 country	→	15 countries
1 berry	→	20 berries

When a noun ends in *f*, change *f* to *v* and add *-es*. When a noun ends in *fe*, change *fe* to *v* and add *-es*. For example:

1 wife	→	2 wives
1 knife	→	9 knives
1 loaf	→	7 loaves

Some nouns have irregular plural forms. For example:

1 foot	→	2 feet
1 tooth	→	10 teeth
1 man	→	5 men
1 woman	→	8 women
1 child	→	7 children
1 person	→	12 people

UNIT 10, Lesson 3, page 190

Non-count nouns

Drinks	Some food		Materials	Subjects	Activities	Other
coffee	beef	meat	corduroy	art	baseball	advice
juice	bread	pasta	cotton	language arts	basketball	equipment
milk	butter	rice	denim	math	exercise	furniture
soda	cheese	salad	fleece	music	hiking	homework
tea	chicken	salt	glass	physical	jogging	information
water	chocolate	soup	leather	education	running	mail
	fish	spinach	metal	science	soccer	money
	fruit	sugar	nylon	social studies	swimming	news
	ice cream	yogurt	silk	technology	tennis	paper
	lettuce		vinyl	world languages		traffic
			wood			weather
			wool			work

UNIT 10, Lesson 6, page 196

Spelling rules for comparatives and irregular comparatives

To make comparative adjectives from one-syllable adjectives, add -er. For example:

cheap ⟶ cheaper
tall ⟶ taller
cold ⟶ colder

If a one-syllable adjective ends in e, add -r. For example:

nice ⟶ nicer
late ⟶ later
large ⟶ larger

If an adjective ends in one vowel and one consonant, double the consonant and add -er. For example:

hot ⟶ hotter
big ⟶ bigger
sad ⟶ sadder
thin ⟶ thinner

For two-syllable adjectives that end with -y, change y to i and add -er. For example:

busy ⟶ busier
pretty ⟶ prettier
easy ⟶ easier

WORD LIST

UNIT 1

active learners, 18
address, 12
applicant, 12
application, 12
attractive, 8
average height, 7
average weight, 7
bald, 7
beard, 7
beautiful, 8
bossy, 14
break room, 16
cafeteria, 17
cheerful, 14
communication, 18
cook, 20
co-worker, 15
curly, 7

customer service
  representative, 16
demanding, 14
department head, 17
discussion, 18
DOB (date of birth), 12
e-mail address, 12
employer, 18
friendly, 15
funny, 15
gender, 12
goatee, 7
good-looking, 8
handsome, 8
heavy, 7
height, 7
hospital,
identification card (ID), 12

inclusive, 24
interesting, 15
interpersonal skills, 18
laid-back, 14
long hair, 7
manager, 22
medical assistant, 21
medium-length hair, 7
mobile phone, 13
moody, 14
mustache, 7
nurse, 20
office, 17
outgoing, 14
participate, 18
personality, 15
physical appearance, 7
practice, 18

quiet, 15
routine, 23
short hair, 7
shy, 14
slim, 7
small-group work, 18
social security, 12
straight hair, 7
supervisor, 14
supportive, 14
talkative, 14
tall, 7
thin, 7
ugly, 8
unattractive, 8
wavy, 7
weight, 7

UNIT 2

accountant, 40
advice, 32
apartment, 28
artist, 40
aunt, 27
balance, 32
bank, 34
book of stamps, 38
brother, 27
business, 36
Certificate of Mailing, 39
Certified Mail, 39
children, 27
Collect on Delivery (COD),
  39
cousin, 27
daughter, 27
Delivery Confirmation, 39
engineer, 40

envelope, 38
expert, 32
Express Mail, 38
family, 26
father, 27
father-in-law, 27
female, 26
fiancé, 27
fiancée, 27
First-Class Mail, 38
game show, 40
grandchildren, 27
granddaughter, 27
grandfather, 27
grandmother, 27
grandson, 27
handle, 32
hair salon, 30
have in common, 34

hazardous material, 39
husband, 27
Insurance, 39
job, 30
keep in touch, 43
letter, 38
mailing service, 38
male, 27
mother, 27
mother-in-law, 27
nephew, 27
niece, 27
package, 38
parents, 27
podcast, 40
pound, 38
prioritize, 32
Priority Mail, 38
Registered Mail, 39

relationship, 26
responsibility, 33
Retail Ground, 38
security guard, 41
sister, 27
sister-in-law, 27
son, 27
standard-sized, 38
take care of, 33
technician, 41
text, 43
tracking receipt, 38
uncle, 27
waiter, 44
wife, 27
work, 32
work/life balance, 32

UNIT 3

ad, 52
ATM, 54
bakery, 55
bank, 54
big, 58
bill, 58
blouse, 62
bookstore, 57
boots, 47
broken, 60
button, 60
buy, 48
cash, 58
change, 53
cheap, 62
cap, 47
check, 56
clearance sale, 48
clothing, 47
clothing store, 48
coat, 47

coffee shop, 62
cost, 58
credit card, 58
deli, 55
discount, 52
dress, 47
drugstore, 55
electronics, 64
errand, 55
exchange, 51
gas station, 55
gloves, 47
grocery store, 55
hardware store, 54
hat, 47
helmet, 47
high heels, 47
hole, 60
interest, 58
jacket, 47
jeans, 47

laptop, 64
laundromat, 54
library, 57
long, 61
loose, 60
mail room, 56
meeting, 56
minimum, 58
mistake, 53
missing, 60
online order, 52
on-the-job training, 56
order, 62
pair of pants, 48
payment, 58
post office, 55
purchase, 58
raincoat, 47
receipt, 48
rent-to-own, 58
return (a purchase), 48

return policy, 53
ripped, 60
sale, 52
sales receipt, 53
sales tax, 53
salesperson, 64
save (money), 63
scarf, 47
schedule, 56
seam, 60
shirt, 47
shoes, 62
shoppers, 48
shorts, 49
sneakers, 47
suit, 47
supermarket, 54
sweater, 47
sweat pants, 47
sweatshirt, 47
swimsuit, 53

swimwear, 53
tax, 52
team leader, 56

tie, 47
tight, 60
umbrella, 47

uniform, 47
windbreaker, 47
zipper, 60

UNIT 4

abbreviations, 78
adult, 72
auto mechanics class, 68
be busy, 80
business class, 68
calendar, 72
clean the office, 75
computer, 70
computer class, 70
computer programming, 70
cook, 74
digital, 72
do the dishes, 75
do laundry, 74
don't feel well, 80
email, 79
emoji, 78
employee, 76
exercise, 71
free-time, 67

get some coffee, 81
get up early, 75
go dancing, 67
go fishing, 67
go hiking, 67
go jogging, 71
go for a bike ride, 67
go for a walk, 67
go out to eat, 67
go running, 67
go shopping, 67
go swimming, 67
go to a meeting, 81
go to the beach, 67
go to the gym, 67
go to the movies, 70
go to the park, 67
go to the zoo, 67
guitar class, 68
hate, 76

have other plans, 80
indoor, 67
interview, 72
invitation, 80
invite, 81
iron, 74
lecture, 72
like, 76
love, 76
lunch, 81
make some calls, 81
message, 78
office, 75
outdoor, 67
polite, 79
professional, 84
punctuation, 78
read, 77
relaxing, 83
résumé, 72

run a business, 68
run some errands, 81
sales, 72
schedule, 73
shift, 76
sick, 76
spend time with family, 77
style, 79
take a walk, 81
take a break, 74
take the bus, 70
use a computer, 77
vacuum, 74
watch TV, 77
website, 72
weekend, 68
work outside, 75

UNIT 5

account, 93
ad, 92
air-conditioning, 92
balcony, 95
basement, 97
bathroom, 92
broken, 87
building manager, 88
bus stop, 95
ceiling, 87
charge, 93
cleaner, 104
clogged, 87
closet, 95
date of service, 93
dining room, 92
dishwasher, 90
door, 87
dryer, 92
eat-in kitchen, 92

electrician, 88
elevator, 96
faucet, 87
fee, 92
fix, 88
floor, 104
furnished, 97
give directions, 101
go straight, 100
go through (a light), 100
heat, 87
homeowner, 98
hot water, 87
investment, 98
kitchen, 95
laundry room, 94
laundromat, 95
leaking, 87
living room, 92
lock, 87

locksmith, 88
mailbox, 87
microwave, 95
own, 98
owner-occupied, 99
(not) working, 87
neighborhood, 96
paint, 90
parking, 97
parking lot, 95
pet, 92
plumber, 88
problem, 86
radiator, 88
rent, 92
rental agent, 94
rental apartment, 92
renter, 98
security deposit, 92
sell, 98

sink, 87
stove, 87
stuck, 87
subway stop, 95
supermarket, 95
take initiative, 104
toilet, 87
traffic, 99
transportation, 92
turn left , 100
turn right, 100
utilities, 92
utility bill, 93
vacuum cleaner, 104
value, 98
voice message, 104
washer, 92
washing machine, 87
window, 87

UNIT 6

anniversary party, 107
Barack Obama, 118
barbecue, 107
be born, 114
be late for work, 124
biography, 123
birthday party, 107
car keys, 121
celebrate, 113
Christmas Day, 112
college, 114
Columbus Day, 112
community, 118
dance all night, 108

dependable, 124
exhausted, 121
family reunion, 107
forget (your lunch), 120
funeral, 107
get a job, 114
get married, 114
get stuck in traffic, 120
gift, 107
government, 118
graduate from
school, 114
graduation, 107
grow up, 114

have car trouble, 120
have children, 114
health insurance, 119
holiday party, 107
holidays, 112
Independence Day, 112
Labor Day, 112
listen to family
stories, 108
look at old photos, 108
lose (your keys), 120
Martin Luther King Jr.
Day, 112
Memorial Day, 112

milestone, 114
miss (the bus), 121
national holiday, 113
New Year's Day, 112
oversleep, 120
parade, 112
politics, 119
president, 119
Presidents' Day, 112
register, 118
retirement party, 107
scan, 118
set an alarm, 124
stay up late, 108

surprise party, 107
take the wrong train, 120
Thanksgiving Day, 112

time line, 119
to-do list, 111
unhappy, 121

upset, 121
U.S. Holidays, 112
Veterans' Day, 112

vote, 118
wedding, 107

UNIT 7

accident, 134
appointment, 128
back, 135
break your arm, 134
break your tooth, 141
burn your hand, 134
call in sick/late, 144
caplets. 132
checkup, 140
chest pains, 126
clinic, 130
cold, 126
cold medicine, 142
cough, 126
cut your finger, 134
dentist, 130
dizzy, 128

dosage, 132
drug store, 132
earache, 126
emergency, 140
emergency room, 127
expiration date, 132
eye drops, 132
fall, 134
feel better, 140
fever, 126
flu, 126
flu shot, 140
get well soon, 141
good luck, 141
have a checkup, 140
have a cold, 132
headache, 126

health problem, 126
heartburn, 126
high blood pressure, 126
hospital, 140
hurt your head, 134
injury, 134
itchy, 128
loss of control, 138
manage stress, 138
medical assistant, 128
medicine, 132
medicine label, 132
miss work, 140
nauseous, 128
over-the-counter (OTC), 132
pharmacist, 133
pharmacy, 133

prescription, 133
rash, 126
refill, 133
respect, 144
shot, 140
sick, 129
sore throat, 126
sprain your ankle, 134
stress, 138
swollen, 128
symptom, 128
tablespoon, 133
take care of someone, 141
upset stomach, 126
wrist, 135

UNIT 8

agriculture, 158
assist customers, 147
availability, 160
candidate, 153
car service driver, 152
clean equipment, 149
computer application
   software, 152
cover letter, 152
computer system
   administrator, 147
customer experience, 149
employment, 159
experience, 152
flexible, 160
food service worker, 147
full-time, 152
gardener, 154
give notice at work, 160

greet visitors, 147
handle phone calls, 147
health benefits, 152
health care, 158
health insurance, 152
help wanted ad, 152
install computer
   systems, 147
job application, 151
job duties, 149
job history, 163
job interview, 148
job market, 159
job requirements, 152
job title, 146
manager, 147
manufacturing, 158
nursing assistant, 147
office assistant, 152

operate a forklift , 148
order supplies, 148
organize files,152
part-time, 152
plan work schedules, 147
prepare food, 147
problem solve, 147
receive shipments, 147
receptionist, 147
record patient
   information, 147
receptionist, 147
references, 152
résumé, 152
salesperson, 148
sales associate, 161
shift, 160
software, 159
software developer, 158

sort materials, 151
speak Spanish, 148
stock clerk, 147
stock shelves, 147
store manager, 147
supervise employees, 147
take care of patients, 147
technology, 158
truck driver, 155
unemployed, 154
unload materials, 147
use a cash register, 148
use a computer, 149
warehouse worker, 147
work as a team, 148
work history, 154

UNIT 9

art, 167
Associate's Degree, 178
Bachelor Degree, 178
be disrespectful, 180
behavior, 180
bully, 180
Certificate, 178
college, 178
college degree, 178
community college, 178
community service, 167
degree, 179
Doctor of Philosophy
   (Ph.D), 178
elementary school, 172

English language arts, 167
financial aid, 178
fool around, 180
for-profit, 178
get along with others, 180
get extra help, 174
grant, 178
guidance counselor, 182
high school, 178
loan, 179
Master's Degree, 178
math, 167
music, 167
non-profit, 178
notice from school, 168

parent-teacher
   conference, 168
P.E. (physical
   education), 167
phone message, 172
plan well, 184
principal, 171
private, 178
PTO (parent-teacher
   organization), 168
public, 178
report card, 182
scholarship, 179
school events, 169
school nurse, 182

school play, 169
school subject, 166
science, 167
science fair, 169
skip class, 180
social studies/history, 167
technology, 167
tuition, 178
university, 178
voicemail, 172
world languages, 167

UNIT 10

apple juice, 200
bag, 187
beans, 189
bottle, 187
bottled water, 200
box, 187
bunch, 187
caffeine, 198
calories, 193
can, 187
carbohydrates, 192
cereal, 189
cholesterol, 192
coffee, 195
cola, 198
coleslaw, 200
commercial, 194
consume, 198
container, 187
convenience, 194
convenience store, 188

cucumber, 189
delicious, 196
dozen, 187
effect, 198
fat, 193
fattening, 197
fiber, 192
fish, 190
fish sandwich, 200
food labels, 192
French fries, 200
fresh, 197
gallon, 187
gram (g), 193
grocery store, 189
half-gallon, 187
hamburger, 200
head, 187
headache medicine, 198
healthy diet, 192
ice cream, 195

iced tea, 200
ingredient label, 192
jar, 187
lemon/lime soda, 198
low-fat, 195
macaroni and cheese, 200
mashed potatoes, 200
meatloaf, 200
menu, 200
milligram (mg), 193
mixed vegetables, 200
non-fat milk, 193
noodles, 200
nutrients, 192
nutrition label, 192
nutritious, 197
onion rings, 200
orange, 189
orange juice, 195
outdoor market, 188
picnic, 191

pint, 187
pork chop, 200
pound, 187
price, 194
protein, 192
quantity, 187
quart, 187
roast chicken, 200
salty, 196
serving, 193
shopping list, 191
soda, 200
sodium, 192
soup, 189
sugar, 192
supermarket, 188
taste, 194
tea, 198
tuna, 189
yogurt, 189

UNIT 11

allergic reaction, 207
ambulance, 208
bleed, 207
burn yourself, 207
call 911, 207
car accident, 214
choke, 207
construction accident, 214
distracted driving, 220
driver's license, 220
electric, 209
electrical cord, 212
electrical outlet, 212
electrical plug, 212
emergency, 206

employer, 219
escape plan, 212
exit, 212
explosion, 214
fall, 207
fall down, 207
fire escape, 212
fire extinguisher, 212
fire hazard, 212
have trouble
  breathing, 207
heart attack, 207
heater, 212
hurt, 215
injury, 215

inspector, 219
matches, 212
medical emergency, 207
OSHA (Occupational
  Safety and Health
  Administration, 218
police, 217
proof of insurance, 220
pull over, 220
registration, 220
report an accident, 220
robbery, 214
rug, 212
run a red light, 220
safety gear, 218

safety hazard, 218
safety procedure, 212
safety tip, 213
seat belt, 221
smoke alarm, 212
speed, 220
steering wheel, 220
swallow poison, 207
tailgate, 220
taxi, 208
toxic chemicals, 218
traffic jam, 217
traffic ticket, 220
unconscious, 207

UNIT 12

ask for a favor, 234
ask questions, 227
be a team player, 244
be on time, 226
call in late, 227
clock in/out, 227
cover someone's
  hours, 234
disabled, 238
earnings, 238
eat at my desk, 229
eat in the break room, 229
employee I.D. badge, 228
Federal tax, 233

first shift, 241
follow directions, 227
full-time, 241
gross pay, 232
health and safety rules, 243
latex gloves, 227
maintain equipment, 227
manager, 228
Medicare, 232
miss work, 234
net pay, 232
orientation meeting, 228
overtime hours, 233
part-time, 241

payroll deductions, 232
pay period, 232
pay stub, 232
rate of pay, 232
regular hour, 232
report a problem, 227
retired, 238
second shift, 241
sick-day policy, 228
Social Security, 232
Social Security benefits, 238
State Disability Insurance
  (SDI), 232
state tax, 232

store equipment, 227
talk to a manager, 229
uniform, 227
vacation-time policy, 228
wear a uniform, 227
wear safety gear, 227
work as a team, 227

AUDIO SCRIPT

UNIT 1

Page 8, Exercises 2A and 2B

Min: Hi, Eva.
Eva: Hi, Min. Are you coming to my party tonight?
Min: Of course. Are you inviting your friend?
Eva: Which friend?
Min: You know—he's handsome and he has short, black hair.

Page 8, Exercise 2C

Min: Hi, Eva.
Eva: Hi, Min. Are you coming to my party tonight?
Min: Of course. Are you inviting your friend?
Eva: Which friend?
Min: You know—he's handsome and he has short, black hair.
Eva: Does he have blue eyes?
Min: No, he has brown eyes.
Eva: Oh. You mean Victor. And he's not my friend. He's my brother! But of course I'll introduce you to him.

Page 14, Exercises 2A and 2B

Erica: Kay, tell me about your new supervisor. What's she like?
Kay: Well, she's outgoing and she's cheerful.
Erica: Yeah? What else?
Kay: She's demanding, but she's supportive too.

Page 14, Exercise 2C

Erica: Kay, tell me about your new supervisor. What's she like?
Kay: Well, she's outgoing and she's cheerful.
Erica: Yeah? What else?
Kay: She's demanding, but she's supportive, too.
Erica: That sounds good.
Kay: Yes, it is. And you know, I'm quiet. But she's talkative.
Erica: That's not a problem. You don't have to talk at all.

Page 20, Exercises 2B and 2C

Kara: Pia, I want to introduce you to my friend. Pia, this is Ron. Ron, this is Pia.
Pia: Nice to meet you, Ron.
Ron: Nice to meet you, too.
Pia: So, are you a nurse, like Kara?
Ron: No, I'm not. I work at the hospital, but I'm a cook in the cafeteria.

Page 20, Listen, Exercise 2D

Kara: Pia, I want to introduce you to my friend. Pia, this is Ron. Ron, this is Pia.
Pia: Nice to meet you, Ron.
Ron: Nice to meet you, too.
Pia: So, are you a nurse, like Kara?
Ron: No, I'm not. I work at the hospital, but I'm a cook in the cafeteria. How about you?
Pia: I work with Kara at the hospital, but I'm not a nurse. I'm a medical assistant.
Ron: Oh, how is it?
Pia: Good. I like it!

UNIT 2

Page 28, Exercises 2B and 2C

Amy: Tell me about your family.
Sam: Well, I don't have a very big family. I have a brother and two sisters.
Amy: Do they live here?
Sam: My sisters live in Senegal, but my brother lives here.

Page 28, Listen, Exercise 2D

Amy: Tell me about your family.
Sam: Well, I don't have a very big family. I have a brother and two sisters.
Amy: Do they live here?
Sam: My sisters live in Senegal, but my brother lives here.
Amy: Really? What does your brother do?
Sam: He works in a hospital. He's a medical assistant.
Amy: And does he live near you?
Sam: Yes. In fact, we live in the same apartment.
Amy: Wow, then he really lives near you!

Page 34, Exercises 2B and 2C

Ming: Tina, is this your sister?
Tina: Yes, it is. That's my sister, Lili. Do we look alike?
Ming: Yes, you do. You look a lot alike. Do you have a lot in common?
Tina: Actually, we do. She works in a bank, and I work in a bank, too.
She's really talkative and I'm really talkative.

Page 34, Exercise 2D

Ming: Tina, is that your sister?
Tina: Yes, it is. That's my sister, Lili. Do we look alike?
Ming: Yes, you do. You look a lot alike. Do you have a lot in common?
Tina: Actually, we do. She works in a bank, and I work in a bank, too.
She's really talkative and I'm really talkative. But what about you, Ming? Do you have any brothers or sisters?
Ming: I have two sisters. And we have a lot in common, too.
Tina: Really?
Ming: Yeah. I have two sisters and my sisters have two sisters.
But I don't have any brothers and . . .
Tina: (chuckling) I know . . . and your sisters don't have any brothers! You do have a lot in common! (laughing)

Page 39, Exercise D

Customer: Hello. I'd like to mail this package.
Clerk: How do you want to send it?
Customer: How long does Retail Ground take?
Clerk: Two to eight days.
Customer: Okay. I'll send it Priority Mail.
Clerk: Do you want Delivery Confirmation or Insurance?
Customer: Yes. Insurance, please.
Clerk: Does it contain any hazardous materials?
Customer: No.

266 Audio Script

Page 40, Exercises 2B and 2C

Oliver: Hello, I'm Oliver Marley, and welcome to They're Your Family Now!—the game show where we ask people questions about their in-laws. Please welcome our first contestant, Mr. Trevor Scanlon.

Trevor: Hello.

Oliver: Now, Trevor, here are the rules of the game. Before the show, we asked your wife Ann ten questions about her family. Now, I'm going to ask you the same questions. You get $100 for every question you answer correctly.

Trevor: OK! I'm ready.

Page 40, Exercise 2D

Oliver: Hello, I'm Oliver Marley, and welcome to They're Your Family Now!, the game show where we ask people questions about their in-laws. Please welcome our first contestant, Mr. Trevor Scanlon.

Trevor: Hello.

Oliver: Now, Trevor. Here are the rules of the game. Before the show, we asked your wife Ann ten questions about her family. Now I'm going to ask you the same questions. You get $100 for every question you answer correctly.

Trevor: OK! I'm ready.

Oliver: Great. Trevor, here's your first question. Where do your wife's grandparents live?

Trevor: Oh! That's easy. They live in San Antonio with the rest of her family.

Oliver: Right! Good start. OK. Here's your next question. How many brothers and sisters does your mother-in-law have?

Trevor: My mother-in-law?! . . . Well, there's Martha, Paula, Henry, Charles, . . . and what's his name? . . . Paul! OK. My mother-in-law has two sisters and three brothers. So that's five in total.

Oliver: That's right! Good job. Next question. What does your brother-in-law Alex do?

Trevor: Oh, wow . . . I know he works in an office . . . Um, he's an engineer?

Oliver: No, he's an accountant!

Trevor: Oh!

Oliver: Better luck on the next one. Here it is . . . When does your sister-in-law Ella work?

Trevor: Oh, I know this one! Ella works at night because her husband works during the day. She watches the baby all day, and he watches him at night!

Oliver: Correct! Well, so far you have three points. We have to take a break, but we'll be right back with They're Your Family Now!

UNIT 3

Page 48, Exercise 2B

Lucy: Hi, this is Lucy Campbell for Eye Around Town, the podcast that tells you what's happening in town. So what's happening today? I'm here at the summer clearance at Big Deals, and the store is full of shoppers. Let's talk to a few of them . . . Excuse me. What's your name?

Erica: Erica.

Lucy: Hi, Erica. Tell us, why are you here at Big Deals today?

Page 48, Exercises 2C and 2D

Lucy: Hi, this is Lucy Campbell for Eye Around Town, the podcast that tells you what's happening in town. So what's happening today? I'm here at the summer clearance at Big Deals, and the store is full of shoppers. Let's talk to a few of them . . . Excuse me. What's your name?

Erica: Erica.

Lucy: Hi, Erica. Tell us, why are you here at Big Deals today?

Erica: Well, I shop here a lot. They have great prices on everything you need.

Lucy: And what do you need to buy today?

Erica: Well, I don't need to buy anything, but I want to buy a new pair of pants for work.

Lucy: Well, I hope you find some, Erica. Next . . . tell us your name, please.

Karen: Karen.

Lucy: Karen, why are you here today?

Karen: I'm here with my daughter. We don't need to buy anything today. We just need to return this dress. It's really easy to return things here if you have your receipt . . . Where is that receipt? I know it's here somewhere . . .

Lucy: Uh . . . OK. And you, sir. Who are you, and why are you here at Big Deals today?

Nick: My name's Nick. I need to buy some shorts for my son.

Lucy: Do you always shop here at Big Deals?

Nick: Yeah. It's so convenient. They have everything here, so I don't need to go to a lot of different stores. I really don't like to shop.

Lucy: OK, well, that's all for today, and I want to look for a jacket while I'm here! I'm Lucy Campbell, and this is the Eye Around Town podcast.

Page 50, Exercise B

1. **A:** I want to buy a few things after work today. Do you want to go to Shop Mart with me?
   B: Sure. I need to return a cap there.
   A: OK. What time do you want to leave here?
2. **A:** Do you want to go shopping during lunch today?
   B: Maybe. I need to get a present for my co-worker. But I don't want to spend a lot of money. I need to check the sales online.
   A: I understand. I need to be careful with my money, too.
3. **A:** All my uniforms for work are old. I need to buy some new ones.
   B: Oh, really? I don't need to wear a uniform to work—regular clothes like jeans are OK.

Page 54, 2A and 2B

Deb: So, what are your plans for tomorrow?

Max: Nothing. I'm going to relax.

Deb: Well, I have a lot to do. First, I need to go to the ATM. Then I need to go to the hardware store. Then I'm going to stop at the deli at the supermarket.

Max: Wow. You're going to be busy.

Page 54, Exercise 2C

Deb: So, what are your plans for tomorrow?

Max: Nothing. I'm going to relax.

Deb: Well, I have a lot to do. First, I need to go to the ATM. Then I need to go to the hardware store. Then I'm going to stop at the deli at the supermarket.

Max: Wow. You're going to be busy.

Deb: I know, And then I'm going to go to the drug store. And after that . . . hey . . . where are you going?

Max: [laughter as if he's joking] I'm going to take a nap. I'm tired just thinking about your errands tomorrow.

Page 60, Exercises 2B and 2C

Anna: Hi, Bessy. Are you going out at lunchtime?

Bessy: Yeah, I need to run an errand. I'm going to Kohn's. I need to return this jacket.

Anna: How come?

Bessy: The zipper is broken.

Anna: That's very annoying. . . . Actually, I need to go to Kohn's, too. I need to return a dress.

Page 60, Exercise 2D

Anna: Hi, Bessy. Are you going out at lunchtime?

Bessy: Yeah, I need to run an errand. I'm going to Kohn's. I need to return this jacket.

Anna: How come?

Bessy: The zipper is broken.

Anna: That's very annoying. . . . Actually, I need to go to Kohn's, too. I need to return a dress.

Bessy: Really? What's wrong with it?

Anna: It's too short. Here. . . . Look at it.

Bessy: Oh, no! Of course this is too short. It's a shirt, not a dress!

UNIT 4

Page 68, Exercises 2A and 2B

Mario: What are you doing this weekend?

Bi-Yun: I'm going to go to the beach with my family.

Mario: Really? Sounds like fun.

Bi-Yun: Yeah. We usually go to the beach on Sunday in the summer. What about you?

Mario: Well, I have class on Saturday. I have a business class every Saturday morning.

Page 68, Exercise 2C

Mario: What are you doing this weekend?

Bi-Yun: I'm going to go to the beach with my family.

Mario: Really? Sounds like fun.

Bi-Yun: Yeah. We usually go to the beach on Sunday in the summer. What about you?

Mario: Well, I have class on Saturday. I have a business class every Saturday morning.

Bi-Yun: You have a business? Wow. That's really neat.

Mario: No, I don't have a business . . .

Bi-Yun: But you're taking a business class, right?

Mario: Yeah. But I don't know how to run a business. That's why I'm taking a class!

Page 72, Exercise 1A

The City Library has several regular events.
The ESL Class for adults meets every Monday and Wednesday from 6 p.m. to 8 p.m.

There is a Job Fair on the fourth Saturday of the month from 9:00 am to 4:00 pm.

The special lecture is once a month, on the second Saturday of the month,

every Monday and Wednesday

from 6 p.m. to 8 p.m.

on the fourth Saturday of the month from 9:00 a.m. to 4:00 p.m.

once a month

on the second Saturday of the month

Page 73, Exercises 2A and 2B

Thank you for calling Atlas Community College's Library. Today is Monday, May 14th, and we are open from 8:00 a.m. to 9 p.m. Today's events:

The computer lab is open from 8:00 a.m. to 8:00 p.m. There is a special résumé writing workshop today. It meets in room 224 at 1:00 pm. There are two ESL Conversation Classes. The morning class meets from 9-11 am, and the evening class meets from 6:30 to 8:30 pm. The Job Interview Workshop series begins today. It meets from 4 to 6 pm.

Tomorrow, Tuesday, May 15th, the library is open from 8:00 am to 9 pm.

The computer lab is open from 8:00 am to 1:00 pm. Computer Skills for Adults meets from 1:00 to 3:00 pm. There is a special workshop on completing a Job Application. It meets at 5 pm.

Page 74, Exercise 2B

Katie: Welcome to the Talk Time podcast. I'm your host, Katie Martin. We all have things that we need to do, at home and at work. And here's the problem: A lot of times we don't like the things we need to do. So, what's the solution? Well, today we're talking to Dr. Collin Goldberg, and he has some ideas. Welcome to the podcast, Dr. Goldberg.

Page 74, Exercise 2C and 2D

Katie: Welcome to the Talk Time podcast. I'm your host, Katie Martin. We all have things that we need to do, at home and at work. And here's the problem: A lot of times we don't like the things we need to do. So, what's the solution? Well, today we're talking to Dr. Collin Goldberg, and he has some ideas. Welcome to the podcast, Dr. Goldberg.

Dr. Goldberg: Thanks, Katie. It's great to be here.

Katie: So, Dr. Goldberg, tell us about some of your ideas.

Dr. Goldberg: Sure. Here's the first one: When you need to do something you hate, do something you like at the same time. For example, if you hate to wash dishes, then do something you love while you wash the dishes. Wash the dishes and watch TV. Or wash the dishes and listen to a podcast. Or talk to a friend on the phone.

Katie: That way you're not thinking about the activity that you don't like.

Dr. Goldberg: Exactly.

Katie: That seems pretty easy. Do you have any other tips?

Dr. Goldberg: Sure. Here's another idea: Put a time limit on the activities you hate to do.

Katie: A time limit?

Dr. Goldberg: Exactly. For example, say it's 1:00 and you need to clean up. Decide what time you're going to finish cleaning, say 3:00. When it's 3:00, you stop.

Katie: That's it?

Dr. Goldberg: Yes. It's an extremely simple idea, but it works. When you have a time limit, you know when the activity is going to end. And that can help a lot.

Katie: That makes sense.

Dr. Goldberg: Right. And here's one more: After you do something you hate, do something you like. For example, if you hate to answer email, but you love to read, then say to yourself, "I'm going to answer email. Then I'm going to take a break and read for half an hour."

Katie: Dr. Goldberg, these sound like really good ideas.

Page 80, Exercise 2B and 2C

Meg: Do you want to get some lunch?

Selda: Sorry, I can't. I have to finish some work.

Meg: Oh. Are you sure?

Selda: Yes, I'm sorry. I'm really too busy.

Meg: Well, how about a little later?

Selda: Thanks, but I don't think so. Not today.

Page 80, Exercise 2D

Meg: Do you want to get some lunch?

Selda: Sorry, I can't. I have to finish some work.

Meg: Oh. Are you sure?

Selda: Yes, I'm sorry. I'm really too busy.

Meg: Well, how about a little later?

Selda: Thanks, but I don't think so. Not today. I have a big meeting this afternoon. Hold on a second. Hello? Oh, hi, Bob. OK. Great. Thanks for calling. Guess what? My meeting was canceled.

Meg: That's great! So now you can go to lunch?

Selda: Yes, I guess I can. Let me get my coat.

UNIT 5

Page 88, Exercises 2B and 2C

Harry: Hello?

Joe: Hi, Harry. It's Joe.

Harry: Oh, hi, Joe. Can I call you back?

Joe: Sure. No problem.

Harry: Thanks. My radiator is broken and I'm trying to fix it.

Joe: You should call the building manager for your apartment.

Page 88, Exercise 2D

Harry: Hello?

Joe: Hi, Harry. It's Joe.

Harry: Oh, hi, Joe. Can I call you back?

Joe: Sure. No problem.

Harry: Thanks. My radiator is broken and I'm trying to fix it.

Joe: You should call the building manager for your apartment.

Harry: That's a good idea. There's just one problem.

Joe: What's that?

Harry: Well, I just got a new job. Now I'm the building manager

Page 94, Exercises 2B and 2C

Rental agent: Hello?

Maria: Hi, I'm calling about the apartment for rent. Can you tell me about it?

Rental agent: Sure. There are two bedrooms and a large living room.

Maria: Is there a laundry room?

Rental agent: No, there isn't. But there's a laundromat down the street.

Maria: I see. Is there a bus stop nearby?

Rental agent: Yes, there is — just around the corner.

Page 94, Exercise 2D

Rental agent: Hello?

Maria: Hi, I'm calling about the apartment for rent. Can you tell me about it?

Rental agent: Sure. There are two bedrooms and a large living room.

Maria: Is there a laundry room?

Rental agent: No, there isn't. But there's a laundromat down the street.

Maria: I see. Is there a bus stop nearby?

Rental agent: Yes, there is — just around the corner.

Maria: Wow! And the ad says it's only $200 a month!

Rental agent: Yes, sorry. That was a mistake. The rent is $2,000 a month, not $200.

Maria: Oh, well, thanks. I guess I don't need any more information. I'm looking for something under $500 a month.

Page 100, Exercises 2B and 2C

Go straight on Warton Avenue for two blocks. Turn left onto Brice Road. Go straight for two blocks. Turn right onto Clarkson Street. Go through one traffic light.

Page 100, Exercise 2D

Go straight on Warton Avenue for two blocks. Turn left onto Brice Road. Go straight for two blocks. Turn right onto Clarkson Street. Go through one traffic light. Your destination is on the left.

Page 101, Exercise 2B

1. there
2. this
3. things
4. theater
5. the
6. third

UNIT 6

Page 108, Exercises 2B and 2C

Rose: How was your weekend? How was the family reunion?

Sam: It was really nice, thanks. My whole family showed up.

Rose: Sounds great.

Sam: Yeah, it was fun. We looked at old pictures and listened to family stories.

Page 108, Exercise 2D

Rose: How was your weekend? How was the family reunion?

Sam: It was really nice, thanks. My whole family showed up.

Rose: Sounds great.

Sam: Yeah, it was fun. We looked at old pictures and listened to family stories. How about you?

Rose: My weekend was pretty good. I had a surprise party on Saturday night.

Sam: Really? Was it someone's birthday?

Rose: No, it wasn't a birthday. I just invited some co-workers from my last job to come over. Then some other friends came over, and—surprise! It was a party!

Page 112, Exercise 1B

1. New Year's Day
2. Martin Luther King, Jr. Day
3. Presidents' Day
4. Memorial Day
5. Independence Day
6. Labor Day
7. Columbus Day
8. Veterans' Day
9. Thanksgiving Day
10. Christmas Day

Page 112, Exercise 1C

Welcome to our company. One of the many benefits we provide for our employees are days off on national holidays. You may not be familiar with the holidays we celebrate in the U.S., so I'll go over them quickly.

1 First of all, we have a free day to start off a year and get a good rest after parties the night before.

2 In May, there is a holiday that celebrates people who have died fighting for our country. It always falls on a Monday, so you get a longer weekend.

3 In the middle of summer, we like to stop and celebrate this country's birthday. You have the day off to go to your favorite parade, have a barbeque, and watch fireworks.

4 In September, there's a holiday to thank all working people. It usually falls on the first Monday of the month. This national holiday recognizes how hard everyone works.

5 There is also a holiday on the 4th Thursday of November. We even give our employees coupons so that they can buy their turkeys cheaper in a nearby store!

Page 114, Exercises 2B and 2C

Amber: Welcome to Star Talk, the podcast where we talk to today's biggest stars. I'm your host Amber Jenkins, and today I'm very excited to welcome actor Daniel Campos!

Daniel: Thanks. It's great to be here.

Amber: So, Daniel, tell us about yourself and your celebrity life.

Daniel: Uh—sure. But my life really isn't that interesting.

Amber: Your life? Not interesting? I don't believe it. I mean, you're a huge star. Now, let's start with your childhood. You were born in California?

Daniel: Yes, I was born in California, and that's where I grew up. I had a pretty normal childhood.

Amber: What about school?

Daniel: Uh, yeah. I went to school. I graduated from high school and went to college.

Amber: And you always wanted to be an actor?

Daniel: No, I didn't. Actually, I wanted to be a plumber when I was a kid. My dad was a plumber, and I wanted to be just like him. I started acting in college.

Page 114, Exercise 2D

Amber: Welcome to Star Talk, the podcast where we talk to today's biggest stars. I'm your host Amber Jenkins, and today I'm very excited to welcome actor Daniel Campos!

Daniel: Thanks. It's great to be here.

Amber: So, Daniel, tell us about yourself and your celebrity life.

Daniel: Uh—sure. But my life really isn't that interesting.

Amber: Your life? Not interesting? I don't believe it. I mean, you're a huge star. Now, let's start with your childhood. You were born in California?

Daniel: Yes, I was born in California, and that's where I grew up. I had a pretty normal childhood.

Amber: What about school?

Daniel: Uh, yeah. I went to school. I graduated from high school and went to college.

Amber: And you always wanted to be an actor?

Daniel: No, I didn't. Actually, I wanted to be a plumber when I was a kid. My dad was a plumber, and I wanted to be just like him. I started acting in college.

Amber: OK, so you had a normal childhood. You went to school. But now your life is very different, right? You probably do lots of interesting things.

Daniel: Uh, not really.

Amber: Oh, come on, tell us. What did you do last night? I'll bet you went to a big, fancy party.

Daniel: No, actually I stayed home. I watched some TV and went to bed early.

Amber: Went to bed early? That's not glamorous at all!

Daniel: I know, I'm telling you, I don't have a very glamorous life. I'm really just a regular guy.

Amber: Well, there you go, listeners—Daniel Campos is just a regular guy. . . .

Page 120 and 121, Exercises 2B and 2C

Maria: Is everything OK? You look stressed out.

Adam: Well, I had a rough morning.

Maria: Why? What happened?

Adam: First, I lost my car keys.

Maria: Oh, no!

Adam: Then I got stuck in traffic.

Maria: When did you get to work?

Adam: At 10:00. I was really late.

Page 121, Exercise 2D

Maria: Is everything OK? You look stressed out.

Adam: Well, I had a rough morning.

Maria: Why? What happened?

Adam: First, I lost my car keys.

Maria: Oh, no!

Adam: Then I got stuck in traffic.

Maria: When did you get to work?

Adam: At 10:00. I was really late.

Maria: That's too bad.

Adam: Wait—it gets worse.

Maria: Really? What happened?

Adam: When I finally got to work, I realized it was Tuesday.

Maria: So?

Adam: So, I don't work on Tuesdays! Tuesday is my day off!

UNIT 7

Page 127, Exercise C

1. I have a cold.
2. I have an earache.
3. I have the flu.
4. I have heartburn.

Page 128, Exercises 2B and 2C

Receptionist: Hello. Westview Clinic.
Roberto: Hi. This is Roberto Cruz. I'm sick, and I need to make an appointment, please.
Receptionist: All right. What's the matter?
Roberto: I have a fever and I'm nauseous.

Page 128, Exercise 2D

Receptionist: Hello. Westview Clinic.
Roberto: Hi. This is Roberto Cruz. I'm sick, and I need to make an appointment, please.
Receptionist: All right. What's the matter?
Roberto: I have a fever and I'm nauseous.
Receptionist: OK. How about Tuesday morning? At 9:00?
Roberto: Yes, that's fine.
Receptionist: All right. What's your name again?
Roberto: Roberto Cruz.
Receptionist: Roberto Cruz. OK, Mr. Cruz, we'll see you on Tuesday at 9:00.
Roberto: OK. Thank you.

Page 133, Exercise C

1. What is the name of the medicine? Milacam
2. How often do I take it? Once a day.
3. What is the dosage? Two tablespoons.
4. What is the expiration date? November 20, 2021
5. How many refills can I get? Two.

Page 134, Exercises 2B and 2C

Manolo: Hi, Val. What are you doing here?
Val: Oh, hi, Manolo. I had an accident. I broke my arm.
Manolo: Oh, no! I'm sorry to hear that.
Val: Thanks. What about you?
Manolo: I hurt my ankle at a soccer game. I think I sprained it.

Page 134, Exercise 2D

Manolo: Hi, Val. What are you doing here?
Val: Oh, hi, Manolo. I had an accident. I broke my arm.
Manolo: Oh, no! I'm sorry to hear that.
Val: Thanks. What about you?
Manolo: I hurt my ankle at a soccer game. I think I sprained it.
Val: That's too bad. I guess you can't play soccer for a while.
Manolo: Oh, I don't play soccer. I just watch.
Val: What? So how did you hurt your ankle?
Manolo: Well, I was at a soccer game. I was hungry, so I got some food. I had a drink and a sandwich in my hands, and I fell down the stairs on the way to my seat.

Page 140, Exercises 2B and 2C

Eva: Hello. Eva Perez speaking.
Sung: Hi, Eva. This is Sung. I can't come in today because I have to go to the doctor. I don't feel well.

Eva: Sorry to hear that. Thanks for calling, and take care of yourself.
Sung: Thanks.

Page 140, Exercise 2D

Eva: Hello. Eva Pérez speaking.
Sung: Hi, Eva. This is Sung. I can't come in today because I have to go to the doctor. I don't feel well.
Eva: Sorry to hear that. Thanks for calling, and take care of yourself.
Sung: Thanks.
Eva: Do you think you'll be in tomorrow?
Sung: I'm not sure. I can call you later after I go to the doctor.
Eva: All right. That sounds good.

UNIT 8

Page 148, Exercises 2B and 2C

Albert: Manny? Hi, I'm Albert Taylor, the store manager. Please have a seat.
Manny: Thank you. It's nice to meet you.
Albert: I have your application here. I see that you're working now. What are your job duties?
Manny: Well, I assist customers and stock shelves.

Page 148, Exercise 2D

Albert: Manny? Hi, I'm Albert Taylor, the store manager. Please have a seat.
Manny: Thank you. It's nice to meet you.
Albert: I have your application here. I see that you're working now. What are your job duties?
Manny: Well, I assist customers and stock shelves.
Albert: OK. Tell me about your skills. Can you use a cash register?
Manny: No, I can't, but I can learn.

Page 154, Exercises 2B and 2C

Albert: So, tell me more about your work experience.
Manny: Well, I came to the U.S. three years ago. First, I got a job as a gardener. Then last year, I got a job as a stock clerk.
Albert: OK. So now you're a stock clerk. Why are you looking for another job?
Manny: Things in my life have changed, and now I'd like to do something different.

Page 154, Exercises 2D

Albert: So, tell me more about your work experience.
Manny: Well, I came to the U.S. three years ago. First, I got a job as a gardener. Then last year, I got a job as a stock clerk.
Albert: OK. So now you're a stock clerk. Why are you looking for another job?
Manny: Things in my life have changed, and now I'd like to do something different.
Albert: I see. By the way, you wrote on your application that you were unemployed two years ago. Can you explain that?
Manny: Sure. I left my job because my mother was sick, and I had to take care of her for two months.

Page 160, Exercises 2B and 2C

Albert: Let me ask you a few questions about your availability. Do you prefer mornings or afternoons?
Manny: Well, I prefer mornings, but I'm flexible.
Albert: All right. Can you work on weekends?
Manny: Yes, I can.
Albert: Great. And when could you start?
Manny: In two weeks. I need to give two weeks' notice at my job.

Page 160, Listen, Exercise 2D

Albert: Let me ask you a few questions about your availability. Do you prefer mornings or afternoons?
Manny: Well, I prefer mornings, but I'm flexible.
Albert: All right. Can you work on weekends?
Manny: Yes, I can.
Albert: Great. And when could you start?
Manny: In two weeks. I need to give two weeks' notice at my job.
Albert: OK. Well, everything looks good. Do you have any questions for me?
Manny: Yes. When can I expect to hear from you?
Albert: Well, I have some other interviews this week. I can let you know next week.
Manny: OK. Thank you for the opportunity to talk with you. It was nice to meet you.
Albert: You, too.

UNIT 9

Page 168, Exercises 2B and 2C

Medi: Carlo brought a notice home from school today. There's a parent-teacher conference in two weeks.
David: Oh yeah? What day?
Medi: Thursday the 19th at 6:00. My mother will watch the kids. That way we can both go.
David: Oh, I have to work that day until 9:00, but I'll try to change my shift.

Page 168, Exercise 2D

Medi: Carlo brought a notice home from school today. There's a parent-teacher conference in two weeks.
David: Oh yeah? What day?
Medi: Thursday the 19th at 6:00. My mother will watch the kids. That way we can both go.
David: Oh, I have to work that day until 9:00, but I'll try to change my shift.
Medi: I hope you can.
David: Me, too. When is Carlo's band concert? I know it's coming up.
Medi: That's Monday the 23rd.
David: OK. I'll definitely go to that.

Page 172, Exercises 1B and 1C

Receptionist: Winter Hill Elementary School.
Elsa: Hello. This is Elsa Vega. May I speak to Mr. Taylor please?
Receptionist: I'm sorry. He's not available right now. May I take a message?
Elsa: Yes, please. I have a question about my daughter Maria's math homework. Please ask him to call me back.

Receptionist: Sure. What's your number?
Elsa: It's 718-555-4343.
Receptionist: OK. I'll give him the message.
Elsa: Thank you.

Page 172, Exercise 2A

Mobile voice mail: Hello. You have reached 718-555-4343. I am not available, but please leave a message after the beep.
Mr. Taylor: Ms. Vega. This is Mr. Taylor. I'm returning your call. Since Maria was home sick today, she won't need to complete next week's unit, but she will need to complete this week's unit. She'll take the quiz on Tuesday. Please call me or e-mail me at jtaylor@winterhill.edu. if you have questions.

Page 174, Exercises 2B and 2C

Mr. Thompson: Hi, I'm Harold Thompson, Carlo's teacher. Nice to meet you.
Medi: I'm Carlo's mother, Medi Duval. Nice to meet you, too. So, how's Carlo doing?
Mr. Thompson: Carlo's a good student. I enjoy having him in class.
Medi: That's good to hear.
Mr. Thompson: He does very well in math. He works carefully.
Medi: He likes math a lot. What about social studies?
Mr. Thompson: Well, he's having a little trouble in that class. He needs to do his homework.
Medi: OK. I'll talk to him.

Page 174, Listen, Exercise 2D

Mr. Thompson: Hi, I'm Harold Thompson, Carlo's teacher. Nice to meet you.
Medi: I'm Carlo's mother, Medi Duval. Nice to meet you, too. So, how's Carlo doing?
Mr. Thompson: Carlo's a good student. I enjoy having him in class.
Medi: That's good to hear.
Mr. Thompson: He does very well in math. He works carefully.
Medi: He likes math a lot. What about social studies?
Mr. Thompson: Well, he's having a little trouble in that class. He needs to do his homework.
Medi: OK. I'll talk to him.
Mr. Thompson: Have you thought about signing up Carlo for homework help after school?
Medi: Homework help? What's that?
Mr. Thompson: It's an after-school program. Older kids from the high school come and help students with their homework. The program is free, and students can get the extra help they need.

Page 180, Exercises 2B and 2C

Tito: Where's Luis?
Anna: He's at a friend's house. Why? What's up?
Tito: Well, his teacher called. He's having some trouble at school.
Anna: Uh-oh. What kind of trouble?
Tito: She said he's not paying attention and skipping class.

Anna: What? Well, we need to talk to him right away.
Tito: Definitely. Let's all talk tonight after dinner.

Page 180, Listen, Exercise 2D

Tito: Where's Luis?
Anna: He's at a friend's house. Why? What's up?
Tito: Well, his teacher called. He's having some trouble at school.
Anna: Uh-oh. What kind of trouble?
Tito: She said he's not paying attention and skipping class.
Anna: What? Well, we need to talk to him right away.
Tito: Definitely. Let's all talk tonight after dinner.
Anna: This is so strange. Luis never has problems at school.
Tito: I know. He's usually a great student.

UNIT 10

Page 186, Exercise C

1. a bag of potato chips
2. a box of cereal
3. a can of soup
4. a bottle of vinegar
5. a jar of mayonnaise
6. a container of yogurt
7. a bunch of bananas
8. a head of cauliflower
9. a pound of grapes
10. a pint of milk
11. a quart of orange juice
12. a half-gallon of ice cream
13. a gallon of water
14. a dozen eggs

Page 188, Exercises 2B and 2C

Agnes: Hi, Yuka. I'm going to the grocery store for some milk. Do you need anything?
Yuka: Uh, let me see. Could you get a can of tomatoes?
Agnes: A can of tomatoes? Sure, no problem.
Yuka: Oh, and I need some onions.
Agnes: How many onions?
Yuka: Two.
Agnes: All right. A can of tomatoes and two onions. I'll be back in a little while.

Page 188, Exercise 2D

Agnes: Hi, Yuka. I'm going to the grocery store for some milk. Do you need anything?
Yuka: Uh, let me see. Could you get a can of tomatoes?
Agnes: A can of tomatoes? Sure, no problem.
Yuka: Oh, and I need some onions.
Agnes: How many onions?
Yuka: Two.
Agnes: All right. A can of tomatoes and two onions. I'll be back in a little while.
Yuka: Wait a second, since you're going, we could use a jar of mayonnaise, a head of lettuce, and a box of cereal. Hey, what are you doing?
Agnes: I'm looking for a pen and paper. I need to write all this down!

Page 194, Exercises 2A and 2B

Your family is important to you. You want to take care of them. You want to give them food that tastes good and that's good for them. Better taste, healthier meals. That's what you get from Baker's Bread. With no added colors or flavors, Baker's Bread is better for you than any other brands. Never frozen, Baker's Bread is fresher than other bread. Try it. You'll taste the difference.

Page 195, Exercise B

A: Oh, you buy Franklin brand coffee. Is it good?
B: Yes, it's excellent. I think it's better than all the other brands.
A: Really? Why?
B: It tastes great and it's not expensive.

Page 200, Exercises 2B and 2C

Waitress: Here are your iced teas. Are you ready to order?
Edgar: Yes. I'd like the meatloaf.
Waitress: And what would you like with that?
Edgar: A side of mixed vegetables.
Waitress: OK. Meatloaf with mixed vegetables.
Edgar: And a hamburger with a side of onion rings.
Waitress: A hamburger with onion rings.

Page 200, Exercise D

Waitress: Here are your iced teas. Are you ready to order?
Edgar: Yes. I'd like the meatloaf.
Waitress: And what would you like with that?
Edgar: A side of mixed vegetables.
Waitress: OK. Meatloaf with mixed vegetables.
Edgar: And a hamburger with a side of onion rings.
Waitress: A hamburger with onion rings.
Edgar: Oh, and could we have some sugar?
Waitress: Sure. Here you go. I'll be right back with your order.
Lina: Excuse me. I want to order something, too.
Waitress: Oh! Aren't you having the hamburger?
Lina: Actually, no. The meatloaf and the hamburger are both for him.
Edgar: Yeah. I'm pretty hungry!

UNIT 11

Page 208, Exercises 2B and 2C

Operator: 9-1-1. What's your emergency?
Olivia: I think a man is having a heart attack.
Operator: OK. What's the location of the emergency?
Olivia: Dave's Sports Shop at 103 Elm Street.
Operator: What are the cross streets?
Olivia: 17th and 18th Avenues.
Operator: All right. What's your name?
Olivia: Olivia Ramos.

Page 208, Exercise 2D

Operator: 9-1-1. What's your emergency?
Olivia: I think a man is having a heart attack.
Operator: OK. What's the location of the emergency?
Olivia: Dave's Sports Shop at 103 Elm Street.
Operator: What are the cross streets?
Olivia: 17th and 18th Avenues.
Operator: All right. What's your name?
Olivia: Olivia Ramos.
Operator: All right, Ms. Ramos. An ambulance is on its way. But don't hang up. Stay on the line with me until the ambulance gets there.
Olivia: OK. I'll just tell the man that the ambulance is coming.

Page 212, Exercise 2B

a fire extinguisher
a smoke alarm
a fire escape
an escape plan
exits

Page 213, Exercise 2C

FIRE SAFETY TIPS for the Workplace
Get out! Stay out! Call 9ll

1 Leave your work area immediately. Do not take anything with you, but alert your co-workers.
2 Don't stop to call 911. Call from a safe location outside of the building.
3 Don't use an elevator to exit the building. Use the stairs.
4 Close any open doors. This will prevent the fire from spreading quickly.
5 Feel every closed door before opening it. Don't open a door that is hot. Try to find another exit.
6 If you smell smoke, stay close to the floor. Cover your mouth and nose with a wet cloth.
7 When you get outside, do not go back to your workplace for any reason. Tell firefighters about anyone still inside the building.

Page 214, Exercises 2B and 2C

Mr. Novak: Did you hear what happened yesterday?
Mrs. Novak: No. What happened?
Mr. Novak: There was a gas explosion downtown.
Mrs. Novak: Oh, my gosh. That's terrible. Was anybody hurt?
Mr. Novak: Yes. Two people went to the hospital.

Page 214, Exercise 2D

Mr. Novak: Did you hear what happened yesterday?
Mrs. Novak: No. What happened?
Mr. Novak: There was a gas explosion downtown.
Mrs. Novak: Oh my gosh. That's terrible. Was anybody hurt?
Mr. Novak: Yes. Two people went to the hospital.
Mrs. Novak: How did it happen? Do they know?
Mr. Novak: No, not yet. They're looking into the cause.
Mrs. Novak: I'll bet traffic is terrible around there.
Mr. Novak: Oh, yeah. It says here a lot of the streets are closed downtown.

Page 215, Exercise 2B

1. here, here
2. art, heart
3. high, I
4. Ow!, Ow!
5. ear, hear
6. high, high

Page 221, Exercises 2A and 2B

Hi, I'm Officer Ramírez, and I'm here today to talk to you about what to do if you're pulled over by a police officer.

So imagine: You're driving along, and everything's great. But suddenly you hear a siren, and behind you there's a police car with flashing lights. That can be really scary. But stay calm and follow this simple advice.

Anytime you see a police car with flashing lights or hear a siren, look for a place to pull over quickly. Always pull over to the right, even if you're in the left lane. Use your turn signal, and pull over to a safe spot.

After you stop your car, roll down your window. Wait for the police officer and stay in your car. Don't get out. If it's dark, turn on the light inside your car. Put your hands on the steering wheel where the officer can see them.

The officer will probably ask for your license, registration, and proof of insurance. Wait for the officer to ask for your documents. Then tell him what you're going to do. For example, say, "I'm going to get my wallet. It's in my purse."

Cooperate and be polite. Follow the officer's instructions. Do not argue with the officer. The officer will give you a warning or a ticket. If you get a ticket, there are instructions on the ticket about how to pay it. You don't pay the officer at that time. Never offer any money or other gifts to an officer.

Page 221, Exercise 2C

Hi, I'm Officer Ramírez, and I'm here today to talk to you about what to do if you're pulled over by a police officer.

So imagine: You're driving along, and everything's great. But suddenly you hear a siren, and behind you there's a police car with flashing lights. That can be really scary. But stay calm and follow this simple advice.

Anytime you see a police car with flashing lights or hear a siren, look for a place to pull over quickly. Always pull over to the right, even if you're in the left lane. Use your turn signal, and pull over to a safe spot.

After you stop your car, roll down your window. Wait for the police officer and stay in your car. Don't get out. If it's dark, turn on the light inside your car. Put your hands on the steering wheel where the officer can see them.

The officer will probably ask for your license, registration, and proof of insurance. Wait for the officer to ask for your documents. Then tell him what you're going to do. For example, say, "I'm going to get my wallet. It's in my purse."

Cooperate and be polite. Follow the officer's instructions. Do not argue with the officer. The officer will give you a warning or a ticket. If you get a ticket, there are instructions on the ticket about how to pay it. You don't pay the officer at that time. Never offer any money or other gifts to an officer.

Finally, don't start your car or leave until the officer gives you permission to go.

Remember, stay calm and listen to the police officer. Police officers want to help and protect you.

UNIT 12

Page 228, Exercises 2B and 2C

Hello, everybody. I'm Michelle Rivera from human resources. Welcome to the Greenville Hotel. I think that you will find this a great place to work. We're going to start our orientation meeting by talking about company policies, and then we'll take a tour of the building.

Let's start with employee responsibilities. We'll give you an employee ID badge at the end of this meeting. You must wear your employee ID badge during your work shift. This is very important.

Also, all employees must follow the dress code. Your manager will explain the dress code for your department. Employees in housekeeping and food service must wear a uniform. Please get your uniforms at the end of this orientation.

Here's another very important responsibility: You must clock in at the start of your shift and clock out at the end of the shift. Please be on time! And you must also clock in and out when you take your break. During your six-hour shift you must take a thirty-minute break. You must not clock in or clock out for another employee.

Page 228, Exercise D

Hello, everybody. I'm Michelle Rivera from human resources. Welcome to the Greenville Hotel. I think that you will find this a great place to work. We're going to start our orientation meeting by talking about company policies, and then we'll take a tour of the building.

Let's start with employee responsibilities. We'll give you an employee ID badge at the end of this meeting. You must wear your employee ID badge during your work shift. This is very important.

Also, all employees must follow the dress code. Your manager will explain the dress code for your department. Employees in housekeeping and food service must wear a uniform. Please get your uniforms at the end of this orientation.

Here's another very important responsibility: You must clock in at the start of your shift and clock out at the end of the shift. Please be on time! And you must also clock in and out when you take your break. During your six-hour shift you must take a thirty-minute break. You must not clock in or clock out for another employee.

Are there any questions? No? OK. Now, some information about our sick day policy. Please open your company policy booklet to page 5 . . .

Page 234, Exercises 2B and 2C

Cam: Hi, Rachel. Can I ask you a favor?
Rachel: Sure. What is it?
Cam: I'm on the schedule for Monday, but I can't come in.
Rachel: Oh, what's up?
Cam: I have to study for a test. Can you take my shift for me?
Rachel: What time do you start?
Cam: 9:30.
Rachel: No problem.

Page 234, Exercise 2D

Cam: Hi, Rachel. Can I ask you a favor?
Rachel: Sure. What is it?
Cam: I'm on the schedule for Monday, but I can't come in.
Rachel: Oh, what's up?
Cam: I have to study for a test. Can you take my shift for me?
Rachel: What time do you start?
Cam: 9:30.
Rachel: No problem. I can use the extra hours. By the way, who's working that day?
Cam: I don't know. Let's check the schedule . . . . Oh, Tim's working that day.
Rachel: Tim? Oh, definitely! I like working with him!

Page 240, Exercises 2B and 2C

Linda: Excuse me, Ron. Can I speak to you for a minute?
Ron: Sure, Linda. What's up?
Linda: I need to talk to you about my schedule.
Ron: OK. Right now you work in the mornings, right?

Linda: Yes. But I'm planning to take classes now. Could I change to evenings?
Ron: Well, let me look at the schedule. I'll get back to you.
Linda: OK. Thanks.

Page 240, Exercise 2D

Linda: Excuse me, Ron. Can I speak to you for a minute?
Ron: Sure, Linda. What's up?
Linda: I need to talk to you about my schedule.
Ron: OK. Right now you work in the mornings, right?
Linda: Yes. But I'm planning to take classes now. Could I change to evenings?
Ron: Well, let me look at the schedule. I'll get back to you.
Linda: OK. Thanks.
Ron: By the way, what classes are you planning to take?
Linda: Business classes. Someday I want to be a manager.
Ron: Oh, that's great. Let me know if I can help.

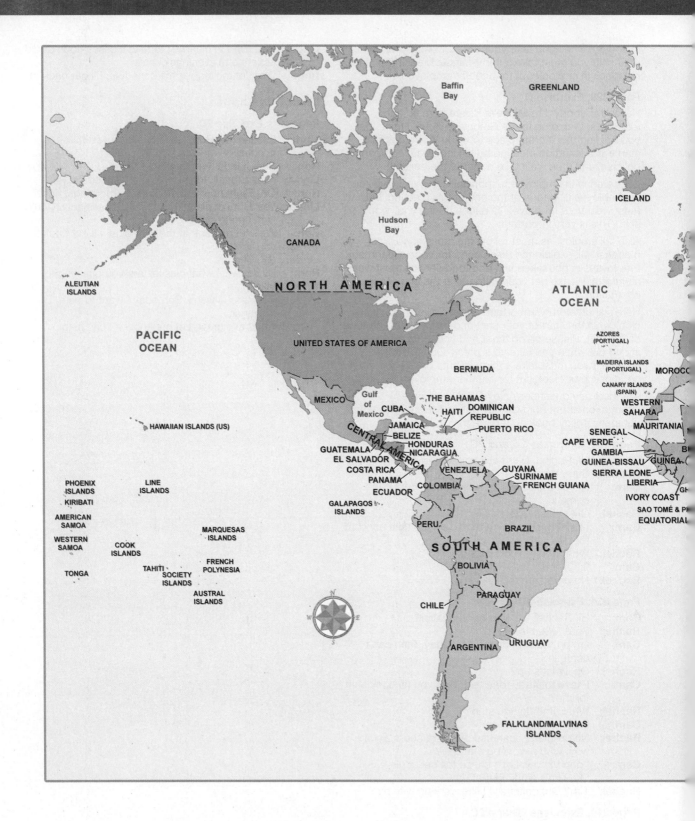

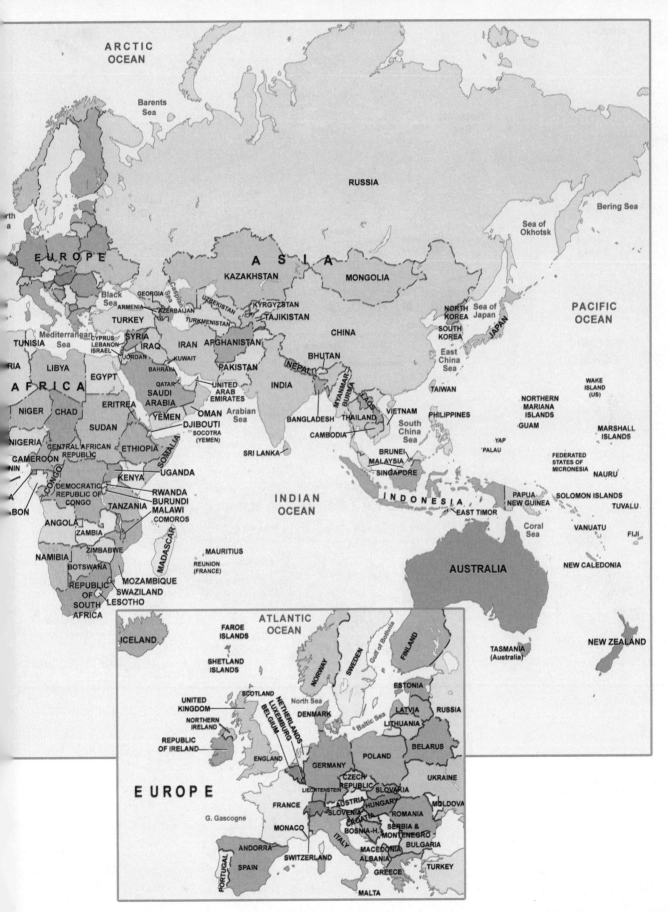

ARCTIC OCEAN

Barents Sea

RUSSIA

Bering Sea

EUROPE

Black Sea

GEORGIA

Caspian Sea

ASIA

KAZAKHSTAN

MONGOLIA

Sea of Okhotsk

ARMENIA

AZERBAIJAN

UZBEKISTAN

KYRGYZSTAN

TAJIKISTAN

TURKEY

TURKMENISTAN

NORTH KOREA

Sea of Japan

PACIFIC OCEAN

Mediterranean Sea

CYPRUS

LEBANON

ISRAEL

SYRIA

IRAQ

JORDAN

KUWAIT

BAHRAIN

IRAN

AFGHANISTAN

CHINA

SOUTH KOREA

JAPAN

TUNISIA

RIA

LIBYA

EGYPT

QATAR

SAUDI ARABIA

UNITED ARAB EMIRATES

PAKISTAN

BHUTAN

NEPAL

East China Sea

TAIWAN

WAKE ISLAND (US)

AFRICA

NIGER

CHAD

ERITREA

YEMEN

OMAN

Arabian Sea

INDIA

MYANMAR BURMA

LAOS

VIETNAM

NORTHERN MARIANA ISLANDS

NIGERIA

SUDAN

DJIBOUTI

SOCOTRA (YEMEN)

BANGLADESH

THAILAND

South China Sea

PHILIPPINES

GUAM

MARSHALL ISLANDS

CAMEROON

CENTRAL AFRICAN REPUBLIC

ETHIOPIA

SOMALIA

SRI LANKA

CAMBODIA

BRUNEI

YAP

PALAU

FEDERATED STATES OF MICRONESIA

NAURU

NIN

CONGO

DEMOCRATIC REPUBLIC OF CONGO

KENYA

UGANDA

RWANDA

MALAYSIA

SINGAPORE

BON

TANZANIA

BURUNDI

MALAWI

INDIAN OCEAN

INDONESIA

PAPUA NEW GUINEA

SOLOMON ISLANDS

TUVALU

A

ANGOLA

ZAMBIA

COMOROS

MADAGASCAR

EAST TIMOR

Coral Sea

VANUATU

FIJI

NAMIBIA

ZIMBABWE

MAURITIUS

REUNION (FRANCE)

AUSTRALIA

NEW CALEDONIA

BOTSWANA

MOZAMBIQUE

REPUBLIC OF SOUTH AFRICA

SWAZILAND

LESOTHO

ATLANTIC OCEAN

TASMANIA (Australia)

NEW ZEALAND

ICELAND

FAROE ISLANDS

NORWAY

SWEDEN

Gulf of Bothnia

FINLAND

SHETLAND ISLANDS

SCOTLAND

North Sea

ESTONIA

UNITED KINGDOM

NORTHERN IRELAND

NETHERLANDS

LUXEMBURG

BELGIUM

DENMARK

Baltic Sea

LATVIA

LITHUANIA

RUSSIA

REPUBLIC OF IRELAND

ENGLAND

GERMANY

POLAND

BELARUS

EUROPE

LIECHTENSTEIN

CZECH REPUBLIC

SLOVAKIA

UKRAINE

FRANCE

AUSTRIA

HUNGARY

MOLDOVA

G. Gascogne

SLOVENIA

CROATIA

ROMANIA

MONACO

BOSNA-H.

SERBIA & MONTENEGRO

ANDORRA

ITALY

MACEDONIA

BULGARIA

PORTUGAL

SPAIN

SWITZERLAND

ALBANIA

TURKEY

GREECE

MALTA

Map of the World **277**

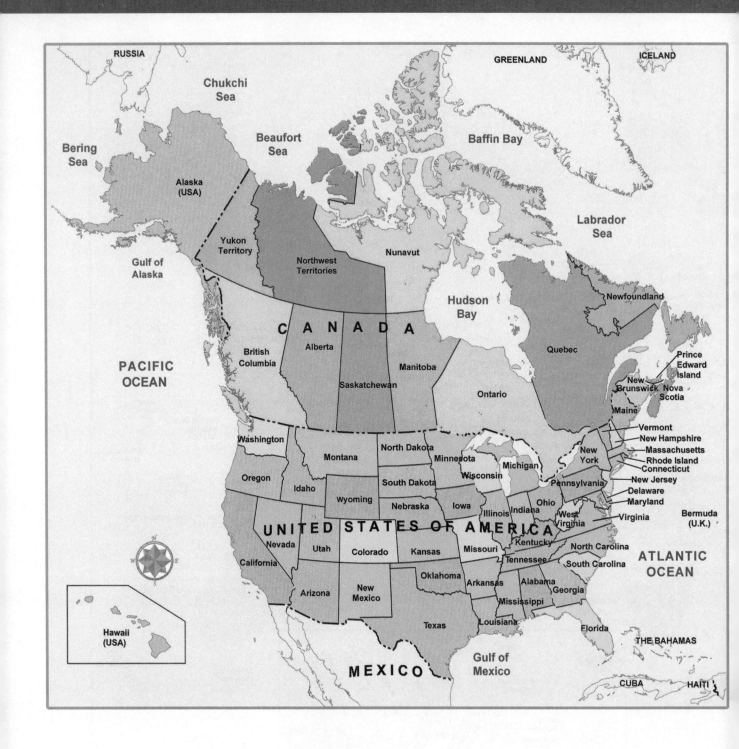

INDEX

ACADEMIC SKILLS

Critical thinking
  categorizing
    clothing, 47
    family members, 27
    food containers, 187
    free-time activities, 67
    health problems, 127
    household problems, 87
    physical appearances, 8
  comparing
    apartment ads, 92
    nutrition labels, 193
    payment methods, 58–59
    resumes, 153
    what people have in common, 34–35
  making connections while studying, 7, 27,
      147
Numeracy: graphs and charts
  of apartment features, 97
  bar graphs, 77
  of clothing types, 47
  of college types, 178
  of family relationships, 27
  of food containers, 187
  of free-time activities, 67
  of gifts at events, 107
  of health problems, 127
  of household problems, 87
  of information for voicemail messages, 173
  of job responsibilities, 227
  of job skills, 151
  of mailing services, 38
  of physical appearances, 8
  of school events, 171
  using information in, 178–179
Numeracy: math skills
  calculating medicine doses, 132–133
  calculating nutrition information, 193
  percentages
    credit card rates as, 58
    of favorite free-time activities, 77
    in job trends, 158
    in receipts, 53
    of renters compared to homeowners,
        98–99
    in store ads, 52–53
    of students attending college, 178
    tax rates as, 238
  understanding pay stubs, 232–233
Reading
  of abbreviations
    in apartment ads, 92
    in ID cards, 12
    in street addresses, 78
    in text messages, 78
  of apartment ads and utility bills, 92
  about caffeine, 198–199
  about college, 178–179
  of community calendars, 72–73
  of emails, 231
  about emergencies, 218–219
  formatting cues in, 138
  getting meaning from context in, 198–199
  graphs and tables in, 178–179
  of grocery ads, 197
  about group work in class, 18–19
  of help wanted ads, 152
  of ID cards, 12–13
  identifying purpose of authors in, 58–59
  identifying supporting details in, 218–219
  identifying topics and main ideas in, 18–19
  of job listings, 152
  about jobs in U.S., 158–159
  of maps
    fire escape plans, 213
    street, 100–101

U.S. and Canada, 278
    world, 276–277
  of medicine labels, 132–133
  of nutrition labels, 132–133
  about Obama, 118–119
  of online order forms, 52–53
  of pay stubs, 232–233
  about payment options, 58–59
  predicting topics of articles in, 78–79,
      158–159
  of receipts, 53
  about renters and homeowners, 98–99
  retelling information after, 32
  scanning for information in, 118–119
  skimming compared to, 98–99
  about Social Security program, 238–239
  of store ads, 52–53
  of street addresses, 12–13, 78
  about stress, 138–139
  summarizing, 19, 33, 59, 79, 99, 119, 139,
      159, 179, 199, 219, 239
  thinking about what you know before,
      238–239
  of timelines, 157
  about U.S. holidays, 113
  of utility bills, 93
  about work/life balance, 32–33
  about workplace safety, 218–219
  about writing styles, 78–79
Study tips
  flashcards
    drawing pictures on, 187
    for job titles and duties, 147
    online, 87
    translating words on, 127
    words that go together on, 227
  making connections, 7, 27, 147
  testing pronunciation, 207
  testing spelling, 47, 107
  testing with partner, 167
  writing sentences, 67
Writing
  of biographies, 123
  capital letters for place names in, 43
  checklists for, 23, 43, 63, 83, 103, 123,
      143, 163, 183, 203, 223, 243
  of dates, 123
  of emails, 78–79
  about emergencies, 223
  about family members, 43
  about free-time activities, 83
  giving reasons in, 143
  of grocery lists, 191
  about home, 103
  of ID card applications, 12–13
  indenting paragraphs in, 103
  about job responsibilities, 243
  of lists, 183
  about nutrition, 203
  punctuation in
    apostrophes, 181, 182, 260
    commas, 43, 123, 183
    in dates, 123
    ending sentences with, 115
    in lists, 183
    periods, 115
    in place names, 43
    question marks, 115
  about saving money, 63
  about school, 183
  spelling
    of adverbs of manner, 259
    of -ing verbs, 258
    of plural nouns, 260
    of possessive nouns, 260
    testing your, 47, 107
  about steps, 23

about study habits, 23
  about study routine, 23
  styles of, 78–79
  of text messages, 78–79, 91
  of translations on cards, 127
  about treating health problems, 143
  using details in, 83, 243
  using examples in, 203
  using topic sentences in, 63
  about work history, 163

CIVICS

Life skills
  calendar and time
    community calendars, 72–73
    expressions of time, 156–157
    free-time activity calendars, 71
    U.S. holiday calendars, 112
    work calendars, 234–235, 237
    writing dates, 123
  emergencies, 205–224
    calling 911 in, 207–209
    describing, 214–215
    fire, 212–213
    identifying types of, 206–207
    medical, 207–209
    writing about, 223
  events, 105–124
    community calendars of, 72–73
    identifying types of, 106–107
    milestone, speaking about, 114–115
    in Obama's life, 118–119
    present continuous for, 90–91
    school, making plans for, 168–169, 171
    simple past for, 110–111, 136–137
    speaking about past, 108–109, 120–121
    U.S. holidays, 112–113
  families, 25–44
    asking about, 40–41
    family trees, 31
    identifying relationships in, 26–27
    separating work and home life, 44
    speaking about, 28–29, 34–35
    things in common in, 34–35
    in work/life balance, 32–33
    writing about, 43
  food, 185–204
    ads for groceries, 197
    asking for quantities of, 188–189
    caffeine in, 198–199
    calories in, 193
    decision making about, 194–195
    in grocery lists, 191
    identifying containers and quantities of,
        186–187
    labels on, 132–133, 192–193
    ordering in restaurants, 200–201
    shopping for, 188–189, 191, 194–195
    writing about nutrition of, 203
  free-time activities, 65–84
    frequency of, 70–71
    identifying types of, 66–67
    likes and dislikes of, 74–77
    responding to invitations for, 80–81
    speaking about, 68–69
    on weekends, 108–109
    writing about, 83
  health problems, 125–144
    doctor appointments for, 128–131
    identifying types of, 126–127
    as medical emergencies, 206–207
    reading medicine labels for, 132–133
    speaking about injuries, 134–137
    writing about treatment of, 143
  homes, 85–104
    ads for, 92
    asking about, 94–97

identifying problems with, 86–87
renting compared to owning, 98–99
renting-to-own, 58–59
speaking about problems with, 88–89
utility bills for, 93
writing about, 103
interpersonal communication
calling to explain absence, 140–141
emojis in, 78
leaving voicemail messages, 172–173
text messages, 78–79, 91, 128, 131
voicemail greeting messages, 173
making plans, 56–57
for school events, 168–169, 171
speaking about, 54–55
at work, 184
money and prices
of college tuition, 178–179
of food, 194, 197
forms of money, 58–59
in online orders, 52–53
on pay stubs, 232–233
in receipts, 53
of rental apartments, 92, 94
saving, writing about, 63
in store ads, 52
of televisions, 58–59
of utility bills, 93
school, 165–184
going to college, 178–179
group work in class, 18–19
identifying subjects in, 166–167
making plans for events at, 168–169,
171
speaking about behavior in, 180–181
speaking about progress in, 174–175
student financial aid, 178–179
voicemail messages related to,
172–173
writing about, 183
shopping, 45–64
for food, 188–189, 191, 194–195
identifying clothes in, 46–47
identifying problems with purchases,
60–61
online, 52–53
payment options in, 58–59
receipts for, 53
for wants and needs, 48–49
small talk, 65–84
about community events, 72–73
about free-time activities, 66–71
about frequency of activities, 70–71
about likes and dislikes, 74–77
transportation, traffic violations in,
220–222

GRAMMAR

Adjectives
+ be, in simple present, 10–11
comparative
-er endings in, 196–197, 261
irregular, 196, 261
spelling of, 261
with than, 196–197
+ -ly, as adverbs of manner, 176, 259
Adverbs
of degree, 62
of frequency, 70–71
of manner, 176–177, 259
Affirmative statements
with can, 150–151
in future, with will, 170–171
with have to, 82
imperative, 102
compound, 222
in present continuous, 90–91

in simple past
with irregular verbs, 116–117
with regular verbs, 110–111
in simple present
with be + adjective, 10–11
with have + object, 10–11
with live/work/have, 30–31
with love/like/hate + infinitive, 76–77
with want/need + infinitive, 50–51
with there is/there are, 96–97
with there was/there were, 216–217
Articles
a, 29, 201
the, 29, 201
Conjunctions
and
in compound imperatives, 222
in compound sentences, 16–17
expressing alternatives with, 162
as unstressed word, 29
but, in compound sentences, 16–17
or
in compound imperatives, 222
expressing alternatives with, 162
intonation of questions with, 161
Contractions
aren't, 10
with be, 10–11, 22, 258
definition of, 10
with do, 258
examples of, 10
he's, 56
I'm, 22, 56
isn't, 10
in present continuous, 210
pronouncing, 149
there's, 96, 190
they're, 10
we're, 56
with will, 169, 170
you're, 22
Infinitives, in simple present
with love/like/hate, 76–77
with want/need, 50–51
Negative statements
with can't, 150–151
in future, with will, 170–171
with have to, 82
imperative, 102
compound, 222
with or, 162
in present continuous, 90–91
in simple past
with irregular verbs, 116–117
with regular verbs, 110–111
in simple present
with be + adjective, 10–11
with don't/doesn't, 10, 30–31
with have + object, 10–11
with live/work/have, 30–31
with love/like/hate + infinitive, 76–77
with want/need + infinitive, 50–51
with there is/there are, 96–97
with there was/there were, 216–217
Nouns
count, 190–191
irregular, 260
non-count, 190–191
examples of, 261
how much with, 191
quantifiers with, 202
plural
count, 190
possessive, 182, 260
quantifiers with, 202
spelling of, 260
possessive

pronouncing, 181
spelling of, 260
using, 182
quantifiers with, 202
in simple present with want/need,
50–51
singular
count, 190
possessive, 182, 260
two-word, stress in, 95
Prepositions, of time, 130–131
Pronouns, object, 177
Questions
adverbs of frequency in, 70–71
with are there/is there, 96–97
choice, with or, 161
with how many, 42, 97, 191
with how much, 191
with how often, 42, 71
information
intonation in, 235
in present continuous, 210–211
in simple past, 122
in simple present, 22, 42
with what/which/when/where, 237
with who, 236
with or, intonation of, 161
pronouncing statements as, 115
with was there/were there, 216
Wh-, 223
yes/no
with be, 22
with can, 150–151
with count and non-count nouns,
190–191
intonation in, 229
with is there/are there, 96–97, 190
in present continuous, 210–211
in simple past, 117
in simple present, 22, 36–37
with was there/were there, 216
Sentences
compound, 16–17
pauses within, 141
punctuation ending, 115
topic, 63
writing, 67
Verbs
action, adverbs of frequency with, 70–71
be
adverbs of frequency after, 70–71
in compound sentences with and and
but, 16–17
contractions with, 10–11, 22, 258
with I, he, we, 56
in present continuous, 90–91
in simple past, 117
in simple present, 10–11, 22
can/can't
in affirmative statements, 150–151
asking permission with, 242
in expressions of ability, 150–151
in expressions of prohibition, 230–231
pronouncing, 149
in yes/no questions, 150–151
do/does
negative contractions with, 258
in simple present information
questions, 42
in simple present yes/no questions,
36–37
don't/doesn't
with have to, 82
in imperatives, 102
in simple present questions, 36–37
in simple present statements, 10,
30–31, 50–51

future tense
  with *be going to,* 56–57
  with *will,* 170–171
has/have
  in simple present questions, 36–37
  in simple present statements, 10–11, 30–31
has to/have to
  in expressions of necessity, 230–231
  pronouncing, 81
  using, 82
imperative, 102
  compound, 222
-ing
  spelling of, 258
irregular
  examples of, 116, 136
  simple past with, 116–117, 136–137, 259
modal, 82
present continuous
  information questions in, 210–211
  spelling of verbs in, 258
  statements in, 90–91, 210–211
  yes/no questions in, 210–211
regular, simple past with, 110–111
simple past
  information questions in, 122
  with irregular verbs, 116–117, 136–137, 259
  with regular verbs, 110–111
simple present affirmative
  with *be* + adjective, 10–11
  with *have* + object, 10–11
  with *live/work/have,* 30–31
  with *love/like/hate* + infinitive, 76–77
  with *want/need* + infinitive, 50–51
simple present negative
  with *be* + adjective, 10–11
  with *have* + object, 10–11
  with *live/work/have,* 30–31
  with *love/like/hate* + infinitive, 76–77
  with *want/need* + infinitive, 50–51
simple present questions
  with *be,* 22
  with *do/does,* 36–37, 42
  with *have,* 36–37
  information, 22, 42
  yes/no, 22, 36–37
will/will not
  future with, 170–171
  pronouncing, 169

LISTENING
Active, at work, 64
To advice on work/life balance, 32–33
About apartments, 94–95
To descriptions of people, 8–9
To directions, 100–101
About doctor's appointment, 128–129
About emergencies, 214–215
About family, 28–29
About free-time activities, 68–69
To get to know someone, 20–21
About grocery shopping, 188–189, 194–195
About household problems, 88–89
To information about people, 40–41
About injuries, 134–135
To introductions, 20–21
To invitations, 80–81
About job skills, 148–149
To likes and dislikes, 74–75
To make plans for school events, 168–169
About milestones, 114–115
About past activities, 108–109
About past events, 120–121
About personalities, 14–15

On phone calls about missing work, 140–141
On phone calls to 911, 208–209
About plans, 54–55
To police instructions, 220–221
About problems with purchases, 60–61
In restaurants, 200–201
About school behavior, 180–181
About school progress, 174–175
About things people have in common, 34
About wants and needs, 48–49
About work availability, 160–161
About work history, 154–155
About work hours, 234–235, 240–241
About work policies, 228–229

SPEAKING
About advice on work/life balance, 32–33
About apartments, 94–97
About child's behavior in school, 180–181
About child's progress in school, 174–175
To co-workers about covering hours, 234–235
Describing people, 8–9
About directions, 100–101
About doctor appointments, 128–129
About emergencies, 214–215
About family, 28–29, 34–35, 40–41
About food quantities, 188–189
About free-time activities, 68–69
Getting to know someone, 20–21
About household problems, 88–89
About injuries, 134–137
About instructions, 102
Intonation in
  in information questions and statements, 235
  of questions with *or,* 161
  in *yes/no* questions, 229
Introducing others, 20–21
About invitations, 80–81
About job availability, 160–162
About job skills, 148–151
About likes and dislikes, 74–77
About mailing services, 38–39
About milestone events, 114–115
About missing work, 140–141
About needs and wants, 48–49
To order food in restaurants, 200–201
About past activities, 108–109, 120–121, 122
For permission, 242
About personalities, 14–17
About physical appearances, 8–9
About plans, 54–55
About policies at work, 228–229
Pronunciation in
  of *a,* 201
  of *can* and *can't,* 149
  of *do you,* 35
  of *-ed* endings, 109
  of *going to,* 55
  of *h* sound, 215
  of *has to/have to,* 81
  linking words together in, 129
  of *of,* 201
  pauses within sentences in, 141
  of possessive *'s,* 181
  of statements as questions, 115
  stress in
    on important words, 21
    lack of (unstressed words), 29
    on syllables, 9, 15, 209
    in two-word nouns, 95
  strong, 149
  syllables in
    definition of, 9
    with *-ed* endings, 109
    with *'s* endings, 181

stress on, 9, 15, 209
unpronounced, 69
testing your, 207
of *th,* 101
of *the,* 29, 201
of *to,* 49, 201
of voiced sounds, 101
of voiceless (unvoiced) sounds, 101, 215
of vowel sounds
  in stressed vs. unstressed syllables, 15
  t between two, 135
of *want to,* 49
weak, 149, 201
of *will,* 169
About weekend activities, 108–109
About what people have in common, 34–35
About work history, 154–155
About work schedules, 234–235, 237, 240–241

WORK SKILLS
Career awareness
  identifying job duties and responsibilities, 146–147, 226–227, 243
  identifying job titles, 146–147, 227
  reading about trends in U.S. job fields, 158–159
Employability skills
  job searches, 145–164
    answering questions about availability in, 160–162
    identifying job requirements in, 153
    identifying job titles and duties in, 146–147
    interviews in, 160–161
    reading about trends in U.S. job fields, 158–159
    reading help wanted ads in, 152
    resumes in, 153
    speaking about hours in, 160–161
    speaking about job skills in, 148–151
    speaking about work availability in, 160–162
    speaking about work history in, 154–155
    writing about work history in, 163
Workplace skills, 225–244
  active listening, 64
  asking about policies, 228–229
  asking for help, 204
  being honest, 164
  being inclusive, 24
  being team player, 244
  calling to explain absence, 140–141
  dependability, 124
  following safety procedures, 224
  listening actively, 64
  log of, 245–246
  overtime hours, 233
  planning well, 184
  professionalism, 84
  reading pay stubs, 232–233
  respecting others, 144
  safety, 212–213, 218–219, 224
  separating work and home life, 44
  speaking about schedules, 234–235, 237, 240–241
  taking initiative, 104
  work/life balance, 32–33

Photos:

Front cover: (front, center): Hero Images/Getty Images; (back, upper left): Asiseeit/ E+/Getty; (back, lower left): Manuel Breva Colmeiro/Getty Images; (back, right): Hero Images/Getty Images.

Frontmatter
Page vi (cell phone): tele52/Shutterstock; vi (front cover images): Hero Images/Getty Images, Manuel Breva Colmeiro/Getty Images, Asiseeit/ E+/Getty, Hero Images/Getty Images; vi (ActiveTeach screenshot): Pearson; vi (MyEnglishLab screenshot): Pearson; vi (CCRS page, bottom, left): Wavebreakmedia/Shutterstock; vi (CCRS page, top, right): Illustration Forest/Shutterstock; vii: Dragon Images/Shutterstock; ix (left): Rick Gomez/Corbis/Getty Images; ix (right): Hill Street Studios/Blend Images/Getty Images; x (left): Nancy Honey/Cultura/Getty Images; x (Paco): Rolf Bruderer/Blend Images/Getty Images; x (Sandra): Fuse/Getty Images; x (Pablo): Kevin Dodge/Getty Images; x (Lola): Leung Cho Pan/123RF; x (Marcos): Sirtravelalot/Shutterstock; x (Ana): Jeff Cleveland/Shutterstock; x (Alba): Daniel Ernst/123RF; x (Sara): Arena Creative/Shutterstock; xii: Mandy Godbehear/Shutterstock; xiii: Eddie Gerald/Alamy Stock Photo; xxii: Courtsesy of Sarah Lynn; xxii: Courtesy of Ronna Magy; xxii: Courtesy of Federico Salas Isnardi.

Pre-unit: Welcome to Class
Page 2 (top, right): Daniel M Ernst/Shutterstock; 2 (center, left): StockLite/Shutterstock; 2 (center, center): Jim West/Alamy Stock Photo; 2 (center, right): Ashwin/Shutterstock; 2 (bottom, left): Geo Martinez/Shutterstock; 2 (bottom, right): Vario images GmbH & Co.KG/Alamy Stock Photo.

Unit 1
Page 5: Ariel Skelley/Getty Images; 8: Paul Burns/Getty Images; 13 (top, right): Daniel Ernst/123RF; 13 (bottom, right): Daniel Ernst/Pavel L Photo and Video/Shutterstock; 14: Cathy Yeulet/123RF; 16 (left): MonicaNinker/E+/Getty Images; 16 (right): Olga Volodina/123RF; 18: Ammentorp/123RF; 20: Pearson/Original Photography by David Mager; 24: Photographee.eu/Shutterstock.

Unit 2
Page 25: Dragon Images/Shutterstock; 28: Rick Gomez/Corbis/Getty Images; 29: Hill Street Studios/Blend Images/Getty Images; 30: Nancy Honey/Cultura/Getty Images;31 (Paco): Rolf Bruderer/Blend Images/Getty Images; 31 (Sandra): Fuse/Getty Images; 31 (Pablo): Kevin Dodge/Getty images; 31 (Lola): Leung Cho Pan/123RF; 31 (Marcos): Sirtravelalot/Shutterstock; 31 (Ana): Jeff Cleveland/Shutterstock; 31 (Alba): kadettmann/123RF; 31 (Sara): ARENA Creative/Shutterstock; 32: NinaViktoria/Shutterstock; 34: JGalione/E+/Getty Images; 38 (1): Lyroky/Alamy Stock Photo; 38 (2): Kari Marttila/Alamy Stock Photo; 38 (3): Alex Staroseltsev/Shutterstock; 38 (4): Jenny Schuck/Shutterstock; 38 (5): Mega Pixel/Shutterstock; 39 (left): AshTproductions/Shutterstock; 39 (right): lofoto/Shutterstock; 40: tele52/Shutterstock; 41: Maskot/Getty Images; 44: Eddie Gerald/Alamy Stock Photo.

Unit 3
Page 45: Shutterstock; 46 (top, left): Jokic/Shutterstock; 46 (top, middle): Atstock Productions/Shutterstock; 46 (top, right): Alexandru Daniel Tantagoi/Alamy Stock Photo; 46 (bottom, left): Dmitry Kalinovsky/123RF; 46 (bottom, middle): LWA/Larry Williams/Blend Images/Getty Images; 46 (bottom, right): Klaus Mellenthin/Westend61 GmbH/Alamy Stock Photo; 48 (top row, left): British Retail Photography/Alamy Stock Photo; 48 (top row, center left): Mega Pixel/Shutterstock; 48 (top row, center right): Erik Isakson/Blend Images/Brand X Pictures/Getty Images; 48 (top row, right): Olga Popova/123RF; 48 (center, right): Primagefactory/123RF; 48 (bottom row, left): Elenovsky/Shutterstock; 48 (bottom row, center): windu/Shutterstock; 48 (bottom row, right): Ruslan Kudrin/Zoonar GmbH/Alamy Stock Photo; 54: ERproductions Ltd/Blend Images/Getty Images; 56: Wavebreak Media Ltd/123RF; 58 (top, left): TatianaMara/Shutterstock; 58 (top, center): Gary Arbach/123RF; 58 (top, right): Sergey Ryzhov/123RF; 58 (Brian): Hill Street Studios/Blend Images/Getty Images; 58 (Cindy): Cosmonaut/iStock/Getty Images; 58 (Craig): Ginaellen/iStock/Getty Images; 60 (bottom, right): Mangostar/Shutterstock; 62: Maigi/Shutterstock; 64: Maskot/Shutterstock.

Unit 4
Page 65: SVRSLYIMAGE/Shutterstock; 66 (1): Elena Elisseeva/Shutterstock; 66 (2): Jack Hollingsworth/Stockbyte/Getty Images; 66 (3): Melanie DeFazio/Shutterstock; 66 (4): Purestock/Getty Images; 66 (5): Comstock/Stockbyte/Getty Images; 66 (6): TongRo Images/Alamy Stock Photo; 66 (7): Kzenon/123RF; 66 (8): Sarah Nicholl/123RF; 66 (9): Laurence Mouton/PhotoAlto Agency RF Collections/Getty Images; 66 (10): Shutterstock; 66 (11): Microstockasia/123RF; 66 (12): Cathy Yeulet/123RF; 68 (top, left): Cathy Yeulet/123RF; 68 (top, center): Shutterstock; 68 (top, right): Goodluz/Shutterstock; 68 (center, right): Pearson/Original photography by David Mager; 68 (bottom, left): LawrenceSawyer/E+/Getty Images; 68 (bottom, center): Iakov Filimonov/123RF; 68 (bottom, right): Choi Ka Hin/123RF; 74: Nicolesy/iStock/Getty Images Plus/Getty Images; 75: Hero Images/Getty Images; 76: Tetra Images/Alamy Stock Photo; 76 (cell phone images): tele52/Shutterstock; 78 (Dan Brown): Luis Santos/Shutterstock; 80: Pearson/Original photography by David Mager; 84: Hongqi Zhang/123RF.

Unit 5
Page 85: Oscar Abrahams/Getty Images; 90: Lisa F. Young/Shutterstock; 91 (cell phone images): tele52/Shutterstock; 92 (top, right): All About Space/Shutterstock; 92 (bottom, left): Yury Stroykin/Shutterstock; 92 (bottom, right): Artazum/Shutterstock; 94 (cell phone images): tele52/Shutterstock; 94 (left): Hero Images/Getty Images; 94 (right): Bilderlounge/Getty Images; 96: Sonya etchison/Shutterstock; 98 (left): Karen roach/123RF; 98 (left, left): Andy Dean Photography/Shutterstock; 98 (right, center): Blanscape/123RF; 98 (right): Andriy Popov/123RF; 104: Dmitry Kalinovsky/123RF.

Unit 6
Page 105: Hill Street Studios/Blend Images/Getty Images; 106 (1): Matka_Wariatka/Shutterstock; 106 (2): Maximkabb/123RF; 106 (3): Image Source/Getty Images; 106 (4): RubberBall Productions/Brand X Pictures/Getty Images; 106 (5): Hill Street Studios/Blend Images/Getty Images; 106 (6): Comstock/Stockbyte/Getty Images; 106 (7): Cathy Yeulet/123RF; 106 (8): AleksandarNakic/Getty Images; 106 (9): Comstock/Stockbyte/Getty Images; 106 (10): XiXinXing/Shutterstock; 108: PeopleImages/E+/Getty Images; 110 (cell phone image): tele52/Shutterstock; 116: AJR_photo/Shutterstock; 118: dpa picture allianc / Alamy Stock Photo; 120: Pearson/Original photography by David Mager; 121: Tyler Mabie/Shutterstock; 124: Hadrian/Shutterstock.

Unit 7
Page 125: Perch Images/Stockbyte/Getty Images; 126 (1): Rene Jansa/Shutterstock; 126 (2): 9nong/123RF; 126 (3): Fuse/Corbis/Getty Images; 126 (4): DianaLundin/iStock/Getty Images Plus/Getty Images; 126 (5): Antoniodiaz/Shutterstock; 126 (6): Pumatokoh/Shutterstock; 126 (7): Tatiana Gladskikh/123RF; 126 (8): SteveLuker/iStock/Getty Images Plus/Getty Images; 126 (9): Danilov1991xxx/Shutterstock; 126 (10): Alexander Raths/123RF; 126 (11): Custom Medical Stock Photo/Alamy Stock Photo; 126 (12): Mangostock/Shutterstock; 128 (left): Stock Asso/Shutterstock; 128 (right): Dmytro Zinkevych/123RF; 128 (cell phone image): tele52/Shutterstock; 130: Takayuki/Shutterstock; 131 (cell phone image): tele52/Shutterstock; 136: Litabit/Shutterstock; 138 (top, right): Cathy Yeulet/123RF; 138 (bottom): BananaStock/Getty Images Plus/Getty Images; 140 (left): Ryuichi Sato/Taxi Japan/Getty Images; 140 (right): Angellce/ iStock / Getty Images Plus/Getty Images; 142: Yakobchuk Viacheslav/Shutterstock; 144: Hongqi Zhang/123RF.

Unit 8
Page 145: Jean Paul Chassenet/123RF; 146 (1A): GoGo Images Corporation/Alamy Stock Photo; 146 (1B): Comstock/Stockbyte/Getty Images; 146 (2A): Wendy Hope/Stockbyte/Getty Images; 146 (2B): Pressmaster/Shutterstock; 146 (3A): Paul Bradbury/Caiaimage/Getty Images; 146 (3B): Andersen Ross/Stockbyte/Getty Images; 146 (4A): Cathy Yeulet/123RF; 146 (4B): Wavebreak Media Ltd/123RF; 146 (5A): Robert Kneschke/Shutterstock; 146 (5B): Diego Cervo/Shutterstock; 146 (6A): Dmitry Kalinovsky/123RF; 146 (6B): Carlos Davila/Alamy Stock Photo; 146 (7A): Flairmicro/123RF;146 (7B): Phovoir/Shutterstock;148: Pearson/Original Photography by David Mager; 151 (1): Ljansempoi/Shutterstock; 154 (2): ARENA Creative/Shutterstock; 154 (3): Diego Cervo/Shutterstock; 154 (4): Ana Bokan/Shutterstock; 154 (center, right): Pearson/Original Photography by David Mager; 158: Mandy Godbehear/Shutterstock; 160: Pearson/Original Photography by David Mager; 164: Vgajic/E+/Getty Images.

Unit 9
Page 165: Shutterstock; 166 (1): David Buffington/Blend Images/Getty Images; 166 (2): David Grossman/Alamy Stock Photo; 166 (3): SpeedKingz/Shutterstock; 166 (4): Shutterstock; 166 (5): AVAVA/Shutterstock; 166 (6): Wavebreak Media Ltd/123RF; 166 (7): Karelnoppe/Shutterstock; 166 (8): Fstop123/E+/Getty Images; 166 (9): Rawpixel.com/Shutterstock; 166 (10): Frederic Cirou/PhotoAlto Agency RF Collections/Getty Images; 168: Pearson/Original Photography by David Mager; 170: Steve Debenport/E+/Getty Images; 172 (cell phone image): tele52/Shutterstock; 173 (cell phone images): tele52/Shutterstock; 174: Pearson/Original Photography by David Mager; 180: Tetra Images/Getty Images; 182: Fuse/Corbis/Getty Images; 184: Matimix/Shutterstock.

Unit 10
Page 185: Rido/Shutterstock; 188 (1): Ariel Skelley/DigitalVision/Getty Images; 188 (2): DAJ/Getty Images; 188 (3): Kostic Dusan/123RF; 188 (center, right): Original Photography by David Mager/Pearson Education; 190: UltraOrto, S.A./Shutterstock; 191: Bluestocking/E+/Getty Images; 192: Bluestocking/E+/Getty Images; 194 (1): Thodonal/123RF; 194 (2): Eurobanks/Shutterstock; 194 (3): Felix Mizioznikov/Shutterstock; 194 (4): Leungchopan/Shutterstock; 194 (5): Noriko Cooper/123RF; 194 (a): Sergey Lapin/123RF; 194 (b): Michael C. Gray/Shutterstock; 194 (c): Peter Cripps/123RF; 195: Pearson/Original Photography by David Mager; 196: AmorSt Photographer/Shutterstock; 197 (pizza): Nolie/Shutterstock; 197 (salad): Robyn Mackenzie/Shutterstock; 197 (chips): AZ/istock/Getty Images; 197 (pretzels): Josh Brown/Shutterstock; 198 (left): Scott Rothstein/Shutterstock; 198 (left, center): Deepstock/Shutterstock; 198 (right, center): Mehmet can/123RF; 198 (right): Patryk Kosmider/Shutterstock; 200 (meatloaf): Jabiru/Shutterstock; 200 (chicken): Slawomir Fajer/Shutterstock; 200 (pork): Jeannette Lambert/Shutterstock; 200 (noodles): Peter Doomen/Shutterstock; 200 (hamburger): Pikselstock/Shutterstock; 200 (fish): Ciaran Griffin/Stockbyte/Getty Images; 200 (mac & cheese): Cathleen A Clapper/Shutterstock; 200 (coleslaw): Lorelyn Medina/Shutterstock; 200 (fries): Pikselstock/Shutterstock; 200 (vegetables): P Maxwell Photography/Shutterstock; 200 (onion rings): Shutterdandan/Shutterstock; 200 (potatoes): Danny E Hooks/Shutterstock; 200 (bottom, right): Pearson/Original Photography by David Mager; 204: Mint Images/Getty Images.

Unit 11
Page 205: Paul Burns/Blend Images/Getty Images; 208: Pearson/Original Photography by David Mager; 210: Terry Alexander/Shutterstock; 214: Racorn/123RF; 216: Loren Rodgers/Shutterstock; 218 (left): Tribalium/Shutterstock; 218 (center): Photobac/Shutterstock; 218 (right): Paul Bradbury/Caiaimage/Getty Images; 220: Bibiphoto/Shutterstock; 224: Jabejon/E+/Getty Images.

Unit 12
Page 225: Nightman1965/Shutterstock; 226 (1): Bilderbox/INSADCO Photography/Alamy Stock Photo; 226 (2): Comstock Images/Stockbyte/Getty Images; 226 (3): Cathy Yeulet/123RF; 226 (4): Jupiterimages/Stockbyte/Getty Images; 226 (5): Maskot/Getty Images; 226 (6): Derek Meijer/Alamy Stock Photo; 226 (7): Hongqi Zhang/123RF; 226 (8): ndoeljindoel/123RF; 226 (9): Taylor Jorjorian/Alamy Stock Photo; 226 (10): Avava/Shutterstock; 226 (11): Fuse/Corbis/Getty Images; 226 (12): Blend Images/ColorBlind Images/Brand X Pictures/Getty Images; 231 (cell phone image): tele52/Shutterstock; 234: Ton koene/Alamy Stock Photo; 238 (top): David Wasserman/Photolibrary/Getty Images; 238 (bottom): Shutterstock; 240 (top, left): Snowwhiteimages/123RF; 240 (top, left center): Elwynn/123RF; 240 (top, right center): Hongqi Zhang/123RF; 240 (top, right): Pixelheadphoto digitalskillet/Shutterstock; 240 (center, right): Hurst Photo/Shutterstock; 244: Yoshiyoshi Hirokawa/DigitalVision/Getty Images.

Grammar Review
Page 247: Daniel M Ernst/Shutterstock; 248 (Ned): Felix Mizioznikov/Shutterstock; 248 (Aki): natu/Shutterstock; 248 (Artur): Avid_creative/Getty Images; 248 (Rohan): Ashwin/Shutterstock; 248 (Lan): Shippee/Shutterstock; 248 (Aya): Flashpop/DigitalVision/Getty Images; 250: Motortion Films/Shutterstock;252: GagliardiImages/Shutterstock.

Illustrations: Laurie Conley, pp. 8, 37, 108, 114 (top), 128, 148 (top row, bottom row left, bottom row right), 157, 158, 171, 208, 249; ElectraGraphics, pp. 11, 44, 52, 53 (left), 64, 71, 72, 73, 74, 84, 91, 93, 100, 104, 113, 124, 132 (top a-f), 133 (center), 140, 144, 148 (bottom row center), 151, 152, 164, 184, 204, 212 (top), 213 (bottom), 214 (bottom), 221 (right, 224), 232, 233, 244, 279, 280-281; Brian Hughes, pp. 77, 189, 193; André Labrie, pp. 33, 34, 54, 88 (top), 120, 180, 228 (top); Paul McCuster, pp. 112, 212 (bottom); Marc Mones, pp. 57; Luis Montiel, pp. 6, 26, 27, 86, 89, 186, 214 (top), 228 (bottom); Allan Moon, pp. 53 (top, center, right); Neil Stewart/NSV Productions, pp. 12-13, 38-39, 132 (bottom), 133; Roberto Sadi, pp. 101; Steve Schulman, pp. 40, 49, 80, 206; Anna Veltfort, pp. 51, 88 (bottom), 111, 114 (bottom), 115, 134, 137, 150, 172, 211, 217